Late Idyll

Late Idyll

The Second Symphony of Johannes Brahms

REINHOLD BRINKMANN

Translated by Peter Palmer

Harvard University Press

Cambridge, Massachusetts

London, England

Originally published as *Johannes Brahms: Die Zweite Symphonie: Späte Idylle*. Copyright © 1990 by edition text + kritik GmbH.

First Harvard University Press paperback edition, 1997

Library of Congress Cataloging-in-Publication Data

Brinkmann, Reinhold, 1934–
    [Johannes Brahms, die Zweite Symphonie. English]
    Late Idyll : the Second Symphony of Johannes Brahms / Reinhold
Brinkmann : translated by Peter Palmer.
        p.   cm.
    Translation of: Johannes Brahms, die Zweite Symphonie.
    Includes bibliographical references and index.
    ISBN 0-674-51175-1 (cloth)
    ISBN 0-674-51176-X (pbk.)
    1. Brahms, Johannes, 1833–1897. Symphonies, no. 2, op. 73, D
major.   I. Palmer, Peter, 1945–   . II. Title.
ML410.B8B7313 1995
784.2′184—dc20   94-29128

Contents

Preface

This book is the product of listening and reading, of the sensuous execution of music and thinking about it, of comparative rehearing (of the relevant symphony in different performances, of other works), and of renewed reading (the score, texts). It is, then, a product of the effort to understand, both historically and from the viewpoint of the present. It is not a book with a theoretical purpose; its analyses are concerned with what Theodor W. Adorno called the "flesh" of music and not with a codification of its bare bones. The author is seeking to reconcile the setting down on paper of aesthetic experiences with historical writings, grasping a historical work in the light of its present-day existence and impact. Brahms's Second Symphony was always a work that he particularly enjoyed hearing, and at the same time was a problematic one: the question of a disparity in value between the first two movements and the last two movements was always acute. This critical perplexity was what prompted and drove him to take up the pen. Certain basic perspectives and levels of experience appear tied up, in the process, with latter-day subjectivity. The author's interest in detecting the somber undertones in this music and their conditioning factors, individual and historical, his sympathy with a broken presentation of serenity, with an "interference" in the idyll—these are also symptoms of a historically informed awareness, symptoms, almost, of a whole generation's tendency toward the problematic. I well remember how the unforgettable Erwin Ratz was incapable of sharing or even of comprehending our doubts regarding the success of the rondo finale unleashed in Mahler's Seventh Symphony, our reservations about music that he, in accordance with his experience of life, had always experienced as a great expression of rejoicing and as artistically perfect. A later, postwar generation heard and interpreted this music no doubt differently. It seems perfectly possible that my interpretation of Brahms's Second Symphony with its transparent estimations of value has a similar basis. Its critical re-enactment reckons with a reader not afraid of music examples who, it is hoped, has the score within reach and who is prepared to consult his or her mind's ear and, if need be, a tape recorder.

Aspects of the analysis have been honed by the lectures and seminars on nineteenth-century symphonic music that I have given at the Hochschule der Künste, Berlin, and at Harvard University. I have pleasant memories of the Brahms Seminar that Friedhelm Krummacher, Christoph Wolff, and I arranged jointly at the Stuttgart Bach Academy in the summer of 1983, where it fell to me to present and discuss the Second Symphony. I am grateful to the friendly members of my 1991 NEH Summer Seminar for College Teachers, "Symphonies after Beethoven," at Harvard University for their animated discussion, and especially to the trombone specialist Andrew Glendening for his remarks and suggestions. Thanks for their kind assistance with my research are also due to my colleagues Elizabeth H. Auman (The Library of Congress, Washington, D.C.), Cornelia Bernini (Thomas-Mann-Archiv, Zurich), Otto Biba (Archiv der Gesellschaft der Musikfreunde, Vienna), Joachim Draheim (Karlsruhe), Ernst Hilmar and Otto Brusatti (Musiksammlung der Stadt- und Landesbibliothek, Vienna), Klaus Häfner (Badische Landesbibliothek Karlsruhe), Bernhard Stockmann (Musiksammlung der Staats- und Universitätsbibliothek Carl von Ossietzky, Hamburg), and J. Rigbie Turner (Pierpont Morgan Library, New York). The (slightly expanded and revised) American edition of this book has profited above all from the critical friendship of David Lewin, to whom this edition is dedicated.

I am indebted to Peter Palmer, whose active and critical participation in the shaping of the English version reached beyond just translating the text; I acknowledge in particular and with pleasure his sympathetic ear for the author's stylistic idiosyncrasies. Special thanks go to Margaretta Fulton at Harvard University Press, who initiated the English edition. And I am most grateful to Mary Ellen Geer for her competent editing of the manuscript.

Allow me a word of explanation regarding this edition and the readership I hope to gain for it. The genre of the work-monograph is relatively
recent in English-language publications on music. Inasmuch as a study
of this kind combines analytical, hermeneutic, source-critical, and historical perspectives in a relatively slim volume, the balance between them
is crucial. Both the range and the intensity of the presentation will therefore be limited. The technical musical analysis must not become too
detailed and certainly not too professional-theoretical, while the historical and interdisciplinary context will be just "touched on" in its ground-
lines, and not extensively traced back and accounted for. Moreover, consideration for the reader makes it preferable to use specific, more easily
accessible methods, especially with regard to musical analysis. In fact I
am *attempting* a happy medium—although I suspect that it will still be
deemed too "specialist." For, much as I sympathize with Joseph Kerman's idea of "musicology as criticism," and while emphatically recog-
nizing the need to conceive musicological studies for a wider readership
(again), I still cannot renounce "analysis" as the basis of the musicolo-
gist's skills. With its quasi-serial retrograde movement, Kerman's question "How we got into analysis and how to get out" is (particularly with
regard to prevailing forms of what Pierre Boulez has mockingly called
bookkeeping analyses) not only brilliantly formulated but also absolutely
correct from a polemical standpoint. Yet I am skeptical about the retrograde part. Adorno's statement that "the key to any meaning in art
lies in its technique" seems, to someone like me whose understanding
of art has been stamped by modernism, an irrefutable claim. The idea
of a musical composition is first of all codified and transmitted as a
musical idea. To perceive it depends on technical analysis, and to convey
this analysis is the purpose of a specially shaped hermeneutic language.
That is what I have attempted in the text and layout of the present book.
The first, German version was intended from the outset as a "lighter"
paperback, written for a series with a wide distribution and addressed
not only to professionals but also to the educated layman. Above all,
however, it was intended to be accessible to students in all branches of
music, and the American edition has retained this objective.

Abbreviations

Billroth   *Billroth und Brahms im Briefwechsel,* ed. Otto Gottfried-Billroth, Berlin and Vienna: Urban & Schwarzenberg, 1935

Frank   "Briefe von Brahms an Ernst Frank," ed. Alfred Einstein, in *Zeitschrift für Musikwissenschaft* IV, 1921–1922, 385–416

Letters   Johannes Brahms, *Briefwechsel,* vols. I–XVI, Berlin 1907–1922, reprint Tutzing: Hans Schneider, 1974

Litzmann   Berthold Litzmann, *Clara Schumann: Ein Künstlerleben nach Tagebüchern und Briefen,* vol. III, Leipzig: Breitkopf & Härtel, 4/1920

Schumann/Brahms   Clara Schumann and Johannes Brahms, *Briefe aus den Jahren* 1853–1896, ed. Berthold Litzmann, 2 vols., Leipzig: Breitkopf & Härtel, 1927

Simrock   *Johannes Brahms und Fritz Simrock: Weg einer Freundschaft: Briefe des Verlegers an den Komponisten,* ed. Kurt Stephenson, Hamburg: Augustin, 1961 = Veröffentlichungen der Hamburger Staats- und Universitätsbibliothek VI

A, B, C . . . Z refer to items in the Documents chapter.

Late Idyll

Genesis and Historical Place

Solidity and Skepticism: Contemporaries I

Let us begin seemingly on the margins, and in fairly general terms. Theodor Fontane, the skeptical bourgeois realist and great North German novelist of a late epoch, who has also been called the "old man *par excellence*," published in 1897—the year of Brahms's death and the year before Fontane himself died—the novel *Der Stechlin*. Stechlin, also known as the Great Stechlin, is a Brandenburg lake near Rheinsberg, north of Berlin, and in the first part of his *Wanderungen durch die Mark Brandenburg* Fontane visualizes it anthropomorphically as a mysterious being. Lake Stechlin looks "enigmatic, like a dumb person with an urge to speak. But his tongue is tied and refuses to obey him, and what he wants to say remains unspoken. . . . He is one of life's aristocrats, entertaining great relationships."[1] In some unfathomable way, Stechlin is bound up with the violent natural occurrences that are happening all over the earth: the Lisbon earthquake, that distant catastrophe of 1755, is said to have caused troubled waters, whirlpools, in reaction to it. But Stechlin, Dubslav von Stechlin, is also the name of the novel's main character. This old gentleman, who owns a *Schloss* and an estate, is a rare case of a person of rank as a character: a man without airs, with a strongly developed feeling for solidity and permanence (the self-awareness of those who were living in the Mark "even before the Hohenzollerns"), but also with the faculty of self-irony, "because it was in his whole nature to place a question mark after everything." "Paradoxes were his passion," we are told. Dubslav is, of course, a Prussian conservative, but one whose humane outlook repeatedly leads or misleads him

1. Fontane, *Wanderungen*, p. 372. The following quotations from the novel *Der Stechlin* are taken from Chapters 3 and 6. Writings consulted on *Stechlin*: Mann, Meyer, Rychner.

into progressive social statements. He has an "image of the right articulation" of the world, yet at the same time he is aware—and this is
indicated by the metaphor of the deeps of the lake which shares his
name—of its hidden pitfalls. "Dark feelings, they're fine things," says
the old skeptic, in response to the smart and fashionable expressions of
the younger generation.

What does all this have to do with Johannes Brahms? In an indirect
or, rather, an underlying sense, a great deal, in my view. I can see an
artistic fellowship of the age at work; that is to say, the works of art
concerned are illustrating a basically shared experience of life in similar
ways. Heinrich Mann stressed the combination of "solidity" and "skepticism" in Fontane, his great forerunner, and this could also be a sum-
ming up of Brahms and his art. *Dauerhafte Musik,* "music built to last,"
was the avowed moral and aesthetic goal of Brahms's compositional
work—work which, for all the assurance and solid craftsmanship, for all
the skill in the "right articulation" (Fontane), was marked by self-doubt
and skeptical questioning, and in the symphony of all genres. The conservative and progressive elements in Brahms could be related dialecti-
cally in a very similar way as in Dubslav Stechlin (the change of para-
digms in the latest Brahms research, with all its one-sided consequences
for the Brahms image, was effected within these very coordinates in the
name of Schoenberg's "Brahms the Progressive"). And the "dark" as a
profound Brahmsian experience is a quite central determinant of the
compositional form and "tone" of his music. Brahms too cultivated
"dark feelings."

Here I am concentrating, first of all, on a very general, historically
conditioned conformity of thoughts and feelings, of artistic attitudes.
Both the writer and the composer, each in his own medium, were reacting to changes in a historical situation, changes which seemed to be
jeopardizing basic preconditions of their outlook on life and their art.
During an epoch that was experienced as a "late" one in history, Fontane
the novelist was creating forms of imperiled individuality which, in regard to substance and outward appearance, I can also discover in the
works of Brahms the contemporaneous musician—albeit more indirect,
more abstract in accordance with the basically nonconceptual character

of the sounding medium of music. This thesis is being proposed in advance of any close analysis and interpretation of the musical art-form. It is meant to attune the reader mentally to the intent and direction of the following study, and also, perhaps, to identify that authorial pre-understanding already intimated in the Preface.

In the literary motif of Lake Stechlin—Fontane calls this the novel's leitmotif—the present author sees something more: for him it is an allegory of the work of art as Brahms, too, understood it and composed it. First there is the special relationship of speech ability and speech inhibition in the author and his work, between talk, the revealing of oneself, and silence, the keeping to oneself; furthermore there is the work's paradigmatic "world-containing" attribute, its representative position in (to cite Fontane again) "great relationships"; then there is the structural connection between all the elements, their seismographically reacting interdependence, as a classicistic formal ideal. And there are also the subterranean currents which can disrupt the smooth surface—in the metaphorical language of *Stechlin,* the secret motors of progress when the lake is stirred up by the "hammering" of "world events," and the "crowing cock" (the red cock, for sure, as a revolutionary symbol) rises up. In the Second Symphony these undercurrents will be manifested as darkenings and structural breaks.

Brahms might also agree with Fontane that artistic quality and artistic effect are determined by the criterion of—in Fontanesque parlance—*rätselhafte Modelung,* "mysterious molding," which turns the actual experience into an artistic product. The "dressing," the linguistic form of the work, whether it be literary, musical, or indeed visual: composition is, for this artistic self-understanding, the Archimedean point of all art. *Hic Rhodos hic salta!*

The above phrase "artistic self-understanding" is intended as a reference to the particular traditional connection of such thinking and forming, and to the decisive role that "tradition" in general plays here. I am driving at a particular refraction in the late nineteenth century's dealings with "tradition": there is an acceptance of being part of a historical sequence, on the one hand, and the resultant burden upon the artistic consciousness, on the other. (Again the polar constellation of "solidity" and "skepticism.") And I am driving at this especially as a personal hallmark of the works of art. *Stechlin* is a dialogue novel (Fontane: "All of it chatting, dialogue, in which the characters present themselves, and with them the story"). "Tradition" is seen encapsulated in its dialogic structure as a literary form of quotation—the way such quotations (which one must know if one is to notice them) are employed, the way they suggest authority and continuity, and yet are themselves relativized again in the speech commentary. The skillful blending of quotations with the "Fontane tone" has been rightly characterized by Herman Meyer as the "realistic-mimetic vigor" of Fontane's formal technique. Such an actualizing reflection on the history of one's art, a confirming of tradition and also a questioning of it—nuanced, frequently broken and mediated—are also peculiar to Brahms's music (and here again the quotation, both direct and indirect, plays an important role). Even stronger than in the novelist, however, is the distinct element of artistic self-assertion on the musician's part with, and against, what is felt to be a "great" musical history, which is both a support and a burden. To personalize the situation: creative writing "after Goethe" did not have the same problematic perspective for Fontane that composing "after Beethoven" had for Brahms. Since his early chamber pieces and songs, this confronting and "inverting" of tradition had meant an enormous creative effort for Brahms. The works and what the composer ironically referred to as their "black border" are evidence of this.

The "Last Great Master Craftsmen": Contemporaries II

In 1845 the young Berlin artist Adolph Menzel painted *Das Balkonzimmer* ("The Room with a Balcony"), an intimate oil-painting measuring only 58 × 47 cm.[2] A piece of chamber music in oils, so to speak. It depicts a bourgeois interior without human figures—more precisely, the corner of a living room, two walls converging diagonally at the rear, a colorful stucco ceiling, polished floor, along with some furnishings that are seem-

---

2. Writings consulted on Menzel: Betthausen, Busch, Forster-Hahn, Hofmann, Wegmann. On Menzel and Brahms see Jensen, pp. 59–60.

ingly casually placed: two chairs, a sofa which is only suggested, one corner of a carpet, and a tall mirror in a wooden frame standing between two lamp-brackets. Draped over the strut of the mirror is a piece of cloth. The warm dark-brown tints of the floor and furniture are set against a white-gray background. There at the back, in the corner of the picture, is the main "event." It comes from the open double-door to the balcony, where a thin curtain of white tulle is hanging. The visual meaning, the pictorial idea appears to reside in the atmospheric interplay of light and movement. A "gentle" draft is blowing the fine-mesh curtain into the room slightly, making it stretch. And through the inwardly moving white veil of the curtain, sunlight is flooding into the room, filtered and yet bright and glistening, reflected in the polished floor diagonally to the vanishing lines of the walls. There are also reflections elsewhere: the left-hand chair and the sofa appear in the wall-mirror, and the mirror also shows a picture in a gold frame evidently hanging outside the painted section of the room, the picture's subject being unrecognizable (or is the picture missing from the room itself?). And of course the correspondence between the two chairs is similarly a "mirroring," a real and concrete one. (It should be noted, however, that the placing of the chairs, back to back at an angle before the mirror, can scarcely have a practical purpose.)

In the literature on Menzel, both popular and scholarly, the *Balkon-zimmer* is described as a small miracle, and with such words as "gracefulness," "charm," "atmosphere," "splendor"; the picture has even been hailed as an "anticipation of Impressionism." To my eye and visual understanding, however, this apparently perfect idyll features a number of curious details. First there is the only partly painted back wall of the room with its coat of white, which does not match the basic color and seems to be leaving an empty rectangle. Either Menzel was portraying a part of the real room in this way, or else this wall was intended to take the right-hand side of the mirror-reflected painting within the painting—in which case Menzel left the work unfinished. Another source of irritation is the sofa: in the mirror this is painted complete with colored stripes and an arm-rest, whereas in the room itself there is merely a rough brown outline. The simple and obvious explanation would be that Menzel failed to complete the picture, but this, it seems to me, will not do, especially because he signed this particular painting. Rather, the idea of the fragmentary is part of the actual painting, the object being gently to question the idyll, the pure coalescence of light and movement—with means just as subtle as the methods used to portray this "atmosphere." The unfinished, the sketchy, is seen as a subtle irritation, an underlying "disturbance" of the harmonious world. This interpretive angle is also of significance for the present book's understanding of Brahms; the musical analysis of the Second Symphony will be guided by an interest in just such elements. The subsequent discussion of melancholy and the final chapter will then steer back to the broader historical perspective.

Now there is also—and this did not apply to Fontane—a direct biographical link between Menzel and Brahms. The two men knew one another personally, though only late in their lives, probably from 1886, and each thought highly of the other. Kalbeck (IV, 261–262 and 422–424; see also Jensen 59–60) already points out some important affinities. Menzel and Brahms both came from a simple bourgeois family, both remained single, both favored a rather coarse and direct mode of expression in social intercourse, and both liked their food and drink, Menzel with his regular eating-place at "Frederik's" in Berlin, Brahms with his table at Vienna's "Red Hedgehog." But both of them led a strict working life, practicing a Protestant bourgeois work ethic, and they felt their artistic existence to be "toil and effort." Both stressed the craftsmanship and technique, the solid and permanent side, the well-made aspect of their art. George Grosz, introducing a Spenglerian nuance with his first adjective, described Menzel as the "last great master craftsman"; music historians place a similar accent in their descriptions of Brahms's "mastery." And there are certainly indications that Brahms himself saw his historical position in exactly that light, as an end—a point to which this book will return in its discussion of melancholy. Menzel's striving for authenticity and Brahms's efforts to create music "built to last" conform to the same workmanlike concept of truth. In Kalbeck's words (IV, 262): "Their art, being a product of *Kennen und Können,* of knowledge and skill, presupposed the closest familiarity with the object on which it demonstrated its idealizing power." Moreover, the two men were alike politically in their veneration of Prussia and their esteem for Bismarck, although Kalbeck, in his naive nationalism (IV, 424), overrates this component. Brahms's obvious patriotism did not have anything like the same importance for his music, as a compositional element or a topic, as Prussian history had for Menzel's life and work (and certainly does not occupy the same space). Yet there is the *Triumphlied* and there are the *Fest- und Gedenksprüche* as politico-ideological manifestations—albeit clothed in biblical texts (see Beller-McKenna's study). And inasmuch as Menzel's thematic concentration on Prussian history and on history in general was an attempt "to restore, through the historical painting, meaning to the chaos of a world whose harmony, he thought, had been shattered" (Wegmann 155), inasmuch as it was intended to create order by contemplating tradition, one begins to perceive a basic parallel to the motives for Brahms's creative activity.

Furthermore, Menzel's repudiation of the large-scale oil painting and concentration on the crayon in his late period may be regarded as analogous to Brahms's lyrical late works, the piano pieces, the chamber works with clarinet (whose Meiningen champion, Richard Mühlfeld, was sketched by Menzel in 1891, as a muse with a classical profile), the *Four Serious Songs,* and his abjuring of large-scale, "world-containing" symphonic form. The most recent art scholarship strongly emphasizes the old Menzel's "ambivalence" toward realistic illustration, his "personal dilemma" regarding the "specific social and cultural milieu of Wilhelminian Germany and the growing complexity of the modern industrialized world" (Forster-Hahn 255), a world where the emergence of photography had an important role for the "observer" who interpreted as he painted. And this "ambivalence" can also be detected in the thinking and creative activity of Menzel's contemporary, Brahms, although—and this needs reiterating—the "absolute" musician is affected artistically in a far more indirect way, and hence his work will also reflect it more indirectly, more "abstractly." The young Menzel's insight into his historical position as a "late" artist could very easily have been formulated by Brahms. In 1836 Menzel wrote to Carl Heinrich Arnold about a contemporary painting: "As regards the composition, it seems to me to bear the full stamp of today's art in general: whereas our great forefathers, for all their profundity of thought, painted with feeling and enthusiasm, we are painting with the hand and with reflection, just the way we write poetry."

Over and above the theme of a biographical and artistic affinity between Menzel and Brahms, these points bring out possible "compositional" similarities between the visual and the musical work of art. (Naturally this is leading to a degree of abstraction where the analytical terminology can no longer be specific to the medium.) And, as a prelude to this book's central interpretation of Brahms, the frequently posed question of what Menzel and Brahms might have discussed and debated when the two of them were belatedly celebrating Menzel's eightieth birthday at length in his Berlin studio is altogether secondary. But the element of "disturbance" that emerges, very subtly, in Menzel's *Balkonzimmer* idyll is a component of the picture which could have an equivalent in Brahms's music. (And to which Theodor Fontane, as we saw, gives literary form in his *Stechlin*.) It also appears in other works by Menzel, as Werner Hofmann (p. 43) was probably the first to remark. Granted, his modernist training (affecting the eye of the spectator, the descriptive categories) and the deliberate selection of the pictures interpreted (while others are overlooked) cast doubts on Hofmann's generalizations. But it is enough, for our purposes, that an important body of important pictures by Menzel is involved here. These are typical of the Menzel whom Fontane, contrasting him with the chronicler of Prussia, called "the other" Menzel who "found his ideal in self-imposed artistic tasks, in the invention of constantly new techniques, and at the same time in solving constantly new problems." Let us look at some typical examples of "disturbances" in his paintings. The one pole is quasi-anecdotal, as guaranteed by the subject and title of the early oil-painting *Die Störung* ("The Interruption") of 1843–1846; similarly in narrative vein but far more dramatic is *Bon Soir, Messieurs!,* showing Frederick the Second's unexpected arrival at Lissa Castle and painted in 1858–1859. At the other end of the spectrum is Menzel's formal conversion of the motif, where the "interruption" assumes pictorial form. Here a drastic example, compared to the subtlety of the *Balkonzimmer,* is Menzel's *Berlin-*

Potsdamer Eisenbahn of 1847, in which the diagonal bisecting of the picture by the railroad reflects the historical conflict between nature and the industrial world in two ways: critically, as an element in the destruction of an archaic landscape (virgin land, primitive arboreal growth) and ancient life-styles (farmstead, sandy lane), but also enthusiastically, in the dynamic progress stirringly evoked by the advancing steam locomotive. The silhouette of metropolitan Potsdam provides the historical dimension, constituting the background from which the "interruption" emanates, both ideologically and formally.

Let another of Menzel's painterly principles be stated in connection with Brahms. It is noticeable that the majority of Menzel's pictures are conceived from a lofty vantage point. Describing the perspective favored by Menzel as the "technique of an imagined bird's eye view," Günter Busch rightly concludes (p. 11): "The foregrounds in Menzel's pictures have a striking tendency to 'rush' toward the bottom edge of the painting and into the bottom corners." In small oil-paintings like *Blick auf den Anhalter Bahnhof im Mondschein* (1846), *Palais-Garten des Prinzen Albrecht* (1846/1876), and *Friedrichsgracht bei Mondschein* (around 1860), but also in the large-scale historical painting *Friedrich und die Seinen in der Schlacht bei Hochkirch* (1856), this perspective and the downward directed "rush" of the picture take on a particular expressive vigor. For the aim of agitating the picture internally goes hand in hand with a coloristic darkening, the painting being focused on a dark—sometimes extremely dark—almost unrecognizable and indefinable fixed point. (Menzel's *Berlin-Potsdamer Eisenbahn* is also presented from such an angle; here the perspective movement forward increases under the impact of the powerful passage of the locomotive.) In *Anhalter Bahnhof* this dark fixed point is a building site, a tangle of boards and other unidentifiable materials seen from the upper story of a middle-class apartment house, whose solid walls are on the painting's lateral borders. The eye of the spectator, however, is drawn into fathomless depths, into a dark abyss. The contrast between the seemingly secure observation point inside and the vague, unpredictable world outside represents an experience that was evidently fundamental to Menzel. And if my interpretation of the *Balkonzimmer* is not completely mistaken, this disturbing experience already extends into the bourgeois interior itself. For Brahms this was a quite common diagnosis, as will be shown subsequently. By means of his concrete subjects the painter is pointing to the industrial revolution as historically conditioning his experiences. Brahms is invoking the same historical situation when, in the letter to Vincenz Lachner that I shall quote later, he accounts for his use of "dark" trombones and kettledrums in his Second Symphony with the cryptic metaphor, "black wings are constantly rustling above us."

What was proposed in the comparison with Fontane is confirmed by looking at Menzel. A writer, a painter, and a musician, three fellow artists of the same generation, found that at the close of the nineteenth century—an epoch they regarded as a later period—basic preconditions of their understanding of life and their art were being called into question. The relevant works of art present these experiences, aesthetically transformed, as "darkenings," "interruptions," "structural breaks." The musical analysis that follows will place Brahms's Second Symphony within this companionship. First, however, we shall read and comment upon the documentation of its genesis.

Documents

The early work-history of the Second Symphony is documented primarily in letters and diary entries by Brahms and his circle of friends. A selection of these documents having some bearing on the composition history and the interpretation is reproduced here in chronological order. (Abbreviations have been expanded and some explanatory notes added in brackets.) In the subsequent text of this study the documents will be referred to by an italic capital letter in parentheses.

A. Brahms to Fritz Simrock, June–August 1877 [Letters X, 37ff.] My place of residence: Pörtschach am See, Carinthia. Since yesterday and the day before I have already written 4 pages C minor for 4 hands!
[14. vi.]
Now I am in the third movement, and if the weather weren't so absolutely lovely you would get it for 4 hands in July for certain.
[30. vi.]

Instead of the last three measures in the 2nd movement of the [First] Symphony I request the setting up of the 5 measures enclosed.
[30. vii.]
The three measures will now have to appear in the 4-hand [edition] as well! Enclosed 3 instead of the last with the fermata!
[13. viii.]

B. Brahms to Eduard Hanslick, Summer 1877 [Kalbeck III, 175]
I am cordially obliged to you, and so as to thank you, if I should have a symphony played to you in the winter, it shall sound so cheerful and lovely that you will think I wrote it specially for you or even your young lady! That's no great feat, you will say, Brahms is a smart fellow and the Wörther See virgin soil, with so many melodies flying about that you must be careful not to tread on any ... What's behind this, though, doesn't want to be finely written up in the newspaper.

C. Brahms to Theodor Billroth, beginning of September 1877
[Billroth 246f.]
Whether I have a pretty symphony I don't know; I must ask clever people some time. But pious I was, at times, in the summer and I would hope of a composition of Edward that it has come off successfully.

D. Clara Schumann to Hermann Levi, 24. ix. 1877 [Litzmann 363]
Brahms is in good spirits, highly delighted with his summer stay, and has finished, in his head at least, a new symphony in D major—the first movement is now written out—of a quite elegiac character.

E. Otto Dessoff to Brahms, March and June 1878 [Letters XVI, 171 and 187]
[21. iii. 78]
When is the D major Symphony appearing? I still don't know any of it except the 1st movement and half of the last.
[probably June 78]
... I heard the [first] movement once at your home, and that was in September [1877].
– Brahms to Ernst Frank, 9. x. 1877 [Frank 402]

Dessoff often comes over [from Karlsruhe to Lichtental] and is very cheery—even if he sees new notes by me.

F. Clara Schumann, Diary 3. and 6. x. 1877 [Litzmann 364f.]
Johannes came this evening and played me the first movement of his Second Symphony in D major, which greatly delighted me. I find it in invention more significant than the first movement of the First Symphony ... I also heard a part of the last movement and am quite over-joyed with it. With this symphony he will have a more telling success with the public as well than he did with the First, much as musicians are captivated by the latter through its inspiration and wonderful working-out ... Saturday the 6th we really did go to Büdesheim. Johannes accompanied us to Oos but then returned to Baden, where he plans to finish writing down his D major Symphony.

G. Brahms to Simrock, 5. x. 1877 [Letters X, 52]
Yes—the lovely new monstrosity—Dessoff claims I never wrote any-thing so fine! But the rehearsal will not be for a lot of time yet.

H. Musikalisches Wochenblatt, 12. x. 1877, 507a
Johannes Brahms will soon have finished a second symphony.
– Ernst Rudorff to Brahms, 21. x. 1877 [Letters III, 170]
The musical journals write that you are working on the conclusion of a second symphony.

I. Brahms to Simrock, 20. x. 1877 [Letters X, 52]
I have been breathing down a copyist's neck in Karlsruhe and must now make a start in Vienna. Actually I would like to rehearse the "D major" with the Hochschule. I shall ask Joachim some time. I was thinking, you see, of going around New Year to Berlin (then to Leipzig).

K. Brahms to Simrock, 8. xi. 1877 [Letters X, 55]
The new symphony is due here on December 9th. But I fear the copyists aren't going to allow it. Then it would be possible on the 30th [De-

cember]. It will at all events be a proper flop, and people will say that this time I took it easy. You, though, I advise to be careful!
– Musikalisches Wochenblatt, 30. xi. 1877, 678b
Johannes Brahms's new (second) symphony in D major is due to receive its first performance anywhere on December 9th at the 1st concert of the Philharmonic in Vienna. Soon afterwards the Master will come to Leipzig.

L. Brahms to Billroth, 9. xi. 1877 [Billroth 250f.]
I am setting the new symphony for four hands. It normally happens at more than the last minute, when I already have the fee in my pocket. This time just for your sake. If only the new piece doesn't, for a change, please merely our more gentle friend [Eduard Hanslick]!

M. Billroth to Brahms, 14. xi. 1877 [Billroth 251]
Bearer of these lines is a trusty man; give him to bring to me what you've finished of [the piano reduction of] the symphony; I'd be glad to read it through during the evening, so as to come to you at 11 o'clock to-morrow morning and play with you. Why, it is all blue sky, babbling of streams, sunshine and cool green shade! By the Wörther See it must be so beautiful. If the instrumentation isn't altogether too chaste, the Viennese will get a quite special pleasure out of this piece!

N. Brahms to Simrock, 22. xi. 1877 [Letters X, 56f.]
The new symphony is so melancholy that you won't stand it. I have never written anything so sad, so *mollig* [soft, with the punning impli-cation of "minor-key"]: the score must appear with a black border. I have given enough warning. Are you really still proposing to buy yourself such a thing? We can always alter the terms, it's my turn to deliver the fair copy in a cover and box [as Simrock had delivered the score of the First Symphony to Brahms].

O. Brahms to Elisabet von Herzogenberg, 22. xi. 1877 [Letters I, 32]
The new one, though, is really no symphony [*Symphonie*] but merely a sinfonietta [*Sinfonie*], and neither do I need to play it for you beforehand.

You need only sit down, with your little feet on the two pedals alternately, and strike the F minor chord for a good while, alternately in the bass and the treble, *ff* and *pp*—then you will gradually get the clearest picture of the "new one."

P. Brahms to Adolf Schubring, 23. xi. 1877 [Letters VIII, 230]
On December 9th here, on January 10th in Leipzig I am doing a new symphony. You must be there!! But it's a quite innocent, cheerful little thing; don't expect anything and drum four weeks beforehand nothing but Berlioz, Liszt, and Wagner, and then its tender charms will be very pleasant for you.

Q. Brahms and Billroth, 4. xii. 1877 [Billroth 252f.]
Brahms: Be good enough to send me at your convenience the last sheet of my "Kattermängs" [Brahms's North German dialect version of *quatre mains/*"four hands"], I'm expecting the score any day.
Billroth: I am sending you herewith the last sheet of your symphony and hope to receive it back soon with the ending. With your permission I would much like to have the whole piece taken down by my copyist, as it is going to be a long time, too long for me at any rate, before it is printed. Even if the G major movement can be mastered with two hands, for me the other movements can't be done that way. I have already entered fully into the spirit of the piece and spent many a happy hour alone with it. I couldn't say which movement I'm fondest of; I find each movement splendid in its own way. A happy, blissful atmosphere pervades the whole, and it all bears the stamp of perfection and the effortless discharge of lucid ideas and warm emotion. Perhaps it is quite a good thing that the performance has been postponed, for the orchestra seems to be dominated by unrest and indiscipline, being tired of the disagreeable grind with *Rheingold, The Deadly Sins* [reference to an oratorio by Adalbert von Goldschmidt], and other things.

R. Brahms to Simrock, 5. xii. 1877 [Letters X, 59]
The musicians are so occupied with the 7 Deadly Sins and Rheingold that there is no time left for rehearsing. They are now requesting the

symphony for the 30th [December], but I've all sorts of things against this.

S. Brahms to E. von Herzogenberg, 12. xii. 1877 [Letters I, 36]
On the 30th I'm to have the F minor [performed] here.

T. Clara Schumann, Diary 23. xii. 1877 [Litzmann 366]
Johannes sent me his second symphony for four hands. But unfortunately it was so hard to read that I couldn't find anybody who could play it with me properly. And yet there was already much that quite enchanted me.

U. Simrock to Brahms, 28. xii. 1877 [Simrock 117]
The four-hand piano reduction of the D major Symphony I found at Frau Schumann's on the second day of the holiday—[Robert] Radecke was struggling with it; and one could hear enough of it already to find it a splendid work—full of sunshine, we are looking forward to Leipzig! The third movement should be irresistible for an audience—and the last seems to lift all its listeners back into heaven, which, moreover, we already found in the first movement.

V. Brahms to Schubring, 27. xii. 1877 [Letters VIII, 231]
On the 10th [January 1878, in Leipzig] I am performing a new symphony. I do hope you will come in good time for this (good rehearsals). You have never heard anything as world-weary—entirely F minor.

W. Brahms to E. von Herzogenberg, 29. xii. 1877 [Letters I, 41]
Here the musicians are playing my latest with mourning bands because it sounds so woeful; it will be printed with a black border.

X. Brahms to Simrock, 30. xii. 1877 [Letters X, 65]
The orchestra has practiced and played here with a voluptuous delight [*Wollust*] and praised me in a way I've never known before! But you must put a black border round the score so that it also shows its melancholy outwardly!

Y. Ferdinand Pohl to Simrock, 27. and 30. xii. 1877 [Letters X, 66]
Brahms's new symphony had its first rehearsal (read-through) on
Monday, today is the 2nd rehearsal. The work is splendid and will be
quickly accepted. The 3rd movement has its da capo already in the bag
. . . Thursday saw the 2nd rehearsal. Yesterday the final rehearsal. Richter
took great trouble over the rehearsals and will also conduct today. It's a
magnificent work that Brahms is bestowing on the world, and so very
accessible as well. Every movement is gold, and all four together constitute a necessary whole. Vitality and strength are bubbling up everywhere,
deep feeling and charm to go with it. Such music can only be composed
in the country, in the midst of nature. The success of the performance,
which takes place in 1½ hours, I shall briefly report below . . .
[Postscript:] It's over! Model performance, warmest reception. 3rd
movement (Allegretto) da capo, repeated calls for more. Duration of the
movements: 19, 11, 5, 8 minutes. Only the Adagio, in keeping with the
profound content, not applauded, but it is still the most valuable movement musically. And now: a toast to the New Year! Brahms is traveling
to Leipzig this evening. Arrival at 12 [noon] and straight to the rehearsal.

Z. Brahms to Joachim, 10. vi. 78 [Letters VI, 139]
Only too willingly I would have been there to hear the performance of
the 2nd Symphony, for I think this piece especially, or a number of things
in it, can with voluptuous delight [*Wollust*] be made to sound well.

Commentaries

I

Johannes Brahms composed his Second Symphony within just four
months between June and October 1877, during his summer stay in Pörtschach on the Wörthersee and his subsequent visit to Lichtental near
Baden-Baden—hence chiefly in the country, and at all events away from
Vienna. The previous year had seen (also in Lichtental), after Brahms
had been wrestling with the "symphonic problem" for decades, the completion of the First Symphony: a significant moment in the composer's

creative career and for his self-understanding. During the winter after the premiere of the First, which took place under Otto Dessoff in Karlsruhe on November 4, 1876, Brahms was busy trying out this work himself in performance; he conducted the First Symphony in Mannheim, Munich, Vienna (not with the Philharmonic but in one of the concerts mounted by the Gesellschaft der Musikfreunde), Leipzig, and Breslau. The spring of 1877 saw—along with the personally difficult but also liberating decision against leaving Vienna for Düsseldorf—Brahms turning, very characteristically, to the one lifelong constant in his creative activity, the composing of songs with piano. Eighteen songs were produced in Vienna (including "Es liebt sich so lieblich im Lenze" from Opus 71), as well as a number of Bach arrangements for piano. Brahms was manifestly drawing breath and gathering his forces after his great artistic exertions.

On June 6, 1877, Brahms traveled to Pörtschach for the summer and arrived there, according to his calendar, on June 9th. There he immediately began work on the piano reduction for four hands of his First Symphony *(A)*,[3] which evidently gave him trouble and took him more than a month. From July he was furthermore supervising the printing of the full score of this symphony and making the last corrections to the notes. At the same time as he was doing this, Brahms started work—in June, according to Kalbeck's statement—on the composition of the Second Symphony, first mentioned *(B)* in a letter to Hanslick (published without the exact date). Aside from the new symphony, Brahms's creative energies during the summer and early fall were devoted to the *a cappella* motet "Warum ist das Licht gegeben dem Mühseligen" from Opus 74 and the duet ballade "Edward," op. 75, no. 1 (*C;* the word "pious" in this letter most likely refers to the motet). In addition he probably produced a first version of the vocal quartet "O schöne Nacht" from Opus 92 as well as the four-part vocal canon "Mir lächelt kein Frühling," WoO 25. Possibly Brahms also began work on the songs "Vergebliches Ständchen" and "Spannung" from Opus 84, which he con-

---

3. The italic letters in parentheses refer to the documents for the history of the work's genesis quoted earlier.

tinued during the two subsequent Pörtschach stays of 1878 and 1879. We have no details of his work on the symphony, of the state and progress of the composition, in the summer of 1877.

– In parentheses: no documents have survived that could furnish evidence of work on the symphony prior to June 1877. (In any case Brahms, that great remover of traces, was usually in the habit of destroying sketches, drafts, and even original fair copies.) All the same, it is not completely misguided to speculate on a possible earlier starting-date for the composition. To spend only four months working on a monumental symphonic score is, even assuming an exceptional concentration, an amazingly short time for Brahms. Works of such dimensions, even when scored for chamber forces, usually took him considerably longer, often several years (which is not to say that he was busy with the same work all the time). Even if his ruminating upon a First Symphony for decades is exceptional, even if the release he experienced on completing it spurred on the composition of the Second directly after, the speed with which he finished it remains an enigma: the conception, sketches, drafts, composition, and copying out—all of it within the brief space of a summer which was by no means solely devoted to the symphony, as the aforementioned extra work on a number of other pieces testifies. Its very proximity to the First Symphony, which will play a role in the ensuing interpretation, could be a pointer to a double conception and hence to the at least partly parallel drafting of the two symphonies. (Moreover, Peter Wollny rightly remarked in a paper for my 1988 seminar on symphonic music at Harvard University that Brahms completed relatively little in the years 1875 and 1876; there would be scope here for undocumented work.) In the coda to the first movement of his Second Symphony Brahms quotes the song he composed in the spring of 1877, "Es liebt sich so lieblich im Lenze," and this could signify both a temporal linkage and a *terminus post quem* (at least for the end of the movement). And it is a completely open question whether there is any chronological significance in the fact that the tuba (instead of the bass trombone) was only introduced during the composition (or the writing down of the full score), as can be discerned from the corrections in the autograph described below. All these things are possible pointers at best, lacking real cogency, and hence conjectural. Even the most important reason for wondering, the assumed brevity of the composition period, is not all that unusual from another perspective. For the Violin Concerto op. 77, which was the next "major" composition after the Second Symphony and in some respects its Pörtschach-born cousin, was evidently also composed in a few months by Brahms in 1878. In sum: there are questions to be asked, possibilities to be weighed, but there is no evidence whatsoever. –

From September 17th onward (Kalbeck III, 176) we find Brahms in Clara Schumann's vicinity in Lichtental, the Baden suburb. The conception of the Second Symphony had been established *(D)*; the first movement and sections of the last movement (and probably of the second and third as well) had been written down, had been played to intimate friends, and had met with spontaneous approval *(E, F, G)*. By mid-October the full score was ready, a copyist was sought, and a first, so to speak trial performance in a not overly taxing situation, with the orchestra of the Berlin Musikhochschule, and a subsequent performance in Leipzig were envisaged *(I)*; evidently the Second Symphony, even more than Brahms had tried to do with the First, was meant to reach the public without any fuss. Yet at the same time the report of a new Brahms symphony was already being published *(H)*. At the end of October Brahms returned to Vienna. There he found the people to copy the orchestral parts and now confidently assigned the premiere for December 9th to a prominent venue: the Vienna Musikverein with the Philharmonic Orchestra under Hans Richter *(K)*. On the other hand Brahms wanted to be assured of the verdict of knowledgeable friends in advance of the premiere. In contrast to what he had done with the First Symphony, he was already preparing the piano reduction for four hands *(L)*, which he played with Theodor Billroth in private on November 15th *(M)* and with the composer Ignaz Brüll before a circle of friends in December (Kalbeck III, 178f.). Clara Schumann, too, was sent the piano reduction in December *(T, U)*. This gave rise to the first overall judgments and to certain pastoral interpretations *(M, Q, U)*. At the same time—perhaps partly in response to these reactions—Brahms embarked in letters to out-of-town friends on a cryptic game with his characterizations of the new symphony (as in *O*), proclaiming it sometimes to be light-mindedly cheerful *(P)* and sometimes to be a deeply melancholic work (as in *N, V,* and *W*). The Viennese premiere was eventually postponed because of the orchestra's excessive workload *(Q, R)*. After some very good rehearsals *(X)* the symphony then enjoyed a great success on December 30, 1877 *(Y)*; the first audience cheered it, and the Press—both local and from farther afield—wrote, with a few exceptions, excellent notices.

As with the First Symphony, Brahms himself took charge of several subsequent performances (Leipzig, Amsterdam, The Hague); after he had carefully checked the text with the help of his friends Joachim and Dessoff, and after he had supervised the printing during another summer in Pörtschach, the full score and piano reduction for four hands were brought out in August 1878 by Simrock in Berlin.

The facts and documents regarding this briefly discussed first phase of the work-history give rise to several commentaries accentuating certain points. They will focus on aspects of the following interpretation.

1. For several weeks in the summer of 1877, Brahms was thinking ahead to the Second Symphony and back to the First simultaneously. When Brahms was preparing the piano reduction of his First Symphony and checking the proofs of the full score, as well as making his final revisions to it, thus giving all the movements another thorough working-over, he was confronted anew, and in the closest way, with the finished composition, its structure, form, and idea, and he had also witnessed its first impact on an audience. And at the same time he was conceiving his next symphonic work. It would be strange if this direct creative connection within the one genre had not left any traces behind it, compositional and contentual. Did Brahms's fresh thinking-through of the First Symphony affect, mold, or guide the beginnings of the Second? Especially in the light of a reception—from the first reactions of friends to the latest scholarly writings—which by common consent has concentrated on a polarity of character, this question remains central to an understanding of the work, and hence to the interpretation that follows.

2. Regarding the details of the composition history there are—as always with Brahms, who was in the habit of destroying his sketches and

drafts—only a few pointers, and these call for some interpretation. This particularly applies to the order in which the individual movements were composed. Undoubtedly Brahms had, as Clara Schumann testifies *(D)*, the whole of the symphony "finished, in his head"—and that means the formal idea of all the movements, down to the compositional detail—when he arrived in Lichtental in the second half of September 1877. From the statements of Frau Schumann and Otto Dessoff *(D, E, F)* it further emerges that he had, at that point, completely notated the first movement in full score, that he played this and parts of the last movement on the piano (no doubt from the full score), and that from October 6th he set about "finishing" the writing down of the symphony. It is, however, a mistake to conclude from these items of information (as has happened once again in the Brahms literature just recently) that Brahms composed the movements, and notated them in the full score, in the order I-IV-II-III. The Brahms autograph score, which is now preserved in the Pierpont Morgan Library in New York, offers a clue. This manuscript uses three different kinds of paper: A for movement I, B for both movement II and movement III, C for movement IV. Each of these batches has, moreover, its own pagination, starting in each case with the number 1: thus movements I (on its own), II and III (together), and IV (on its own) are numbered separately. It can at least be seen from the paginations that Brahms began to write down the second movement in full score before the first movement was completely notated (or else the page numbers could have run on), that the entire third movement was written down after the second, and that the writing of the fourth was begun before the third had been notated to the end of the movement. And these data support the view that sections of both the second and the fourth movement (at least the two openings) had been written down in full score when Brahms told Clara Schumann about the finished manuscript of the first movement at the end of September *(D)*. So he evidently arrived from Pörtschach with three segments of full score, which suggests—although one must be cautious—a certain parallelism, or meshing, in the writing down of three movement openings back in the summer. The hypothesis that the full score had already reached an advanced stage by the end of September also makes it easier to understand how Brahms was then able to complete the whole symphony in October in a relatively short time.

Here a further glance at the autograph score may be helpful. For at first Brahms used only three trombones for the low brass writing in the orchestra, if I am deciphering correctly the original indication in front of the corresponding systems on page 2 of the score. (Amid the crossings-out it is difficult to reconstruct how to read it.) At some time or other during the composition Brahms then added a tuba to the brass as the lowest bass instrument and amended all the instrumental indications accordingly.

Now in this autograph score, the original instrumentation without the tuba only appears in the two outer movements; the second movement includes the tuba from the start of the autograph. (The third movement in its entirety dispenses with the low brass.) This might confirm the hypothesis, just touched on, that movements I and IV came into existence prior to movements II and III. One may conclude more cautiously that the final instrumental form of both the first movement and the finale was only decided during the writing down of this autograph, whereas the instrumentation for the two inner movements was established before Brahms wrote out the full score. And there seems to be a further difference between movements I and IV. For in the autograph the tuba seems to have been added at the revision stage (including the extra rests) throughout the first movement, and the writing, which was originally purely for trombones, has often been modified, especially in the third trombone part. The prominent measures 33ff., in particular, are affected by this (see the discussion below). In the fourth movement, too, the tuba at first appears to have been a later insertion. But here the source-critical situation is somewhat more complicated because of manifold deletions, including what are obviously corrections of oversights. At the beginning of the movement, in front of the accolade, the system underneath the trumpets is, *ante correcturam,* assigned to "Timpani a.d.," the one below it to "1. 2." trombones, and the one below that to trombone "3" alone. This has been corrected in its entirety, and the three systems below the trumpets are now, *post correcturam,* assigned to—reading from top to bottom—"1. 2. Trombones / 3. & Tuba / Timpani a.d." It is thus possible, and indeed likely, that only the three trombones were at first envisaged for the finale as well. Now the low brass certainly enters at a very late stage in the last movement, not until measure 202, which is directly before the Tranquillo episode. And here there are only notes, and no names of instruments. But the writing for the low brass is four-part. The writing down must therefore have happened after the correction to the accolade at the beginning of the movement.

There is a possible technical explanation for adding the tuba. For, under conditions in the mid-nineteenth century, the sound-determining brass writing in the coda to the finale (mm. 353ff.) calls for the tuba instead of the trombone so as to produce all the low notes on one instrument, without alternating between bass trombones of different pitch. And the second movement requires the tuba from the beginning, or, to be more precise, from the low b in measure 3. The first autograph version of the opening movement, on the other hand, was plainly conceived without the tuba; wherever, in the final version, the tuba seems called for (instead of the bass trombone), as for the low pedal-note a in mm. 266ff., 274ff., or in all passages with four-part low brass, these are later amendments based on the new instrumentation.

The entire matter remains, however, ambiguous. It might be assumed that the decision to use the tuba was made before the writing down of the brass parts in the second half of the finale. Whether, at that point in time, the beginning of the second movement, with its tuba indication, had already been written down is not clear from the sources. The important thing is that the original idea of the symphony, and particularly its first movement, started out from a scoring with three trombones. Or, conversely: the timbral conception of a pure "choir" of trombones is obviously connected primarily with the character and tone of the first movement. The addition of the tuba, which other considerations motivated in other movements, then prompted a rethinking of the low brass sound in the first movement as well. And once again measures 33ff. were particularly affected by this.

This may be the place for further discussion of the question—it already touches on compositional issues—of why Brahms employed the tuba at all. An initial answer could probably be sought in the tonal quality, agility, and blending-power of the low brass instruments and the way these qualities developed in the second half of the nineteenth century. This leads in both directions: to the ophicleide, the tuba's coarse and clumsy forerunner, and to the bass trombone, which often dominates the trombone choir unintentionally. (A contrabass trombone, known to Brahms from Wagner's *Rheingold* score, was ruled out from the start: this instrument was relatively primitive in its speech and agility and scarcely lent itself to Brahms's symphonic purposes.) The tuba is, in Central European symphonic music and especially its Viennese tradition, a relatively late instrument. Even Bruckner did not use it until his Fifth Symphony; his Third and Fourth manage with three trombones despite the augmented brass. One early instance: Niels V. Gade wrote for four-part low brass using the alto, tenor, and bass trombone and the "bass tuba or contrafagotto" in his First Symphony, published in 1844, but it is not known whether Brahms was acquainted with this work (Gade does not figure in his library). On the other hand the tuba was already prominently represented in orchestral works by the "Neo-German" School, such as the second (1855) version of Wagner's *Faust Overture*, Liszt's *A Faust Symphony* of 1854–1857, and his *Dante Symphony* of 1855–1857 (with its two tenor trombones, bass trombone, and tuba), whose score was in Brahms's possession. And similarly, around the middle of the century Berlioz had already replaced the ophicleide—it also appears in Mendelssohn's *A Midsummer Night's Dream* overture— with the tuba in revisions of his earlier works, not to mention the tuba's appearance in opera scores up to Wagner's *Ring*: sound effects with which Brahms was thoroughly familiar. (He owned a score of *Rheingold*, with its contrabass tuba, from 1875 onward.) Tchaikovsky, too, probably used three trombones and a tuba as early as his Second Symphony, op. 17, of 1872 (first version; I have only the final version of 1880 at hand), and certainly used them from his Third Symphony, op. 29, of 1875 onward (Brahms owned the score, which was published in 1877). Yet in his First Symphony, completed in 1876, Brahms with his three trombones still does not go beyond Beethoven's Fifth Symphony and Schumann's Fourth, and he uses them, like Beethoven in his Fifth, only in the finale, saving them for the most pronounced moment. Only Brahms's Second

Symphony uses the fourth low brass instrument. In his Third Symphony he reverted to three trombones (without a tuba), though in this case from the beginning, whereas his Fourth Symphony again reserves the sound of the three trombones for the last movement with its singular formal model and its archaically pathos-charged tone.

For the characteristic sound of the Second Symphony, however, especially that of its first two movements, Brahms's ear evidently required the augmented dark-sounding brass—and this is a pointer to the interpretation below. It was the sonorous and symbolic character of the trombones that he wanted primarily; as he acknowledged later in his letter to Lachner (as glossed below): "I cannot manage without the trombones." I know of no models in the prevalent symphonic literature of the age for the idea of possibly as many as four trombones. Schubert may have thought about four trombones for the one particular moment of the "Andante" passage in the first movement of his last symphonic fragment, D. 936A—the sketch indicates this at all events. (And Andrew Glendening has put forward the illuminating proposition that the passage is an homage to Beethoven linking up with his *Equali* for four trombones, which were of course played and sung in Schubert's hearing in the funeral procession to the cemetery at Währing.) But naturally Brahms was not acquainted with this fragment. He might well, however, have known Heinrich Schütz's "Fili me Absalon" from Winterfeld's reprint (the book is in his library). But evidently it was for the aforementioned technical reasons that Brahms favored the tuba. The bass trombones of the time, if not restricted solely to supporting the trombone "choir," obviously did not blend well with the string basses; passages in parallel with the double basses were a particular problem. Berlioz, in his *Treatise on Instrumentation*, expressly advises against using the trombone to reinforce double basses, "with whose tone color, moreover, it in no way agrees"; and in his capacity as editor of the *Treatise*, Richard Strauss helpfully adds that "the softer bass tuba or, even better, the low horns are excellently suited to supporting the basso cantante" (Berlioz 302). Such considerations—which might have been raised in the Second Symphony in such passages as movement I, mm. 33–36 (with its parallel cello at this very delicate moment), movement II, mm. 1ff., 27ff., 86ff., and

movement IV, mm. 363ff. (also mm. 369–372 with the solo entry)—
would be a plausible motive for introducing the tuba instead of the
possible low trombone. A further motive might have been the aforesaid
deficiency in certain low registers on the bass trombone: the low sustained d and a, precisely the notes that were so important for Brahms
in this symphony, were lacking on both the contemporaneous bass trombone in B-flat and the one in E-flat. Practical considerations, presumably
the instrument's technical shortcomings, thus ruled out the trombone
as the lowest instrument. So Brahms was obliged to resort to the tuba.
For this, to be sure, he did not need to look to other composers for
immediate models, because movements II ("Denn alles Fleisch, es ist wie
Gras"), III ("Herr, lehre doch mich, daß ein Ende mit mir haben muß"),
and VI ("Denn wir haben hier keine bleibende Statt") of the *German
Requiem* which he completed in 1866 already have three trombones and
a tuba. These are movements which, especially where the three trombones and the tuba are heard, speak of last things, of death and the Day
of Judgment. (Incidentally, the autograph of the *German Requiem* suggests—at least on inspection of a microfilm—that, in this case as well,
the tuba was added to the three trombones belatedly. The same signs of
corrections are apparent as in the autograph of the Second Symphony.
Thus Brahms was thoroughly familiar with the process of adding the
tuba when he revised the score of his Second Symphony.)

To sum up, then, it can be stated that the tuba—so unusual in
Brahms's symphonic music—entered the score of the Second Symphony
only by way of complementing the original pure trombone "choir,"
which was genuinely connected with the sonorous and expressive
character of the first movement in particular. And it is significant in
this context that the ultimate, long-held fortissimo chord for low brass
(finale, mm. 425–427), an extremely prominent sound in the nature of
a reference, is entirely reserved for the isolated three trombones,
whereas the tuba at this point merely reinforces the short tutti strokes
in the rest of the orchestra.

3. Brahms's first presentation of the D major Symphony in a rendition
of the two outer movements, as well as the continuous pagination of the
two middle movements in the autograph, opens up another perspective.

Both these things seem to reflect the fact that in Romantic symphonies the outer movements on the one hand, and the inner movements on the other, stand closer together, with a marked emphasis on the large-scale outer movements. With Mendelssohn, Schumann, and Brahms (his First Symphony is a particularly good example of this), the first and fourth movements generally convey the work's "idea" and constitute the pillars of the symphonic form; the second and third movements, which are usually character pieces, are lighter in tone, dimensions, and demands, often proceeding (to quote Eduard Hanslick's review of the premiere of Brahms's Third Symphony) "at a leisurely pace upon a middle level of feeling, allowing tender and graceful sentiments to unfold in tranquillity" (Hanslick 1886, p. 363). But with Brahms's Second Symphony caution is needed in this area as well. Obvious though it is that Brahms, in order to give some idea of his new symphonic whole, was concentrating on the great outer movements, although at least part of the second movement already existed, and clearly though he was thereby confirming the pattern of the Romantic symphony, it is in this very respect that the Second Symphony is unusual: its second movement is the only Adagio in any of Brahms's four symphonies. Thus the D major Symphony that people have interpreted so cheerfully and lightly contains the weightiest slow movement in Brahms's symphonic music. This, too, is worth thinking about.

4) An interesting point is the immediate work-milieu of the Second Symphony, to which Brahms himself refers in his letter to Billroth *(C)*: the F minor ballade "Edward," op. 75, no. 1, which he composed in Pörtschach and sent to Clara Schumann in the middle of August (Litzmann III, 361), and the D minor motet *Warum*, op. 74, no. 1, which his own work-catalogue (Orel 540) records his composing in "summer 77 Pörtschach" (although using old models from his Mass of 1856). The commonly held view is that the two works are gloomy antitheses to the optimistic D major Symphony and scarcely compatible with its expressive character, belonging rather to the world of the First Symphony. It seems doubtful, however, that this creative juxtaposition is purely accidental. The text of Job in the first section of the motet has as one of its themes the questioning of optimism, of cheerfulness, by the "Mühse-

ligen" (the "struggler")—an epithet which Brahms was fond of identifying with himself; and this leads afresh to the possibility of underlying connections. An explicit reference by Brahms himself will also contribute to the motet's reappearance in the subsequent overall interpretation of the D major Symphony. And Brahms seems to be referring to the key of the duet ballade when he represents the as yet unknown symphony in a number of letters as a dark-tinted work in F minor *(O, S, V)*.

5. These strange characterizations of the Second Symphony, the equivocal Brahmsian toying with meanings that was addressed above, are intrinsically the most salient feature of the foregoing documents. This starts early on with Clara Schumann's comment, evidently deriving from a hint by Brahms, that the first movement was "of a quite elegiac character" *(D);* it is pursued in the ambiguous phrase about the "lovely monstrosity" *(G)* and culminates in the letters prior to the premiere from mid-November onward. On the one hand there is the belittling tendency: "this time I took it easy" *(K)*, "no symphony but merely a sinfonietta" *(O)*, "a quite innocent, cheerful little thing" *(P);* and on the other hand, at first interwoven with this *(O)*, then dominant, there is the opposite, tragic characterization: F minor, *Weltschmerz,* melancholy *(N, S, V)*. Typical is the style in which the information is couched, the ironic accent: the edition "with a black border," the Philharmonic playing with mourning bands *(W, X)*. Such subterfuges are by no means unfamiliar in Brahms, who enjoyed disguising himself in certain situations and from certain angles of his life; the striking thing with regard to the Second Symphony is the intensity and amount. There are several possible ways of deciphering the meaning of this particular mask of irony. The first—and this is the interpretation currently favored—is to assume a jocular attempt on Brahms's part to lead his friends astray, with a view to planting false expectations in their minds; the second would be to assume that Brahms was aware of the transparency of his maneuver, especially in the light of the exaggerations. A third interpretation has not been considered in any of the literature on Brahms, and it is this: the irony might signify the imparting of an element of truth and Brahms's fractured relationship to serenity, to the undividedly pastoral world. But then the question will arise of the "melancholic" ele-

ments in the actual music, and what was simply a biographical pose will turn into a question of comprehension—one affecting both the composer and the score of his symphony.

6. If the movement lengths at the premiere, as recorded by Ferdinand Pohl *(Y)*, are accurately gauged and also in accordance with Brahms's own ideas on tempi, they could provide some clues to interpretation. The accompanying table (see p. 30) compares these movement lengths at the premiere performance with the times on some recordings that were at my disposal. (Where the recording does not observe the repeat of the first-movement exposition, the corresponding time has been added. Times are given to the nearest five seconds.)

An interpretation of these timings is not without its pitfalls. One must assume of Pohl, the chronicler of the first performance, that he rounded the times down or up to the nearest minute, thus setting a margin of error of minus/plus half a minute; moreover, extreme tempo modifications in individual passages (such as the coda of the first movement) are possible, and these would plainly extend the length of the movement, in spite of a basic tempo that was faster overall, making it seem particularly difficult to convert movement times into metronome figures. That, over and above this, every performance and recording has its own particular set of circumstances, from location and recording conditions to orchestral peculiarities and what is loosely called the "current form" of the conductor, goes without saying. And naturally interpreters and their views undergo changes, and specifically with regard to the tempo (Furtwängler in 1945 compared to 1948 and Karajan in 1963/1964 compared to 1978 are proof of this, in their contrasting ways). As always, it would be dangerous to draw hasty conclusions and above all to generalize. Yet, with careful argument, it is possible to discuss some general tendencies.

The first point to strike one is that none of the more recent interpretations shows the same tempo proportions as the premiere performance; the closest are Karajan in 1978 (with slightly slower outer movements) and Bruno Walter (though his second movement is much faster). Taken collectively, the range of the tempi is astonishing—in either direction in most of the recordings (like Maazel with his extremely slow first move-

Performance/Recording	Year	Length of movement (minutes/seconds)			
		I	II	III	IV
Richter, Vienna Philharmonic	1877	19	11	5	8
Mengelberg, Concertgebouw Orchestra (Tel. TH 97005)	1940	17:40	9:15	5:00	9:00
Furtwängler, Vienna Philharmonic (EMI Angel WF-60051)	1945	19:20	10:15	5:50	8:40
Furtwängler, London Philharmonic (Richmond B 19020)	1948	20:20	10:50	6:10	9:00
Toscanini, NBC Symphony (RCA Victor LM 1731)	1952	19:40	8:25	5:20	8:45
Walter, New York Philharmonic	1953	19:50	9:10	5:15	8:15
Klemperer, Philharmonia Orchestra (Electrola 1 C 153-50035)	1956	20:10	9:00	5:15	9:00
Karajan, Berlin Philharmonic (DG 2530044)	1963/ 1964	20:40	10:40	5:10	8:55
Szell, Cleveland Orchestra (Columbia D 3S 758)	1967	20:15	9:10	5:35	9:20
Horenstein, Danish Radio Orchestra (Unicorn 72001)	1972	20:20	10:40	5:10	9:55
Kertesz, Vienna Philharmonic (Vox SVBX 5125)	1973	19:50	10:00	4:55	9:00
Böhm, Vienna Philharmonic (DG 2563588)	1976	21:00	11:45	5:35	9:50
Maazel, Cleveland Orchestra (London CS 7007)	1976	22:10	9:40	5:30	9:35
Karajan, Berlin Philharmonic (DG 2563966)	1978	19:50	10:20	4:50	8:30
Bernstein, Vienna Philharmonic (DG 2560106)	1983	20:40	11:55	5:30	10:05

ment and relatively fast second movement). Furtwängler in 1948, Böhm, and Bernstein are conspicuous by their general tendency toward the slow extreme, Mengelberg in his first two movements by a tendency to the fast extreme. In individual movements the following conductors come close to the premiere timings: in the first movement, Furtwängler in 1945 but nobody else (the nearest being Toscanini, with Walter, Kertesz, and the 1978 Karajan lagging behind); in the second movement the figure is matched by the 1948 Furtwängler and, only just, Horenstein and the 1963/1964 Karajan; in the third movement the Karajan of 1963/1964 and 1978, Mengelberg, Horenstein, and Kertesz, as well as Walter and Klemperer, are evidence of a more uniform idea of the tempo (though in view of a total duration of only five minutes, differences of seconds are already relevant); in the fourth movement Bruno Walter alone attains the fast "Allegro con spirito" of the premiere, the 1978 Karajan being the only other conductor to approach it.

This much is clear, therefore: the first movement is evidently being played in the twentieth century altogether more slowly (with the sole exception of Mengelberg), no doubt because of the "non troppo" attached to the Allegro heading—perhaps also because of an unquestioned view of the movement-type at the outset; the second movement is generally taken more quickly (with Bernstein and Böhm, the extreme cases, taking the opposite course), again probably as a result of the appended "non troppo"; on the other hand the finale was played very much faster at the end of December 1877, there being scarcely a single conductor today who realizes the "con spirito." This is symptomatic of a standardizing view of the work. Brahms's Second Symphony, played as the reflection of a serene and tranquil pastoral atmosphere, is conceived as going entirely at a medium tempo: no real Allegro in the first movement but rather an affectionate Moderato, similarly no drastically gripping finale con brio, and also—avoiding the opposite—no great Adagio pathos or extreme depth of expression in the second movement.

In the first movement in particular, the modifications to the basic tempo are interesting. With nearly all those recordings that take about twenty minutes, thus differing from the quicker tempo at the premiere relatively little, this is the result of a very slow start (mm. 1–43, and similarly at the beginning of the development); at measure 44 (and in the development at the fugato, around m. 200) there is generally a distinct increase in tempo. Thus the horn passage at the beginning is hardly envisaged as Allegro, and what is the authentic basic tempo appears to be adopted for the flourishing string passage from m. 44 onward (it would be quite possible to discuss a formal argumentation in favor of this). Although this is no proof whatever that, at the premiere, the first movement was played more quickly from the beginning, the matter is worth considering. The model for the beginning and its historical background need bearing in mind here. The subsequent analysis of the movement will return to this point.

II

The four symphonies of Johannes Brahms are, like some of his other works, to be placed in pairs. Both external and internal factors support this. The dates of origin already reveal groups of two. As regards the First and Second Symphonies this was shown at the start; the Third and the Fourth were—after a symphonic rest—composed in similar proximity to each other between 1883 and 1884/1885. Regarding the mutual relationship of the first two symphonies Philipp Spitta remarked as long ago as 1892: "The first two symphonies form the imaginative contrast that is often noticeable in Brahms and must be regarded as a pair that has sprung up from the self-same, deeply hidden root" (Spitta 425).

Previous accounts of Brahms's symphonic music have accepted, and one-sidedly dwelt on, the contrast that Spitta mentions; as against this, however, it is worth pursuing his more far-reaching suggestion of a common "root" for these two so apparently antithetical works, which means first embarking on the interpretation of the Second Symphony from the way it followed the First, and hence from what was initially the same set of problems. And crucial to such an undertaking is an accurate reading of the First Symphony in terms of the history of ideas, a precise and concrete definition of its historical perspective. (The reader so inclined is asked to pursue this apparent detour over a number of pages.)

Symph. no. 1

Excursus: "Nature" versus "History"

The earliest reactions of Brahms's contemporaries to his First Symphony already underlined the point that its internal musical logic reflected a "course of ideas" (Robert Schumann's "Ideengang"), whose origins could, furthermore, be defined in terms of the history of the genre. Richard Pohl wrote, when reviewing the premiere, of the confident "feeling that underlying this is a quite definite logical train of thought, that a poetic content is finding musical expression," and the finale repeatedly reminded him of Beethoven's Ninth "not only in the tragic accents, but even in a melodically related principal idea. That Brahms," Pohl continued, "who has forged altogether the firmest direct link to Beethoven, would sympathetically tend that way in the symphony, too, was foreseeable; but which way he will now turn in his second symphony, which is sure to come, we are all the keener to find out after the impression his first one has made on us." Theodor Billroth also remarked at once that "the whole symphony is founded on a series of moods similar to Beethoven's Ninth." And for the music historian Friedrich Chrysander, to name a third witness (all the quotations are taken from G. Schubert, 194ff.), the "act of referring to Beethoven, the connection with the last, or Ninth, Symphony of that Master" was a conscious act on the part of the composer following in his footsteps. Chrysander saw the "art-historical significance" of Brahms's First Symphony as lying, from this angle, in a compositional-cum-aesthetic problem: "how to create a counterpart to the last sections of the Ninth Symphony which would achieve the same effect in nature and intensity, without resorting to song." The "return of the symphony that combines playing and singing to the purely instrumental symphony" is how Chrysander expresses the Brahms-Beethoven constellation in this work. The idea of a "counterpart" is fascinatingly accurate, but the merely internal-aesthetic concept of a "return" to the instrumental realm fails to reach the truth. Brahms wanted, and composed, more than that.

To begin with, this much is evident: Brahms in his First Symphony was taking up a Beethovenian matrix, that "plot archetype"[4] of nine-teenth-century symphonic music which might be paraphrased as the resolution of a conflict of ideas through an inner formal process aimed toward a liberating ending—in a nutshell, the "positive" overcoming of a "negative" principle. In his *Eroica* Symphony, and even more in the Fifth and Ninth, Beethoven was clearly composing models of a radical form of evolution, shaping the symphonic comprehension of time and the world as a concluding process in a way that made music history, more than any of his other innovations. Here two things need stressing: the individuality of the respective realizations of this formal model (the impression of a developmental form resulting from the encroachment on the theme in the first movement of the *Eroica;* that process driving through every movement of the Fifth, to the breakthrough in the finale's C major march; the layout of the closing movement of the Ninth as an act of elevation in music and the freedom text), and also the concrete historical meaning which this formal model is carrying. For Beethoven's symphonism is here dealing musically—and this can be stated irrespec-tive of the debate as to whether his music is described more adequately with Kantian or with Hegelian categories—with the great ideas of his age, which were heralded by the French Revolution. It communicates these ideas as aesthetic ones, presenting them in musical form. (Hegel states in his *Vorlesungen über die Geschichte der Philosophie* ["Lectures on the History of Philosophy," section 3, part 3] that in the philosophies of Kant, Fichte, and Schelling, "the Revolution [is] recorded and ex-pressed in the form of thought to which the mind has latterly progressed in Germany"; here I am adding, in an un-Hegelian way with regard to music, the form of artistic, musical thought.) And if Brahms took up this specific formal imprint in his First Symphony, that must also mean—however consciously—a coming to terms with the ideas sup-

---

4. An apt coinage by Anthony Newcomb (see the Bibliography). "Plot" is that prin-ciple which turns a mere succession of events into a narrative, a "story": "Plot . . . is the design and intention of narrative, what shapes a story and gives it a certain direction or intent of meaning" (Brooks xi).

porting it. Yet Brahms lived more than half a century later than
Beethoven. Is the subject of Brahms's symphony still the same as the
subject of Beethoven's Ninth? Certainly it is one taken from the same
dynamic century of the evolution of middle-class ideas. But, for all the
historical continuity at the end of that century, after the decades of res-
toration, and in a phase of conservative consolidation, can it still give
the same answers to presumably analogous questions? If Brahms's adoption of the symphonic formal model is taken as indicating the continuity *thesis*
of the problems, then the specific form and concrete meaning of the
individual work will be the decisive criterion for determining the place
within the history of ideas. In terms of our connection, it will suffice to
attempt a necessarily succinct account on the basis of an interpretation
of some musical data in the finale of the First Symphony.

The above finale has—with its bipartite slow introduction, seemingly
ambiguous and equivocal sonata form (with a rondo allusion at the start
of the development and a substituted principal theme in the reprise), its
coda stretta and two "external" interpolations in the reprise and coda—
a thoroughly unusual form. But it does actually make sense to speak of
sonata form: precisely the modification to the established model is an
example of "plotting," clarifying the movement's meaning and this symphony's "idea."

At its commencement the finale, like the trumpet fanfare at the start   *Finale*
of the finale to Beethoven's Ninth, takes up the initial conflict of the   *of*
entire symphony, clearly forming an arch with the first movement.   *Symph #1*
There, a slow introduction of gigantic dimensions sets the "negative
principle" in both tone and structure, and the extremely taut and skillful
main Allegro itself wages the conflict in the thematic discourse of intro-
ductory motto and principal theme. In the finale's great Adagio introduction, this conflict is presented at first by similar means (key, chromaticism, apparatus, timpani, expressive character), concentratedly
recalling and actualizing, as it were. In the process the motivic elements
prefigure the later Allegro theme, still tied in with the minor of the initial
situation. But in contrast to what happens in the first movement, this
"negative" setting is not treated anew in the Allegro section as well. Nor
does the main Allegro theme itself—like its model, the "Joy" melody

after the recitative in Beethoven's Ninth—appear as the end of a lightening process, as a resolution. Instead there already suddenly enters within the actual slow introduction, and thus ahead of the principal theme, something entirely different, an opposite world. The sphere of the diminished seventh chord is abruptly cut off, and over a fading drum-roll, reinterpreting the third in A-flat major on the low instruments, pure C major appears in the noble sound of the trombones, which are heard for the first time in the symphony at this point, along with string tremoli, the whole passage pianissimo—a completely new configuration, a previously unheard tone which, being so out of the ordinary, encases the central event of this focus of attraction: the great "alphorn" call on the first horn. (As early as September 12, 1868, Brahms had quoted it in a letter to Clara Schumann [Schumann/Brahms I, 597], with the underlying text: "Hoch auf'm Berg, tief im Tal, grüß ich dich viel tausend mal" ["High up on the mountain, deep in the valley, I send you many thousands of greetings"].) Though prepared motivically in the woodwinds in mm. 27/28, it seems like an epiphany in the context of the symphonic finale.

The horn call is followed by something which is equally novel in this work, a chorale-like passage intoned by the trombones now dominating the sonority, which Brahms had obviously saved to emphasize these two formal elements. Only now, after the formulation of the opposite world, does the main Allegro movement appear with its communal song theme in C major, in the rich, broadly flowing sound of the strings—that great melody which could be sung as a chorus and which points as clearly as a signpost to the "Joy" melody in the finale of Beethoven's Ninth, reproducing it down to details of syncopation and the one prominent interval of the sixth. The C major theme (as the counterpart to the initial motif in C minor at the start of the introduction) is therefore part of the overcoming of the conflict, which is presented as a key-conflict, already achieved with the horn call and the chorale; it is part of the positive opposite world. Within this world, on the new level, a new antithesis is now worked out. But by having the principal theme of his finale quote the melody from Beethoven's finale without giving it the same function, Brahms is indicating his altered standpoint.

Here a word is needed about the formal disposition of Brahms's finale. Its central Allegro (between the introduction and the stretta coda) has been occasionally interpreted—most recently by Giselher Schubert, pp. 234ff.—as being a sonata lacking a development section, and thus as tripartite in essence but bipartite in effect. Two seemingly "abnormal" elements obviously pose problems: in m. 186, following the exposition, the return of the principal theme in C major (which seems to militate against reading this as the start of the development), and in m. 285, the principal theme's absence (which seems to prevent one from reading this measure as the start of the recapitulation). The Allegro does in fact commence with an exposition which is orthodox even by classical standards: a fully-rounded principal theme in C major, stated twice (mm. 62ff., 78ff.) and followed by development-like passages (mm. 94ff.). The modulatory paragraph (mm. 114–118) is extremely concise and quotes the alphorn call, switching, as in the introduction, from flute to horn. Finally, there is an animato second theme (mm. 118ff.), lighter in character, and the tutti epilogue (mm. 148ff.). An exposition repeat is expressly not written down.

And here commences an ambiguous, yet unequivocal game with the formal conventions. Form becomes more and more the "representational means," as Schoenberg later put it with regard to tonality; form is "used" to state a meaning in notes.

Instead of modulating to the dominant, G major, the exposition ends in E minor (m. 183). Several measures with the head of the main theme follow, and the complete main theme reappears (m. 186)—in C major, as at the start of the exposition. From the direct evidence of the ear this could be taken for an exposition repeat. But such a view is belied first by the richer instrumentation (though in most performances, and especially the celebrated ones, the extra woodwind and timpani are almost completely covered by the dominant string sonority), and then, conclusively, by the thematic variation from m. 201. What follows is a veritable development. The appearance of the (almost) complete main theme in the fundamental C major key, though unusual at the start of a development section, is not unfamiliar in Brahms: in the finales of both his Second and his Third Symphony the development begins in a similar way. (The first movements of the first three symphonies still observe the *una/seconda-volta* repeat of the exposition; only the Fourth Symphony, with its passacaglia finale, transfers the formal principle of disguising the start of the development to the opening movement. Beethoven had prominently realized this ingenious playing on the listener's expectations at exactly the same place in the sonata structure as early as his Opus 59, No. 1, the first Rasumovsky Quartet, and this was indeed in the opening movement, which likewise does not prescribe or write out any repeat of the exposition. With Beethoven, however, the deception is revealed with a violent jolt after a mere four or five measures; his formal conception is essentially more dramatic.) If, then, the aural impression of a "repeat of the exposition" proves to be a deliberate trick in Brahms's case, there is still no mistaking the fact—eminently plausible for a final movement in the classical tradition—of a sonata form overlaid by a rondo element.[5] The repeat of the main theme at the start of the development, in the fundamental key of the movement, would correspond to the repeated ritornello A in a rondo. (This approximation to the rondo is interesting from the angle of the middle and late Brahms's comprehension of the sonata, his overall position in the history of the symphony, and above all the change this was possibly heralding in the function of the finale.) In the finale of Brahms's First Symphony, the above state of affairs does not jeopardize our reading the second section of the Allegro as, in principle, a development section. The start with the original main theme in C major seems designed above all to accommodate the particular "plotting" of the development, with its focus of attraction.

In this genuine development (which extends the development-like part of the exposition) the repeated main theme is, as Giselher Schubert has shown (p. 238), expressly brought closer and closer to the alphorn call by means of developing variation over a number of steps, and finally, at the development's climax in mm. 285ff., the theme is converted into the horn call (Example 1).

<hr>

5. Hence Donald Francis Tovey, with his invariably sure musical instinct, took up the allusion to rondo form at this moment in the finale: "as if the movement were, in spite of its elaboration, to be a rondo" (Tovey 198).

In terms of the construction and formal function as well as the historical meaning, this is an extraordinary moment. Although, in the process, the alphorn call appears above the fundamental note c, it does so at first (m. 285) in the diminished seventh chord, resolving toward A minor; only with the e in measure 287 is C major achieved, as a sixth-chord. The last motivic development proceeds parallel to this: the horn call begins in measure 285 with the notes of the minor third c–b–a, still concealing within it the c–b–c–a of the start of the principal theme, and the discarded motif's intermediate position between the principal theme and the call theme is made clear rhythmically; only in mm. 286–288, with the notes e–d–c–g, does the original motivic shape appear; the note e is used as a common axis. Thus within the actual focus of attraction the principal theme and the call theme are related to each other in the variants of the alphorn motif. At the same time, the bass line is permeated by an augmentation of the same procedure that serves as a groundwork, the rhythmic form being reminiscent of the opening bass figure in mm. 1–2 of the slow introduction. In the same context it is also revealing that the achieved alphorn call is heard on its original horn only from measure 289. At the actual focus of attraction the call—in both its motivic variants—is uttered by the first violins, the instruments of the principal theme which is expected but does not appear at this point.

This passage is not only the structural culmination of a purely thematic process. It marks the dynamic climax of the evolution of the entire form, and the alphorn call is sounded at the point where, as a result of the development, one expects the start of the recapitulation, and with it, in line with the orchestral climax, a powerful main theme heard in the full orchestra. The string tone and the first variant of the call are still distant reminders of this main theme, but instead of reappearing it is emphatically replaced. Here the alphorn call transcends an adaptation of a Beethovenian theme, quelling it, effacing it. And the result is that, in the coda stretta, where all the preparation (from mm. 367ff., on the lines of mm. 183/184, and with the start of the principal theme in the basses) leaves one expecting a third (or, including the possibility of measure 285, fourth), now triumphal appearance of this historically fraught theme, the adaptation is reduced to a simple intensifying figure (mm. 391ff.), and the chorale replaces it for good. Instead of the symphonic main theme it is thus the chorale, formally interpolated again, which becomes the hymnic highlight of the whole. And one important point: this double substitution with the alphorn call and chorale is highlighted audibly.

The symphony's emphatic chorale ending itself is prepared in more ways than one. First and foremost it is a quotation of the trombone chorale in the finale's slow introduction, where it similarly begins in A major, aiming for the subdominant of the C major cadence. But the chorale chanting and symbolism seem already prefigured in the first movement, in the hymnic accents of measures 232ff. in the development. Their melodic fall of a fifth, whereby the upper note is fringed with the sixth, suggests a deliberate echo of the calm after the storm toward the end of the fourth movement of Beethoven's *Pastoral* Symphony, where an analogous chorale-like passage (mm. 146ff.) prepares the "shepherds' song" in the finale. This has three perspectives. First, in the light of the two concluding movements of Beethoven's Sixth Symphony, Brahms's Second seems like a pastoral answer to the "stormy" tone of his First. In the second place, pastoral religiosity as a possible opposite symphonic world can be dated right back to Beethoven—a different Beethoven, to be sure, from the one who composed the historically fraught Ninth Symphony. And third, the hymn in both cases is instrumental communal song. So Chrysander's phrase about a "counterpart . . . without resorting to song," which for Richard Taruskin (p. 247) is "the most pointed critique of the Ninth," in the sense of an instrumental correcting of the aesthetically problematic vocal finale, falls somewhat short of the target. In his First Symphony at least, Brahms could not manage without alluding to the vocal collectivity.

  – In parentheses: the formal layout of Brahms's closing Allegro is, in this perspective, posited as being effectively tripartite. Crucial to this is the view that the focus of attraction in mm. 285ff. has the function and formal authority of a recapitulation as a felt event, and that to appraise the movement as being a sonata without development is a contradiction in itself. Arguments in favor of a bipartite layout are constituted by the C major theme at the start of the second paragraph, the way that the alphorn passages before the second subject correspond, which is to say in mm. 114ff. and 285ff. respectively, and the immediately following second theme. Then (as Giselher Schubert reckons) measures 186ff., taken in themselves and without proceeding from a development, would comprise a quasi-textbook start of a recapitulation with the main theme in C major; the ensuing development-like passages and the modulating alphorn quotation from the exposition would, in this "recapitulation," be extended into a large-scale development with its own internal climax; the second theme would follow in orthodox fashion again in mm. 302ff., and the epilogue would lead to the stretta coda. But such an attempt at a textbook integration would not do justice to the movement's musico-functional purpose and its perspective from the standpoint of meaning.

The deviations in the formal sections and above all their changes in function would be stronger and mightier than their orthodox links. In the tripartite interpretation, on the other hand, the "recapitulation" occurs where it is expected to, as the climax of a developmental evolution, but with the "event" of a thematic transformation and substitution. This important moment appears to be prepared twice over—first of all directly, through the thematic evolution, and also from a distance, through the two anticipations of the call motif in the exposition in the formally parallel places: before the second theme (mm. 114ff.) and, altogether abridged, before the main theme's second appearance (mm. 184–185). Nevertheless, the interpretation of the meaning and its historical exegesis do not depend on whether one decides to divide the movement into two sections or three. –

The two aspects that were discussed last—the strategy of a new theme to replace the symphonic main idea, and the instrumental realization of the vocal collectivity in the tutti close—indicate a connection but also a contrast with another source of inspiration for this C major finale: Schumann's Second Symphony, in C major. Brahms, as we know, thought particularly well of it. Historically and compositionally this is an extremely ambitious work with a complex network of relations, and in the final rondo-sonata movement the emphatic entry of a "new" (though repeatedly prepared) theme at that point in the form where the start of the recapitulation is expected particularly stands out. This was something Brahms could adopt as a formal idea. But in contrast to the effective breakthrough of the alphorn call in the Brahms finale, what appears in Schumann's, after the music has quieted down and after a number of general rests, is a lyrical song-like melody (mm. 280ff.) expressly played on solo instruments, and its closing confrontation and monumentalizing union with the entire symphony's fanfare motto (its Berliozian *idée fixe*, in the guise of a Haydnesque motif) makes a forcible impact. This was a striking, touching, and revealing attempt to blend the intimate lyricism of the Romantic song—Schumann's most personal domain—with the aesthetic requirements of the large-scale symphony. The idea, embodying as it does a central problem of the Romantic hierarchy of genres, could in its historical intermediate position have a

Schubertian inspiration, while altogether anticipating an important element in Mahler's symphonic music.[6] Brahms adopted the formal model
provided by Schumann, not the meaning contained by it. He introduced
in an analogous position the grand note, the collectivity. And within it,
he distanced himself from Beethoven through the meanings connoted
by the alphorn and the chorale. The lyrical nerve-center of Schumann's
finale, on the other hand, is of course a deliberate, and deliberately intimate, biographically transmitted Beethoven quotation, the "Nimm sie
hin denn, diese Lieder" from the song cycle *An die ferne Geliebte*—a
double homage, as in the *Fantasie* for piano, op. 17.

It is hardly to be supposed that Brahms's idea of replacing the principal theme of his finale was prompted directly by Berlioz. All the same,
with the benefit of hindsight one can, like Mark Evan Bonds,[7] point to
the parallel of *Harold in Italy,* this being a work that Brahms put on the
program in his last season as conductor of the concerts of the Vienna
Gesellschaft der Musikfreunde. The remarkable final movement begins,
of course, with a distinct reference to the finale of Beethoven's Ninth
and ends with a noisy brigands' march. The hero represented by the
viola vanishes utterly, perishes. Berlioz's plot for *Harold* can be compre-
hended as a challengingly anti-heroic correction of the Beethovenian

6. In the opening movement of Mahler's First Symphony, at the powerful "breakthrough" in the recapitulation, the song-like main theme—the Wayfarer's song—is replaced by the horn passage that first appears in the development after the reminiscence
of the slow introduction, and thus resembles a second exposition. So in this Mahler
symphony the horn call and chorale are allocated to the climaxes of the opening movement and finale (with Brahms it is the recapitulation and coda of the finale), the increasing bond between the two being indicated by similar "breakthrough" structures
before the climax of the movement. One is also readily reminded of Richard Strauss's
symphonic poem *Don Juan,* where Juan's second theme is substituted for the lyrical love-
theme in the recapitulation—a musical thought with (programmatic) connotations, similarly derived from the development and similarly entrusted to the horn.

7. See the Bibliography. Bonds is preparing a major publication on the symphonic
reception of Beethoven that will demonstrate the "misreading" (Harold Bloom) of
Beethoven in works by, among others, Mendelssohn *(Hymn of Praise),* Schumann
(Fourth Symphony), Brahms (First Symphony), and Mahler (Fourth Symphony) as well
as Berlioz.

archetype (Bonds, passim). The aesthetics underpinning such "negativity," which—in the spirit of the dawning modernist movement, *die Moderne*—set the grotesque and the ugly on a par, at the least, with the beautiful (Victor Hugo's writings are pertinent here), are, as Schumann's reaction already proves, foreign to the Viennese symphonic tradition before Mahler. Brahms's First Symphony—where, metaphorically speaking, Beethoven similarly vanishes in the end—is still wholly within the ambit of the heroic note, the theory of the sublime. It is set with Beethoven versus Beethoven, as criticism in the positive sense of the word.

Twice over in Brahms, then, the "Beethovenian" theme is substituted, repudiated in an eventful way. It never manages to develop a principal theme's recapitulatory function; and marking the finale's, and so the symphony's, climax is denied it. Other themes with other connotations, the alphorn call and the (Protestant) chorale, take its place. The alphorn call and chorale present an antithesis to the tragic note in the first movement and the introduction to the finale. Or to sum it up further: nature and religion intervene to resolve the dramatically sharpened conflict on a higher plane. But in contrast to what happens in the finale of Mahler's First Symphony, this new plane is not achieved in a sudden radical "breakthrough" but is set initially, in the slow introduction to the finale, as a positive counterpart alongside the stated antagonisms, and only then—and one more time, progressively recovered—as a result and an event.

Both the association with and the detachment from Beethoven can thus be understood as a deliberate and emphatic act. (One is almost tempted to say that Brahms's First Symphony was written as a musical essay on this tradition.) For all that the Brahmsian finale demonstratively copies Beethoven's Ninth with its principal theme and symphonic "plot," it distances itself from it no less tellingly. It is no cantata consisting of variations on the "Freude" melody, no musical discourse on the subject of freedom, but a movement whose objective is gained from suppressing the analogous principal theme, from concentrating on two formally and materially external elements whose expressive connotations are clear. Brahms's formal disposition has the likely subject of freedom withdrawing in the end, turning into a preliminary to the natural horn call; and the closing stretta is not, as it is in Beethoven, a final and most intense invocation of the idea of "Freude," of Joy, but the statement of a religious hymn.

To put the matter more simply (which must be permitted us here): it is no longer the humanist fervor of freedom and brotherliness but nature and religion that resolve the issue for Brahms. Beethoven at the beginning of the nineteenth century was concretely relating his symphonic music to history, shaping a program of ideas that had very precise structural analogies in the processual form of music and its drive toward a goal, as also in the explicit formulation of this goal itself. Beethoven's formal volition was finally aiming at change, reformulation, new foundation, even in the postulate of a utopia. Brahms in the end was relating the program of ideas in his—formally at first analogous—First Symphony to what was beyond history, unchanging, constant, essentially at rest: the nature-metaphor, the chorale. He was a contemporary of the late nineteenth century who had become a skeptic. And Brahms creatively expressed this at first with emphatic reference to Beethoven and eventually in an equally emphatic alienation from Beethoven.

To adopt the viewpoint and terminology of recent literary and art historians, Brahms's reception of Beethoven expresses an "anxiety of influence."[8] The First Symphony marks that point in Brahms's symphonic wrestling with the overly powerful model (Harold Bloom's "the

---

8. The following remarks refer primarily—in the context of recent methodological discussions on the foundation of reception research in music—to Harold Bloom's first and most influential book on this subject, *The Anxiety of Influence*. What seems particularly useful in our connection is Bloom's concept of "misreading" (though the term itself might be problematic), which describes the relation between the later artist and an apparently overpowering model as an act of self-liberation through "profiting" reinterpretation. The ability to "misread," to reformulate, distinguishes (in spite of all a successor's "anxieties") the independent, authentic artist from the epigone: "Poetic Influence—when it involves two strong, authentic poets—always proceeds by a misreading of the prior poet, an act of creative correction that is actually and necessarily a misinterpretation" (Bloom 30). The adoption of Bloom's illuminating idea need not involve his deconstructionist basic position. Here it is neither possible nor necessary to discuss that position.

strong poet") where, after working to a careful plan over several decades, he achieves and demonstrates a liberating self-detachment from his hopeless symphonic inheritance, which was littered with failures. By re-interpreting, by emphatically "misreading" the Beethovenian symphonic "plot," Brahms was clearing and paving the way for his own symphonic idiom. Thus the Second Symphony, after the First Symphony's act of liberation, begins at the point where the latter ended: with, as it were, the undisguised nature-metaphor; the symphony freely formulates what the First gained as a result and was pointing the way to. And yet it is only apparently free; the nature-melos of its beginning still has the Beet-hovenian background attached to it. So with Brahms there is no tri-umphant self-confirmation. Signs of the "anxiety of influence" linger on, and there is no chance of a great, emphatic fulfillment for this nine-teenth-century latecomer, either in the symphony or in other genres. The Second Symphony does indeed have a "black border" *(W)*. And a lyrical taking-back characterizes, in the end, the late works of Brahms. Harold Bloom has observed (p. 7) that the "anxiety of influence," the experience of being strongly influenced artistically, is a "variety of mel-ancholy." It is significant how frequently and earnestly Brahms himself applied this word to himself and his music. (Nietzsche, when he used it in polemics against Brahms, could hardly have suspected this.) Here melancholy signifies more than just a personal self-diagnosis, private and artistic. It is—as well as that—a historical signature. In the context of an interpretation of the Second Symphony the concept will, by virtue of analytical findings and documentary evidence, come into consideration again.

One sidelight to complement the remarks above: a quite similar "crit-ical" stance toward tradition on the composer's part can already be found in the early Brahms. The relationship of his Piano Sonata in C major, op. 1, to Beethoven's Opus 53 (the *Waldstein* Sonata) and Opus 106 (the *Hammerklavier*), to which it patently refers compositionally, similarly constitutes a positive association and, at the same time, a critical correction (see Brinkmann 1987, pp. 86–88). Again the reference to tra-dition is meshed with a critique of tradition. Incidentally, this is also the case with the early Eichendorff song "In der Fremde" from Brahms's

Opus 3, which expressly refers to the first song in Schumann's *Liederkreis*, op. 39. The version of the poem, the identical key of F-sharp minor and identical rhythmic-melodic model for the vocal line represent an adaptation on Brahms's part, while the style of writing and the type of song indicate a conscious distancing from the prototype.

There is a piece of evidence, on Brahms's part, which proves that such strategies of self-assertion were deliberate. Anna Ettlinger, the remarkable young woman from Karlsruhe who met Brahms at Hermann Levi's house between 1864 and 1872, recounts a revealing episode in her memoirs:

> Once, when I was talking about the song "Dunkel, wie dunkel" and said: "Yes, I now know how you went about composing the start of the song—you inverted the start of the *Appassionata*," he [Brahms] replied, smiling: "You've discovered my secret! That is what I have always done, I've always taken something of Beethoven's and inverted it." (Ettlinger 66)

Inverted Beethoven

Of course, this was primarily a reply, half-indulgent, half-mocking, to the naive supposition that the simple arpeggiated triads at the beginning of the song "Treue Liebe," op. 43, no. 1, were inconceivable without Beethoven's sonata. But, as always with Brahms's ironically defensive remarks, there is more to it than that. The generalizing and exaggerating, the "always done," "always taken something of Beethoven's," and especially the stress on the "inverting," are signs that this had touched a nerve in Brahms's self-understanding. Brahms, it seems, is trying to say (and one notices his enjoyment of this statement) that if he was following the path taken by Beethoven, he had turned him upside-down in the process. The "inversion" of Beethoven's Ninth: that is the intention of the finale to Brahms's First Symphony, and the musical image is also appropriate inasmuch as an inversion always preserves the relation to the original subject.

Brahms's First Symphony also proves to be a key work within the symphonic music of its time, in the context of the ideas of this late period of the symphony. It was a <u>nature-metaphor</u> that Mahler would take as the starting-point for his First Symphony (which transforms the opening

of one of Beethoven's symphonies, the Fourth, into the entrance of nature *[Natureingang]* and is explicitly headed "Like a sound of nature").
The same composer was to paraphrase the finale theme of Brahms's First
(and with it, the sphere of Beethoven's Ninth) at the beginning of his
Third Symphony, in a movement which Mahler characterized as "Pan
awakens" and "Summer marches in." Schoenberg's "Pan-icky" portrayal
of nature, as the inner form of his *Gurrelieder,* comes within the same
context. That the early Mahler, like Bruckner, employed the chorale as
a hymnic climax in the symphony, and much else, could also be mentioned at this point.

Mahler in this context posits "nature" as the aesthetic principle supporting his symphonic writing, and he expressly distances himself from
the mere realistic imitation of nature. In his letter of November 18, 1896,
to Richard Batka he writes: "I always feel it is curious that most people,
when speaking of 'nature,' are constantly thinking just of the flowers and
birds and scents of the forest, et cetera. The god Dionysos, the great Pan
are never acknowledged. So—you already have, there, a kind of program,
that is to say a sample of how I make music. It is always, everywhere,
just the sound of nature! It seems to me this was what Bülow once
described to me with the suggestive phrase 'symphonic problem' . . . But
now it is the world, nature as a whole which has, as it were, awakened
from inscrutable silence to sounding and tinkling." "Symphony" meant,
for the early Mahler, "using all the technical means at hand to build up
a world." This symphonic "world" is conceived of in the letter to Batka
as "nature," "nature as a whole"; thus a "sound of nature" is not the
imitation of a bird-call but the realization in sound of the "nature"
principle as a musical language, set down in the symphonic score.

All these musico-artistic invocations of nature and religion in the
second half of the century come within a larger context in the history of
ideas. "Nature," here, should be seen as offering an opposition; it denotes
an anti-historical, anti-civilizing force. In the process it is both external
nature, beautiful, grand, and unspoiled, and also a reference to man's
"inner" nature, his true self, visualized as being "natural" in origin. And
"nature" means the supposed unity of the two in distinction to the
developing particularity of the modern middle-class form of existence.

(Brahms's horn call seems a symbol, a realistic musical representation of this principle.) It is, first of all, a contrast to the predominance of "history," the optimistic definition of human subjectivity through autonomous historical thinking. What the first half of this "historical" century saw as the guarantor of a liberating knowledge was perceived during the second half as being dubious and indeed destructive in its consequences. Wilhelm Dilthey's summary, skeptical question of 1903 voices this profound uncertainty (behind the positive part of it there remains Kant's proud definition of the Enlightenment as "man's emergence from his self-incurred under-age state"): "A seemingly irreconcilable contradiction arises when historical awareness is pursued to its ultimate consequences. The finite character of every historical phenomenon ... and thus the relativity of every kind of human conception of the way things cohere is the last word in the historical world-view, with everything in a state of flux and nothing enduring ... The historical world-view is liberating the human spirit from the last chain that the natural sciences and philosophy have not yet severed—but what way is there of quelling that anarchy of beliefs which is threatening to break out?" (Dilthey 9).

The pessimistic attitude to the historical approach was, toward the end of the century, one element of the fear embracing all areas of life that "modern culture was heading for a profound crisis," a conviction held by "many thinkers and artists since at least 1870" (Iggers 168). Brahms's melancholy comment on the tragedy of a man who can do too much and knows too much, and who thus seems to be losing hold of the way things cohere, expresses the same experience, the same disquiet. And his symphonic answer with (to use a Nietzschean term) the "super-historical" forces of nature and religion as the supposed guarantors of coherence is a product of just this situation. The digression on "Melancholy" in the subsequent analysis will consider it with regard to Brahms from a different perspective.

Here one can touch upon the range of problems only as interpretive background. Out of the multitude of possible references for the dichotomy of history and nature, let a continuous tradition do service for the rest—a tradition which runs from Droysen via Burckhardt to

Nietzsche and which may be suspected of deriving its increasing skepticism toward history from the aggressive pessimism of Schopenhauer. In the positive, definitional meaning "nature" and "history" are presented as complementary "concepts by which the human mind grasps the world of appearances" in Johann Gustav Droysen's *Grundriß der Historik* (section 1). In Kant, and right through Goethe, they are understood as a priori forms of perception and stand for "space" and "time," accentuating coexistence, constancy in change, the figure of the circle on the one hand, and succession, the changing within constancy, development, and process, on the other. (I shall return to these categories below as generalizations of musical conditions as well.) In Jacob Burckhardt's *Reflections on History*, which are permeated by his distrust of an idealist philosophy of history, in the concept of his Basle lectures, history is understood as "the breach with nature caused by the awakening of consciousness" (p. 31). If the essence of history is "change," this has to be faced by working out "the *recurrent, constant,* and *typical* as echoing in us and intelligible through us" (p. 17). The beautiful, "exalted above time and its changes" (p. 21), is therefore superior to history: "Poetry achieves more for the knowledge of human nature (than history does)" (p. 65).

It was Friedrich Nietzsche, a pupil of Burckhardt's (he attended the latter's lectures in 1870, and both of them digested, with varying degrees of radicalism, Schopenhauer's vehement critique of history), who, in the critical diagnosis of his age contained in his second *Untimely Meditation* of 1873, entitled "Of the Usefulness and Drawback of History for Life," denounced the decadence of one-sidedly historical political thinking, the "excess" of history inspired by the historical school, that "hypertrophic virtue" in which the nineteenth century placed so much trust. As a remedy and compensation for the man "without myths" of his time, Nietzsche invoked—and this is a reflection of Jacob Burckhardt's ideas—what he called the "unhistorical" and "super-historical," those "powers which divert the attention away from Becoming toward what gives existence the character of the eternal and identical, toward art and religion" (section 10). ("To retranslate man into nature" is, in Nietzsche's late text *Beyond Good and Evil,* section 230, still regarded as "a strange and crazy task, but it is a *task.*") In the subsequent, third

Untimely Meditation entitled "Schopenhauer as Educator," art, in a way that recalls Goethe, is expressly invoked as a "rationalist" *(aufklärerisch)* means of "perfecting nature": "This is the basic thought of *culture,* insofar as the latter is able to present each one of us with just one task: *to promote the creation of the philosopher, the artist and the saint within us and without us and by this means to work at perfecting nature.* For just as nature needs the philosopher, so too it needs the artist, for a metaphysical purpose, namely its own self-enlightenment, so that eventually it will be confronted with a pure and finished creation, which is something it never gets to see clearly in the commotion of its Becoming—in other words, its self-knowledge" (from paragraph 5).[9]

Nietzsche's paradigm for this range of values in the realm of art, of music, was not of course Brahms but (still) Richard Wagner. Wagner in his post-1849 writings (thus after the collapse of the German Revolution) had renounced "history" (current affairs as well as the historical in general), at least in what he said. This happened chiefly in *A Communication to My Friends* of 1851, where it took the form of an artistic reorientation and prescriptive self-interpretation, with history and myth as avowed opposites, the former being renounced and only the latter being given a positive slant. (Wagner's projected Barbarossa drama and his realization of the *Siegfried* drama are cited as the two points of reference within his own oeuvre.) But Wagner had already (as in his poem *Die Not* of March 1849) introduced the concept of "nature" as an antithesis to the sociohistorical concept. Nature versus culture, nature versus civilization, nature versus history—this, coming now via Feuerbach's anthropology, is the ruling constellation in Wagner's post-revolutionary writings. It appears at the center of *Art and Revolution,* from the end of July 1849, and in the first chapter of *The Art-Work of the Future* of fall 1849: "When the

9. On the context of Nietzsche's views with regard to natural philosophy, compare Löwith, also Granier (see the Bibliography). William J. McGrath has argued convincingly that Nietzsche's invectives against the "liberal faith in history, progress, and justice" (p. 62) deeply affected the Pernersdorf circle around Lipiner and Kralik, to which the young Gustav Mahler belonged. On the connection of Nietzsche's nature postulate with the historical disposition to melancholy (and to the "idyll" principle) see Heller, pp. 82ff.

learned physician no longer has a remedy, we finally turn in our despair once more to—*nature*. Nature and nature alone can achieve even the unravelling of the great universal destiny . . . Nature, human nature will proclaim this law to those two sisters, culture and civilization: as long as I am contained within you, shall you live and prosper; but as long as I am not within you, shall you die and wither!" (R. Wagner III, 31).

Thus the Brahmsian solution or, rather, Brahms's nature-linked reformulation and redefinition of the symphonic form-and-content problem "after Beethoven" (and before Mahler) leads to some central themes of the late nineteenth century in German culture generally, to a fresh vision of the theme of the century. Thomas Mann in his novel *Doctor Faustus*, which, amid later omens of a historical catastrophe, sums up the development of the German middle class from the early nineteenth century on, has his composer Adrian Leverkühn demanding as a program the "taking back" of the Ninth Symphony. In music it was the skeptical Johannes Brahms who, toward the end of the century of the bourgeoisie, expressed this taking back as a composer through his serious modification to the symphonic archetype, realizing it to the full in the tragic note of the passacaglia in his Fourth Symphony. (From partially outside of the Viennese symphonic tradition, and influenced by Eugène Sue's Paris as well as the aesthetics of Victor Hugo, who set the grotesque on a par with the sublime, Berlioz doubtless went before him. The "negative" ecstasy of the divided finale to his *Symphonie fantastique* with its combination of the Dies irae and witches' dance—an ironic reflection on the double fugue in the finale of Beethoven's Ninth—was quite rightly interpreted by Robert Schumann as the burlesque signature of an era in disarray. *Harold in Italy* followed, as shown by Bonds, with a heavily anti-heroic, and that means anti-Beethovenian, plot.) But more will be said on this subject in the last chapter.

In this connection there is, once again, Richard Wagner to consider. The year 1876 saw the premiere of Brahms's First Symphony, whose form-process is channeled into a prominently featured nature-metaphor as the positive antithesis to the dramatic conflict of its beginning. And the same year saw the first Bayreuth Festival and the premiere of the complete *Ring* cycle, at the beginning of which a *principium ante prin-cipium,* a primordial start is set: the nature-metaphor of the flowing Rhine as the symbol of a world that is still undisturbed by conflicts. Both composers, Brahms along with Wagner, however far apart they may be in other respects, thus enter, from the viewpoint of the history of ideas, into a historical configuration. (And the fact that the Viennese premiere of the Second Symphony had to be postponed because the Philharmonic was too busy rehearsing *Rheingold* at the beginning of December 1877 is, as a historical gloss, almost ironic.) The two masterpieces deal musically with what most deeply affected the men and women of their age; they both bear witness to the same historical situation.

III

This brings us to the historical place of our Second Symphony (to which we are finally returning). It begins, as already mentioned, at that preg-nant point which the First Symphony had attained while grappling with and diverging from Beethoven's symphonic "plot archetype"—as a na-ture-metaphor.[10] The unmistakable "tone" at the very beginning defines this point:

- the horn sound, using the natural notes of the instrument to begin with, harmoniously alternating with a bright woodwind passage, the two underlaid by the drone of the string basses;
- simple, clearly articulated melody, with arpeggiated triads and dia-tonic steps in the upper voices, thirds and sixths;

---

10. The point that between the First and the Second Symphony there may also be a formal compositional caesura, and with it a "consolidation" of formal strategies, espe-cially in the internal weighting of sonata movements, has been recently made by James Webster, pp. 62f. The "ideological" symphonic finding-oneself (by grappling, above all, with Beethoven) would thus be matched by an aesthetic and compositional finding-oneself (preceded, says Webster, by "a convincing synthesis of Beethovenian, Schuber-tian, and more recent styles"). I was unable to make use, in the main text of this book, of the essays in the 1983 *Brahms Studies,* which only became available in 1991.

- "four-square" periods with correspondences between the rhythmic motifs, a vibrant oscillating rhythmicality about the lightly agitated 3/4 beat;
- sound, repose, balance, manifestly a world without conflicts. The Romantic nature-topos is patent.

(Antonín Dvořák's Sixth Symphony of 1880 is similarly in D major and clearly follows in Brahms's footsteps, but more brightly, almost unproblematically, with an allusion to Smetana's *Vltava* toward the end of the first movement, and with the same restlessness in the theme of the rondo finale, "Allegro con spirito," as in the fourth movement of Brahms's Second Symphony. It is revealing that the Dvořák D major Symphony, too, presents the pastoral life, "nature.")

And Brahms's contemporaries immediately heard and interpreted the music in this way: "Why, it is all blue sky, babbling of streams, sunshine and cool green shade!" *(M)*. Thus his "lovely monstrosity" seems, at first sight, to be liberated from that "symphonic" burden, that body of ideas from the start of the century that was governing the generic history of symphonic music. But while this symphony "liberatedly" represents Brahms's most personal position (as he himself was keen to suggest— see Kalbeck III, 175), it still presupposes a tradition, albeit a discarded one. It does not *arrive at* a contrary position, as the First Symphony does; it *is* a "counterpart" as a whole and from the beginning. (Here I am adopting Chrysander's concept in an expanded form.) And traces of that act of liberation are also plain to behold within it.

An early critique (*Neue Zeitschrift für Musik,* January 25, 1878) aptly applied the concept of the idyllic to the Second Symphony. But in constituting an idyllic-pastoral counterpart to the social character of Beethoven's Ninth, it is still at the same time a large-scale symphony. Hence one would have to call it a monumental idyll. To be sure, this concept of the idyllic will need corroborating from several viewpoints, both compositional and aesthetic-historical.

Let us now go on to discuss one particular aspect, an initial correction of the superficial picture. Kalbeck already raised the question (III, 213f.) of how to interpret an evident connection between the principal themes of Brahms's Second and Beethoven's *Eroica* Symphony. The similarity is indeed striking (far more so than the similarity Hanslick thought he could see between Brahms's Violin Concerto and the *Eroica*). It affects, in the same 3/4-time, the triadic arpeggiation as well as the rhythm, and it goes on for exactly as long as the unbroken diatonicism is uppermost in Beethoven, which is to say until the C-sharp encroaches on the thematic structure (Example 2).

The Brahmsian "nature" melos, which is disturbed by no such encroachment, is doubtless constructed periodically in units of four measures against the background of the Beethoven theme. But Brahms simply shifts the level of the thematic conflict from a direct, dramatic breaking-up to a structural conflict in a configuration (see the analysis of the theme below). Couldn't this, too, be called a "counterpart" (in miniature)? At all events the different thematic realization of a similar formal idea indicates a historical detachment within the same composing tradition: Beethoven's strikingly direct, head-on presentation as compared to the intricacy of the Brahmsian style, pensive and ambiguous. Now this would be an isolated link between the openings of the two symphonies, were it not for several other factors. One of these concerns a similar thematic link in the first movements. Both the rhythmic figuration and the character of two violin themes are closely related—in Brahms, a thematic shape in the fourth section of the exposition, and in Beethoven the third thematic idea of the main subject (or the second in the transitional group); in both movements sixteenth-notes are first arrived at here, with the increase in rhythmic intensity, although these figure the preceding eighth-note in Brahms, whereas they are part of the subsequent one in Beethoven (Example 3).

In both opening movements, these rhythmically analogous figurations of half/quarter-notes in the principal theme, on the one hand, and eighth/sixteenth-notes in the later violin motif, on the other, represent the angular points of the temporal movement which the 3/4-time comprises.

Equally important are some formal analogies between the two opening movements. At the start of the development, two passages of varying thematic character alternate in Beethoven, leading to a fugato: first motif *b* in the main subject (mm. 166ff.) is developed, then motif *a* (mm. 178ff., reinforced with motif *c*), and then motif *b* again (m. 220), and the fugato evolves out of this (mm. 236ff.). In Brahms, the thematic alternation and the placing of the fugato are similarly designed, within a smaller compass: the development begins with the first four-measure phrase of the main theme (on the horn), and the counter-phrase works up the quarter-note motif derived from the "motto" *x*. This is repeated, and with m. 197 the first stage of the intensifying fugato is arrived at.

Finally, in both symphonic movements the horn has a central function (Kalbeck already remarked on this). Among numerous complex illustrations of the point (Brahms: opening of the movement, start of the development and recapitulation, coda; Beethoven: end of the development, middle of the coda), let us just pick out the entry in the coda, which is of importance to a formal grasp of these two movements. In Beethoven, it is at the climax of the coda and of the whole movement (m. 631) that the horn presents for the first time the unbroken principal motif, heralding the goal of the process. In Brahms, the long horn solo provides a bridge to the end of the movement, with its flowing melody for strings (mm. 454ff.). This identifies the difference between them, the "processual" function of the active horn emerging more and more from the background in Beethoven, compared to the function of "architectonic" articulation in Brahms, where the contemplative horn color finally gives way to the string sound. (That Brahms's third movement—mm. 63ff.—also contains echoes of typical staccato gestures in the strings in the scherzo movement of the *Eroica*—the opening measures and so forth—is a point to be mentioned in passing.)

This relationship of the Brahms symphony to music history, again to the Beethoven tradition, though in a more discreet way, makes it clear that the natural note at the beginning of the work has, in fact, only the semblance of spontaneity. Even the nature-idyll is determined reflectively; there is, in Brahms, no naive immediacy that has escaped from the idea and obligation of history. The detailed analysis of the first movement which this prelude foreshadows will demonstrate that, even now, the degree of reflection has not yet by any means been described adequately. (From the viewpoint of the First Symphony, a thought can be inserted in anticipation at this juncture: whereas, in the slow introduction to the finale, Brahms's First confronts two principles with each other, its form achieving a positive triumph over this antagonism, the opening of Brahms's Second follows the opposite route from the pastoral note to its gradual clouding-over. The basic conflict appears afresh, albeit in a more relaxed and personal form, and less dramatically, less obviously weighed down with history.)

One could now go on to compare the Second Symphony's thematic framework and the types of movement with other works by Brahms. It could, for instance, be shown how thematic formations in the pastoral first movement, in particular, were taken up and altered, in their turn, in the Violin Concerto, op. 77, composed a year later—a work which, not fortuitously, is also in D major. Authors such as Hanslick (1886, pp. 265ff.), Kalbeck (III, 213ff.), and Floros (p. 203) have drawn attention to particular links of this kind. Kalbeck especially, prompted by Hanslick, has also seen Beethoven's *Eroica* as providing the background to both these works. Here one can only suggest the appeal of attempting to describe the Second Symphony—including both structural and functional aspects of its themes, and their importance to the tone and character—as the middle work in this chain of three. That the Violin Concerto is one step further removed from the *Eroica* (and the heroic spirit in general) than the symphony seems patent.

At this point, however, the question of tempo merits attention once more. If (as shown above) the motivic material and figurative rhythms of the Brahmsian main idea, on the one hand, and the subject's smallest rhythmic figure, on the other (bound up with further parallels), are concretely related to the motivic-rhythmic writing in the first movement of Beethoven's *Eroica,* then the problem of tempo will be posed from a fresh, historio-comparative standpoint. Beethoven's "Allegro con brio" movement of 1804 acquired the tempo marking of dotted half-note = 60 in 1817 (after Mälzel's invention of the metronome). Without discussing whether the age difference of a good twelve years in Beethoven could mean a slight shift in interpretation, and without even touching on the much debated general problem of the Beethoven metronome figures, one can still state the following: first, that the metronome markings concern the basic tempo, which is subject to occasional modification (rigid mathematical time-beating is not demanded); second, that the markings set an exceptionally fast (viewed in the light of today's practice) basic "con brio" tempo; and third, that they indicate the 3/4 downbeat as the envisaged movement's unit of measurement, and not the quarter-note.

In terms both of composition and of the history of ideas, Brahms's Beethoven reception was described above as being, in general, a modifying one, and this could also apply to the Second Symphony's tempo-range in its assumed relation to the *Eroica.* The Allegro heading is the same but changes from "con brio" into "non troppo": plainly the tempo is meant to be slower than in Beethoven. Thematic contours are taken over, and for Brahms, too, the downbeat sets the basic measurement, but the type of motion and movement seem transformed. This assuredly means a faster tempo for Brahms than is generally the custom today. But it is significant that, compared to Beethoven, Brahms "lacks" the animatedly pulsing eighth-notes as background accompaniment to the main theme: his type of movement, having been recast as a nature-topos, is conceived more as a flowing motion than as an energetic forward thrust.

– In parentheses, and linking up with the digression on the First Symphony, an idea with wider implications may be interpolated at this point. It seems useful, if not imperative, to regard the typical differences in movement and motion between the two symphonies of Beethoven and Brahms as representing a change in the historical situation. Beethoven's radical processual form, which aims at change, and at path-breaking reformulation, articulates a new experience of "time" within the aesthetic medium. A study of the history of knowledge by Wolf Lepenies has described the "end of natural history" and the "temporalization of all the hypotheses connected with the conception of the 'chain of beings'" as marking a basic transformation in European thought around 1800. Developing Arthur O. Lovejoy's reference to the "temporalizing of the chain of being," this account characterizes the "change from the eighteenth to the nineteenth century" by stating that "a growth in experience of previously unknown dimensions can only be worked up henceforth through temporalizing techniques" (Lepenies 1976, pp. 44, 121, and passim). The particular issue at stake here is the experience and understanding of "history as process," in contrast to the circular tradition of natural thought models. The "temporalization" of artistic structures and forms which is operative in the works of Beethoven's "new road," and which Lepenies only marginally touches upon (1976, p. 106), can be thought of (in turn following Hegel's proposed analogy between political and intellectual processes) in conjunction with that shatteringly new experience of historical "time" which Reinhart Koselleck has identified as the result of the epoch-making event of the French Revolution. "Since the second half of the eighteenth century there has been a growing number of signs pointing to the concept of a new time, in the emphatic sense of the term. Time is not just the form in which every history is acted out; time itself takes on a historical quality. It is no longer within time but through time that history is then accomplished. Time is made dynamic, a force of history itself" (Koselleck 321). Beethoven's aforementioned radicalizing of the principle of "form as process" shortly after 1800, first adumbrated by Carl Dahlhaus (1974), is, as an artistic strategy, the expression in musical language of this revolution in thinking. And after its partial realization at the start of the First Symphony and in Beethoven's Violin Sonata Opus 30, No. 2, the piano sonatas of Opus 31, and the *Eroica* Variations, op. 35, this principle gains the upper hand in the *Eroica* Symphony and sets about defining a new symphonic paradigm. If Brahms was decidedly modifying Beethoven, and his *Eroica* Symphony in particular, by projecting an entry of nature at the start of his Second Symphony and conjuring up, both in the sound and in the type of movement and motion, the "static," indeed "spatializing," natural idea of time, then this also signifies a skeptical reaction against the optimistic and utopian promise of that forward-looking, perspectivist idea of history which Beethoven's formal process implies. –

This has brought us back to Brahms's Second Symphony and Beethoven's *Eroica*. If, from the interpretive angle, one also takes seriously the form of a modifying compositional linkage with regard to the tempo, and if one takes the duration of the movements at the premiere of the Brahms symphony as tending to confirm this, one arrives at a basic tempo which is somewhere between the tempo of the *Eroica* Symphony (certainly the Brahms will be distinctly slower) and the currently accepted tempo (certainly faster than this). Beethoven's measurement is dotted half-note = 60, whereas the 19 minutes for the Brahms opening movement in 1877 (Hans Richter) amount to roughly dotted half-note = 38 (the many imponderables call for great caution!), while the approximately 17½ minutes taken by Mengelberg already come to about dotted half-note = 41. Hence a basic tempo of dotted half-note = 40 for the start of the movement would be something like the pace that would be in keeping both with a "modifying" Beethoven adaptation and with the verdict of the premiere, or with analysis and historical data. But the imprecise formulation of this paragraph is a pointer to the difficulties involved in a really exact definition.[11] Mengelberg's time of 17½ minutes

---

11. Christian M. Schmidt, with whom the present author had an opportunity to discuss his general views, made a case recently (see the Bibliography), starting out from the *Eroica* Symphony and insisting on a balance in the duration of the four movements, for dotted half-note = 50, and thus a total length of 14½ minutes for the first movement (with the exposition repeated). To be sure, Schmidt does not discuss the premiere data, neither does he cast doubt on the usual length of the second and fourth movements today, and—the decisive thing analytically—he does not incorporate the factural differences, the differences in the writing between the opening of the Beethoven movement

for the first movement, for instance, would give a basic tempo of dotted half-note = 41 (quarter-note = 123). In practice, however, the conductor starts the movement at quarter-note = 118–120, takes mm. 44ff. at roughly 146, is down to 120 for mm. 82ff. (second subject), speeds up somewhat with his 126 for the sixteenth-notes of mm. 127ff., adopts the same tempo at the start of the development, accelerates to 140 in the fugato, reverts to the initial tempo of 120 in the recapitulation, and performs the string theme in the coda (mm. 477ff.) more slowly than that, at 116. All the same, his average tempo is quicker overall, which roughly corresponds to the figures favored above, although the beginning could be played somewhat faster at the expense of the accelerando in the development.

Mengelberg's tempo modifications (which he shares, in principle, with most of his fellow conductors) land him, at one important point, in a dilemma which also affects the opening of the movement. If mm. 1ff. (compare Example 4) are taken at quarter-note = 118 and mm. 44ff. (compare Example 10) substantially faster at quarter-note = 144, then the start of the recapitulation, which combines the two passages simultaneously, will call for either a firm decision (in favor of 118 or 144) or a compromise (a medium tempo). Mengelberg takes the recapitulation initially at the slow pace he adopted for the start of the movement, rigorously fitting the eighth-theme from m. 44 to this standard and thereby relegating it to a wreath-like accessory. But also conceivable (and even sounder analytically) would be a balance between the two passages and hence an energetic formal concentration through the reprise. To be sure, this calls for approximately the same tempo for the main theme and its variant with eighth-notes in the exposition—a further argument in favor of an initial tempo that is quicker from the outset.

That the idea of a faster tempo changes one's view of the music and affects the analysis of it will be obvious. The horn writing at the beginning seems considerably leaner, more "classical"; in the development

---

and the Brahms movement. From the standpoint of these more complex considerations, his findings appear correct in their drift, but much too exaggerated.

section, certain passages (such as the E minor passage for trombones in mm. 224ff.) become considerably more drastic, more pointed; and the "sempre tranquillo" episode just before the end of the movement has less of a cozy Biedermeier sound to it. It is this view upon which the following analysis will be based.

Analysis

"The musical *strength of the ideas* in Brahms"

LUDWIG WITTGENSTEIN

Theme

The Second Symphony is—like Brahms's symphonic music in general—conceived thematically from the outset. The working with themes and thematic components (that is to say, phrases and motifs), the derivation, contrasting, and combination, spreads a network of relationships not only over the individual movement but across the entire work. Unity within the diversity of *Gestalten* (forms) communicating with one another is a central aesthetic category. The beginning of a movement, especially the beginning of the symphony, expounds the principal musical thoughts, setting a "theme" for the composition in both meanings of the word: as *Gestalt* (on whose elements the whole then lives), and as musical content (upon which the whole then discourses, the way one refers to a speech having a theme). Thus an anatomy of the thematic beginning of a symphony already identifies essential features of the whole work.

First Aspect: Unity in Diversity = 2 thematic procedures

The beginning of this movement (Example 4) is designed as a configuration (in contrast to Beethoven's *Eroica* Symphony, where one might speak of a constellation, for there an encroachment—which leaves an imprint—is made upon the conventional thematic *Gestalt*). Here, two elements enter into a special relationship, whose tension includes factors that divide and factors that unite.

In the string basses there begins a motif *x* which is expanded into a
four-measure phrase and repeated a number of times, a motif characterized by an oscillating semitonal turn to which a descending fourth is
appended. The motivic action fills the measure with three quarter-notes.
Above it, as though on a second level, there is a very clearly articulated
eight-measure phrase, the antecedent of a 16-measure period (although
this is enlarged at the end and remains open). The instrumentation
makes this construction transparent: it separates the horizontal levels
into strings and winds, and it differentiates the period through the
double sequence of horn and high woodwinds. The eight-measure unit
is divided into a phrase and counterphrase of four measures each, and
these in their turn are combinations of two-measure motivic groups; the
elementary units are, ultimately, single-measure motifs which either are
variously related to one another as a two-note sequence of half-note and
quarter-note (*m1 m2*),[12] or else already represent a variant of the three-
note bass motif *x*. The small-scale articulation (one tie per measure)
supports this disposition. The rhythmic alternation (*m/x*) and the motivic changes of direction (*m1/m2*) are attractively asymmetrical. The

12. In depicting motifs, variants are indicated by prime signs, inversions by open-top
brackets, as shown in Example 5.

changes of harmony inherent in the melody as such (I-- V I / I + V I V I) are not parallel either; it is noticeable that the phrase itself remains consistent tonally, and only at the beginning of the counterphrase is there a deviation from harmonic change with the measure. An interesting feature is the little line of development pursued by the bass motif *x* from measure 1 via 4 (inversion) to 6 (a single ascending line), which, if the bass is included, produces three different versions of motif *x* in measures 4/5/6 (Example 5).

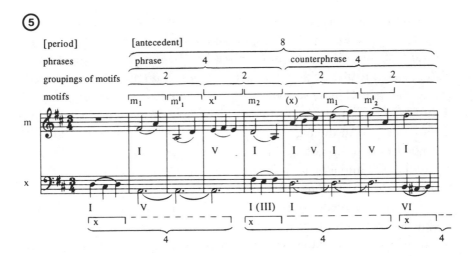

This is the initial material of the symphony, a small stock of basic elements and of larger components made up of these elements, and almost all the work's thematic formations are derived from them or set in relation to them.[13] The continuation of the main theme already shows one of the principles of this "thematic work": variational unfolding in direct succession (Example 6).

In measure 10 the first horn initially begins with the theme motivically

---

13. The following thematic analyses owe much to the analytical studies by Klein, Komma, Korte, Reti, Schachter, Toch, and Wörner (see the Bibliography). Although the present chapter will take these studies for granted, it will not adopt everything in them. And there is no question here of proving every analytical detail mentioned.

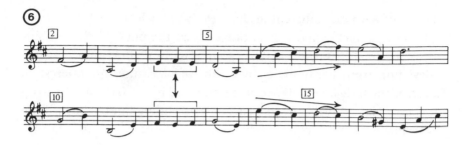

unchanged, but in E minor. In measure 12, however, the variant of *x* is inverted in relation to the analogous m. 4, and instead of the leading-upward of mm. 6/7, *x'*and *m1* are seen to be directed down in mm. 14/15 (there are also slight intervallic changes to *m1* and *m2*); more and more the quarter-note sequences of *x* take hold of the writing, and in mm. 19/20 the semitonal turn in *x* is lengthened rhythmically (making it more like *m*) in the high strings, before the action finishes oscillating for good in quarter-notes. This gradual and, as it were, vegetative conversion of the initial material is one way of meeting the classical aesthetic concept of diversity founded on unity.

Another way of doing so is the motivic relating of distant formal segments (paragraphs, movements) to the initial proposition—a technique which is used in this symphony particularly lavishly, in part overtly and in part more covertly. Example 7 illustrates how pregnant passages in all four movements originate in *x* and *m*. The terse, motto-like motif *x*, in particular, is involved in new thematic formulations. As a defining element the original pitch contour is retained in every instance (with or without the appended fourth, including inversions), while changes occur in the rhythm, character, and function.

First movement:

– In m. 66 (Example 13) a scherzo-like 6/8 version of the doubled motif (plus fourth) is placed against the beat; but, whereas in mm. 64/65 the harmonic change, sforzati, and phrasing clearly disrupt the triple time corresponding to the three-note motif, in m. 66 the double motif is accentuated differently internally through the beat: 𝄽𝅘𝅥𝅘𝅥𝅘𝅥 𝅘𝅥𝅘𝅥𝅘𝅥;

– the derivation of the energetic string figure in mm. 127ff. (Example 17)

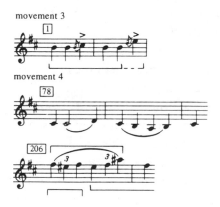

is, motivically, very similar, but the rhythmic version of *x* (here minus the fourth) conforms entirely to the quarter motion;

– at the end of the exposition (mm. 156ff.), the quotation of the second theme (strings) acquires a playful flute "counterpoint" in triplets which is obtained from *x,* and which has the inverted and normal forms of the motif tumbling over each other (something will be said later about this passage's metrical function and the upbeat in m. 155).

Third movement:
– Although somewhat more covert, the construction of the Ländler-like main theme in the third movement (Example 26) is still immediately perceptible, deriving as it does from the inversion of the basic motif *x* (plus fourth). The doubling of the first and third notes, the appoggiaturas, and the rethinking of meter and rhythm and of the articulation result in a completely new picture.

Fourth movement:
– This doubling of the first note is taken up in the sonorously swaying second theme of the last movement (mm. 78ff., Example 32); here the syncopation, different continuation (minus the fourth), and animated string sound set up a further change of character;
– finally, the triplet figuration in the "Tranquillo" section of the development (mm. 206ff., Example 34) also originates in *x* (minus the fourth). The relating ear might, as it becomes more and more alert to subtle connections, assume a linkage via the flute part at the end of the first-movement exposition (mm. 156ff.), especially as the "Tranquillo" episode also starts in the woodwinds with the flute dominant.

Harder to recognize are some repercussions of the *m* motifs which are also enumerated in Example 7. In the opening movement the derivation of the F-sharp minor second theme's accompanimental figure is immediately obvious; this figure emerges, a little beforehand, from the basses in m. 59, and it appears in m. 67 as a continuation of the scherzando theme, which derives from *x* (see Examples 13 and 14). On the other hand, it is only via an intermediate stage that one can see how the heavily dotted unison theme in mm. 118ff. (Example 16) refers backward. And although it is quite possible to explain the evolution of the one-measure motif *m1* in the second movement (mm. 33ff., Example 24), the tracing back of relationships to elementary intervals already marks the limit of what is analytically plausible.

More complicated, but quite recognizable as compound formations, are those themes which connect several starting-points. They are presented synoptically below (Example 8):
– the violin theme in m. 44 of the opening movement (Example 10 and third system in Example 8) builds the semitonal turn in *x* (here as a–g–

sharp–a) into its florid eighth-note figuration of the main theme *m*, and then adds a falling fourth in quarter-notes with d‴ as the top note;

– the main theme of the finale (Example 30 and second system of Example 8) is quite clearly an expanded and figured version, a "coloration" of *x* + *m* (conversely, one can also describe *x* + *m* as the hidden framework behind the finale's main theme). But at the same time it incorporates the aforesaid violin theme from m. 44 in the first movement (Example 10): rhythmically in the first measure, through the figuration in mm. 2/3, with the falling fourth starting from the same d‴ in mm. 4f.;

– the opening movement's second theme (mm. 82ff., Example 15 and fourth system in Example 8), while obviously deriving from *m* (the third in m. 2 and the third-filler a–b–c-sharp in m. 6), includes at the same pitch the *x*-turn a–g-sharp–a from m. 44 (Example 10) and also adopts the falling fourth from that measure;

– a correspondence is achieved between the second themes of the two outer movements (Examples 15 and 32, as well as the fourth and fifth systems of Example 8) not only through the sonorous strings in the same register—playing in thirds in the one case, sixths in the other; for in addition, the second theme of the finale (mm. 78ff.) is, in its second measure, a filling-up at the corresponding pitch of the "rolling" motion of the third in the opening movement's second theme (mm. 82/83); moreover, it was already shown how the second theme of the finale begins with a variant of *x*, following on from the main theme of the third movement (Example 26); its first two measures are, to conclude, clearly oriented rhythmically to the model of the main theme of the finale itself (system 2 in Example 8).

Of course all the reformulations that have been presented here become, in their turn, points of departure for further derivations and cross-connections. In Brahms's Second Symphony this is done with great refinement and consistency. If the two thematic procedures— local step-by-step change, and the global, "mirroring" setting of relationships—are viewed together from this perspective, one can readily see that there is scarcely a measure in the work which is not "thematic": everything appears reconciled to everything else. According to the postulates of classical German aesthetics, this formal principle of (to use Goethe's terminology) "metamorphosis" and "repeated mirroring" serves to give a large, multi-sectional composition an inner unity, while at the same time permitting a rich diversity of ideas and characters. It is the ability to combine the two that constitutes—within the realm of thematic composing—this symphony's particular aesthetic character.

At this point Schumann can be referred to again as a direct model. His D minor Symphony already takes the principle of thematic unity to extremes in a way that far exceeds Beethoven (the latter's Fifth Symphony, for instance), deriving all, or nearly all, its musical ideas from the one nucleus set at the beginning (and combining this with a multiplicity of other strategies for integration, such as a distinct reflection of Berlioz's *idée fixe*). Compared to that work's almost didactic-seeming insistence on unity, to be sure, Brahms appears more relaxed, less strained in his D major Symphony, especially in the final movement. Schumann's efforts, which are markedly increased in his work's second version of 1851, were devoted to producing a well-nigh seamlessly coherent whole—the instrumental masterpiece depending on itself, and thus "absolute." It is significant that the aged Brahms preferred the "lighter" first version of 1841: "The look of the first score has always delighted me. It is moreover a pleasure to see how ideas arrived at serenely and lightly are expressed just as lightly and naturally. It's the same—without pursuing the comparison—as with the G minor Symphony of Mozart . . . all quite self-evident and as though it couldn't ever be otherwise, nowhere a glaring color, nothing arbitrarily imposed, and so forth. Conversely, you always had the feeling with the second edition that the enjoyment is not so simple, that the eye and the ear must always be contradicting" (letter to Heinrich von Herzogenberg, October 1886, Letters II, 2, p. 127). For all his skill in thematic integration, Brahms in his D major Symphony still wanted to avoid any "arbitrarily imposed" straining for effect.

There are also other unifying elements with Brahms, such as the types ✗ of texture and voice-leading. The prominent sounds—which are also typically "Brahmsian" in other ways—are the parallel thirds and sixths, often specifically in the woodwinds. "Bohemian thirds" was Adorno's name for them, and the sound this name denotes is linked with a specific kind of "music-making" *(Musikantentum)*. This too begins at m. 6 in the main theme of the opening movement. Just a handful of examples: first movement, mm. 82ff., the second theme for strings; second movement, mm. 35ff., in the "grazioso" section; third movement, opening measures, again in the woodwinds; fourth movement, mm. 28/29 in the flutes, mm. 86ff. and 289ff. in the second theme, similar to the first movement in its sonorous string tone, mm. 206ff. as a characteristic of the "Tranquillo" episode, and finally from mm. 353ff., dictating the first section of the coda.

Second Aspect: Configuration = meter, phrase overlap.

At the beginning there is, as described, a thematic configuration. This concept borrowed from dramatic theory presupposes the independence of the "figures" that are coordinated with one another. The horn phrase *m* in the theme is designed to occupy four measures as a tonally self-contained phrase unit, while the bass motif *x* is made a four-measure unit by being lengthened. The two components are, however, combined in such a way as to produce a five-measure structure (an irregularity in terms of classical musical poetics). The dislocated overlaying gives rise, both harmonically and metrically, to a disagreement between the two components—the configuration sets up a tension, a conflict. (And the lengthening of x into a four-measure unit was undertaken for precisely this purpose.)[14]

The two figures differ in their internal construction; the basic shapes *(Gestalten)* seem, in this form, designed to contradict when heard simultaneously. The four-measure unit x in the bass consists of a one-measure skirting of the tonic keynote d by the leading-note, and of three measures of dominant foundation. The first two measures of m figure the tonic triad (from the third via repeated fifth—thus with a dominant tendency—to the keynote), the third measure of m turns toward the dominant, and the fourth measure restores the tonic. Hence in measure 2 of the compound structure, the dominant (in the bass) and tonic (in the upper part-writing) are superimposed. To put this another way: through the bass note a, the tonic entry of m is converted *(umfunktioniert)* into a dominant six-four chord. Its resolving of the suspension then also occurs in m. 4—in, so to speak, an irregular place for m. And the end-measure 5 of m is already the initial measure of the next component. A playing with ambiguities has begun.

This applies all the more to hypermetrical orders, that is, the metrical implications of groupings of measures. x, as the step opening up from the tonic to the dominant, is in itself downbeat, with a heavy first measure and a light second measure. m defines, in itself, the beginning of its tonic, which is measure 2, as heavy. Hence the configuration of the two again produces an ambiguity for m. 2: the light *(x)* and heavy *(m)* coincide. The full horn texture in m, to be sure, seems more lasting, and it gives the second measure *in toto* considerable weight. Hence m. 1 seems, after the event, metrically like a lighter upbeat. But a state of suspense remains—this is precisely what seems strained for. For once again, just as with the thematic work, this formal principle of the beginning is being developed locally and globally.

---

14. The topic of ambiguity as a formal principle of this symphony (and other nineteenth-century works) is discussed by Epstein (pp. 67–68, 162ff.), who has some very good observations to make. The structural configuration has already been interpreted (pp. 55f. above) as a transforming reaction to the beginning of the *Eroica* Symphony.

The motivic content, harmonic articulation, and hypermetrical placing of the figures bring about, against the background of the constant dislocation differential, an oscillating of the texture in the entire opening paragraph. This shows the configuration in a changing light. The motivic material and phrase structure of the two components generally remain the same, but the conflict-points in the overlaying process become different harmonically, intensive, to varying degrees. *x* is actually the dynamic component in the writing; wind phrase *m* maintains a harmonically self-contained I-- V I or II-- (V/II) II structure, this phrase being given new meaning by the changes to *x*, or following them. The modifications to intervallic steps within, and in the order of, the four *x* components already indicate this (counting in semitones):

⌐d a⌐	3↓	⌐f-sharp d⌐	3↓	⌐b e⌐	–	⌐e a⌐
5↓		4↓		6↓		6↓

There follows a brief description of the start and end of the respective overlappings.

mm. 1/2   *x:* leading-note turn around d with falling fourth, hence tonic-dominant. This means the layering of tonic *(m)* and dominant *(x)* in m. 2.

mm. 5/6   *x:* turn of major seconds around f-sharp with falling major third, hence tonic (third and keynote), but slightly tending toward the independence of f-sharp (mediant, third degree). This means the confirmation of the tonic close of *m* in measure 5, and the pure tonic in measure 6.

mm. 9/10   *x:* leading-note turn around b with rising fourth, hence clearly cadencing on the dominant (secondary dominant b with leading-note a-sharp to the supertonic E minor). As a result of this change the second measure of *x*, which is the E minor measure 10, now clearly becomes a strong measure; the relations in mm. 1/2 are reversed. This means that in measure 9, *m* is reconstrued as a false close toward B minor, and in measure 10 it follows the dominant process of *x*, sequencing toward E minor, with the harmonic-metric structure of *x* now reinforcing the entry of *m*.

mm. 13/14   *x:* leading-note turn again, this time around e with rising
            fourth, hence a dominant harmonic progression again (this
            time from the secondary dominant to the dominant). This
            means that the agreement of *m* and *x* in measure 13 is only
            ostensible, being differentiated with regard to function; *m*
            rounds off its subdominant E minor version to the relative
            tonic, and *x* is the dominant. The A major thus arrived at
            is then spun out on both levels.

Taking into account the internal points of conflict in the two components (for instance, the dominant A major over the tonic D major in m.
8, and the secondary dominant B major over the secondary tonic E minor
in m. 12), the result is a constant fluctuation of the harmonic and the
hypermetrical meanings. Though seemingly serene and confident, the
symphony begins in a surprisingly unstable, ambiguous fashion.

   This kind of playing with metrical meanings, undermining the hypermeter, and with contrasts between rhythmically or metrically differently formed units, both horizontal and vertical, governs the whole
symphony. It is continued above all in the various internal time divisions of the exposition and in the layerings and contrastings of the first-
movement development—whose form refers, moreover, at central
structural points, to changes in the initial model just described, providing signposts. It permeates the baffling ambiguity of the hypermeter
in the second movement, and it is exposed to view in the metrical
contradictions of dances in the third movement. The Second Symphony could be called Brahms's Art of Meter.

First Movement:
Allegro non troppo, 3/4, D major

The first Allegro uses—and this is axiomatic for Brahms—first-
movement sonata form. This states its relation to symphonic tradition,
the Viennese sonata "spirit" to which the movement is addressing itself,

and also sets forth the general layout, comprising an ①exposition with several themes, a functionally and structurally ②contrasted development, followed by a ③summarizing recapitulation (and also, in this symphony, a coda), but it tells one little about the movement's individuality. How the model for the movement is filled out, the concrete particularity of it against the given generality in the background, will now be described. ⎫ *outline* Five aspects will be highlighted in the process: the peculiar opening of the movement, the richness of themes and characters in the exposition with its internal shadings, the specific shaping of the development, two particular features of the recapitulation that diverge from a mere replica of the exposition, and finally the function of the coda with the emotional and structural goal of the movement, and the strangely restrained ending. This will entail a consideration of the formal idea of the whole, of the meaning and historical position of this music.

The Opening of the Movement

There are in every composition outstanding moments from which its individual character can be experienced and determined particularly well. In thematically conceived works of the tonal era, the beginning and ending are often productive starting-points for an interpretation; the way music begins (either starting off strongly, opening imperceptibly, gradually getting into its stride, or seeming just to carry on) and ends (closing firmly, running its course, stopping, or pointing to something beyond) is graphic evidence of its inner form. Both apply to the opening movement of Brahms's Second Symphony: it begins remarkably and it ends remarkably. The opening is in several stages, strangely hesitant at first, and only after an extremely dimmed low point does it start to unfold, as though from cessation, from immobility. And the end of the movement has a plagal tinge with its pronounced G minor, softly, in the penultima's low register. Effects as striking as these never happen by chance with Brahms.

At the start there is heard directly, with no introduction to frame it or lead into it, the aforesaid main theme pastorally swaying internally, a nature-image in notes (see Example 4).[15] It forms a quasi-period, and it is, from an instrumental angle, clearly articulated in the symmetrical four-measure changing of horns and woodwinds over the string bass line, but harmonically and metrically ambiguous, unstable from the beginning because of the overlaying of groups of measures in the thematic configuration. And what comes at the end of the upper-part unit of sixteen measures is not—as asserted by the transpositions of the constant bass model—the tonic D major rounding it off; instead the consequent opens to the dominant. But it engenders no cogent continuation into new spaces; it does not develop. Rather, the harmonic movement from m. 17 onward remains stationary on the level of the dominant. The architectonics of corresponding groups of measures are discontinued; the wind writing goes on fluctuating in the same way (mm. 19–21 = 17–18) over a long pedal-point a, eventually being widened from a quarter-pulse to a progression by the measure (mm. 20–23). Also in m. 17, with the entry of high strings into the sound, there is a coloristic announcement of the change in character. On the unstressed part of the measure, the first violins and violas enter as octaves in the background, at first (mm. 17–18) covertly and then (mm. 19–20) overtly syncopated. They detach themselves, in a high register with the lengthened motif x (mm. 19–21), from the receding winds and now, taking up the quarter-note motion, dominate the sound until they alone are left. There follows an even descent in arpeggiations of the A-major chord, and finally a persistent revolving in the middle and low register (with cellos instead of violas), diminuendo, contracting (m. 30), breaking off—which is certainly an astonishing thing to happen: the complete taking back of a symphonic first movement after a few measures. The beginning of the symphony trails off, comes almost to a halt before it can proceed to unfold.

15. Elmar Budde drew my attention to the main theme's typological affinity with a melody for the Catholic Marian hymn "Milde Königin gedenke" (melody by P. Alberik Zwyssig, composed 1841; see Wilhelm Bäumker, *Das katholische deutsche Kirchenlied in seinen Singweisen,* vol. 4, Freiburg im Breisgau, 1911, No. 260). The similarity of the melodic *gestus* is indeed striking. The character-type is that of the pastoral.

Measures 32ff., which fulfill these events, are crucial to an understanding of the work. Through their unmistakable tone, the mixture of harmonic and coloristic darkening at an early formal point of concentration, they impress themselves indelibly on the attentive ear, casting their shadow backward and forward across the whole movement.

Minimal changes to the string octaves announce this extraordinary moment through successive clouding-over. In m. 27 the cadentially established A major triad is transformed by the g into a chord of the seventh (compare the g-sharp in m. 22), in m. 30 F-sharp minor is heard, and in m. 31, where the music breaks off, there comes with a chromatic step the diminished triad b–d–f. By m. 32 the previously large-scale orchestral writing has contracted into the single note d (Example 9).

And it is precisely now that the emphatically new element appears: an isolated, muffled timpani roll, pianissimo, whose expressive connotation is directly communicated, followed by three somber chords in the low brass (three trombones, tuba). With slow, deliberate motion they slip, by the measure, from the widely spaced diminished seventh chord of g-sharp–d–f–b via the D minor six-four chord to the same diminished chord within a narrow compass, as though circling upon itself, in the grip of a quiet urgency. Imaginative listeners may perceive in the timpani roll of mm. 32ff. a distracted echo of the d–c-sharp–d in m. 1; David Lewin argues a case for regarding the tuba's subsequent g-sharp in m. 33 as the intermediate link between the d–(c-sharp)–d timpani roll and the a–g-sharp–a–d in mm. 40–44. And of course: in mm. 292–295, just before the recapitulation, there reappears on the low strings the constellation of d–c-sharp–d–g-sharp, grounding an intensified form of the violin theme from m. 44.

Max Kalbeck (pp. 172–173) saw in this passage starting at m. 33 the "key to the singular start of the Adagio," drawing a parallel technically with the "dialogue" of the outer parts, expressively with the "brooding" intonation. And from this premise regarding the start of the second movement, he related the First Symphony's slow introduction to this trombone passage. This product of sensitive rehearing deserves consideration, even if one does not go along with Kalbeck's subsequent speculation that the Adagio was originally intended for the First Symphony.

Trombones a/a 5th

The <u>entry of trombones</u>, the "principal of that family of wind instruments" which Berlioz (p. 302) described as "epic," is nearly always very
consciously calculated in nineteenth-century symphonic music, their
sound often being reserved for particular moments. One has only to
recall the way they appear for the first time in the finale of Beethoven's
Fifth Symphony and, as instruments of solemnity, serve to ground the
triumphal march. Or the way Schubert, in his "Great" C major Symphony, opens up to their echoing motif-call quite new effects into the
distance, and how, in that symphony as a whole, precisely the trombones
create the somber heart of the Romantic orchestral sound. Brahms similarly uses trombone color with great precision and subtlety. In the First
Symphony it first appears, as discussed earlier, in the introduction to the
finale, where it is a resoundingly positive rejoinder to the tragic accents
of the first movement, bound up with nature's summons and the style
of a chorale. But it is a completely different matter here in the Second.
Stamped by the expressive character of the diminished seventh chord
and by its status in the formal disposition (harmony, color, and texture
are mutually conditional in their meanings), the trombone and timpani
sound forms the somber antithesis to the idyllic nature-metaphor of the
beginning, realizing more directly, eventfully, what the structural configuration in that section was surreptitiously hinting at: an emphatic
questioning of the pastoral world, a firm denial of the possibility of pure
serenity. Moreover, in this work Brahms introduces the trombones conspicuously early on. It seems as though he wanted to make its dual
perspective clear from the outset.

Three times the four-measure sequence of kettledrum and low brass,
<u>pregnant with meaning</u>, rings out, impressing itself over a period of
twelve measures, and then a striking fresh start occurs. It appears at m.
44 (compare Examples 9 and 10) as a decided contrast to what went
directly before it, on every compositional level: florid string colors instead of the deep, somber brass; music in a major key, consonance,
brightness instead of the ponderous diminished chords; sprightly eighths
as the smallest rhythmic unit instead of soberly moving dotted half-
notes; pulsating accompanimental figures in the inner parts, overall
rhythmic concentration, forward movement, an upswing to the melodic

gestures instead of their previous slowing down, halting, a breaking off. But, just as with the introduction of the kettledrum and trombones, this complete renovation of the texture does not happen abruptly but is mediated by various means. The technique, which is very characteristic of Brahms, can be categorized with the concepts already used earlier: local, step-by-step change, and the establishing of a global, mirroring relationship.

Where the contrast is laid out within the local sphere, roughly between measures 32–48, three techniques are working in conjunction: the instrumental combining of both sides, the harmonic change in the three brass phrases themselves, and the motivic anticipation of the violin melody in m. 44.

At first it is hardly noticeable that the cellos are already doubling the tuba part in the four-part brass writing from m. 33, for here the deep string color is still almost wholly concealed. In the second group from m. 37 the texture is only three-part, with the tuba dropping out; the cellos, now heard together with the third trombone, come more to the fore. And in the third group, finally, the cellos are an independent part, first (m. 41) as the bass of only two trombones, and then in full four-part harmony as the harmonically characteristic seventh, g. And parallel to this, the kettledrum ceases rolling at its third appearance in m. 40 and blends with the double bass pizzicato at the dominant pitch a, which inaugurates the cadential formula. On the opposite side the trombone sound, now static, extends underneath the new string texture until m. 45. If the cellos become increasingly prominent after m. 33, and the strings are thus gaining in importance, the trombones are gradually withdrawing, until eventually (mm. 42–45) they are just background orchestral filling; their seeming approach to motif *m1* (mm. 44–45) disappears almost unnoticed, augmented and broken off, behind the violins dominating overhead.

The autograph shows that this is the result of a carefully considered working-out and correction. For, amid the heavy deletion in the fifth system from the top, it can be seen in mm. 33–35 that, *ante correcturam,* the first and second horns, also playing *piano,* were given the same notes as those which in the final version are played by the first and third

trombones. These two horn parts have been deleted. (In mm. 37–39 the
horns are resting from the outset.) Here it is not absolutely clear whether
the original horn parts were deleted either (1) before, or (2) when they
were replaced by trombones, or whether the two horns were doubling
the two trombones before the correction. Possibility (1) could be supported by the absence of horns in mm. 35–37. Possibility (2) is suggested
by the fact that the notes for the third trombone in the autograph have
obviously been written over rests, which means they were added in connection with the deletion of the horns. (The rests for the tuba in mm.
37–39 are also later additions.) All this fits in with a manifestly similar
process of correction in the low strings in the same passage. There, in
mm. 33–39, all six bass notes (g-sharp–a–b/b-flat–a–g-sharp) are written,
ante correcturam, in the double bass system, and a "col B[asso]" marking
in the cello system in m. 33 directs the cellos to double the basses; then
in m. 40, the pizzicato appears only in the cellos prior to the correction,
with a rest for the basses. This version has been revised instrumentally.
The "col B" marking in the cellos at m. 33 has been deleted, and so has
the pizzicato note a for the cellos in m. 40. Instead, the original double
bass system in mm. 33–40, the bottom part in the texture, is now assigned
to the cellos, and the lowest system on the page, which was originally
empty, is used between mm. 33–40 to accommodate the basses, which,
post correcturam, are resting in mm. 33–39 and take over the pizzicato a
in m. 40. Thus the reading of mm. 33–35, *ante correcturam*, would be a
repeatedly mixed four-part texture of three trombones, two horns, cellos,
and double basses, the first part being realized on the first trombone and
first horn, the second on the second trombone, the third on the second
horn, and the fourth part on the third trombone and low strings. The
bass tuba takes over, after the correction, the function of the double
basses, which are thus able to drop out; the third trombone is given the
second horn's sustained d. And in order to make the altered disposition
unmistakably clear, the new distribution of the low brass instruments is,
in the left-hand margin of this page of the autograph, expressly stated
once more. (The parallel passage in the recapitulation, at mm. 347ff., has
also had the instrumentation amended, and that could indicate a revision
date after the movement had been completely written down.) If one

regards the deletion of the horns (in connection with the low brass writing's filling-in) as pertinent and analogous to the reduction of the string basses, the trend toward developing a pure trombone(-tuba) sound is visible overall. (The Brahms letter to be quoted later, with the stress it places on the trombones, points in the same direction.) The effect of this sound as a somber contrast is vigorously developed at its first entry and can then be modified step by step.

Parallel to this there is the harmonic transformation in the brass writing. In mm. 34–36 the four-part diminished seventh chord with the contrary motion in the outer voices seems to revolve back on itself; no resolution appears urgently expected. (Functionally one can posit a shortened ninth chord of the dominant-of-the-dominant.) In mm. 37–39 there appear three chromatically downward gliding triads with functional gradation and cadential tendency (minor subdominant, dominant six-four chord, incomplete dominant-of-the-dominant). Finally, in the third group (mm. 41ff.), after the kettledrum/bass process and with the cello part given independence, the purely dominant cadence follows. Overall, therefore, a step-wise transition of the three chordal groups into the D major diatonicism has clearly been composed, a preparation for the change in the writing.

The most distinct agent and herald of the contrast is the motivic anticipation in each of the last measures of the kettledrum/trombone groups. Here (m. 35, m. 39), with varying instrumentation, register, and pitch, the motto-like bass motif *x* from the beginning of the symphony is blended in. Its breaking-off gestures at the end of the phrase and, ultimately, its warm-up broadening in mm. 42–43—where it is now already dominating the trombone sound—are advance signs of the fresh start in m. 44. There the motif, again as an a–g-sharp–a, is integrated into the first portion of the violin melody. Thus measure 44, viewed in direct succession, appears a contrast as much as a goal.

(This, too, is the product of second thoughts, of a correction. For the three trombones were extending in the autograph beyond m. 45, as far as the first quarter in m. 48; parallel to the bassoons, but richer in motion, they filled in the background sonority. This was deleted by Brahms. He reserves the trombone tone for the great, telling moment and therefore keeps the intermediate passage as brief as possible. Thus the sound of high violins extinguishes the somber trombone sound, swallowing it up.)

The motivic anticipation affects, too, the further formal procedure. It can basically be described as a mirroring and intensification. The violin theme in m. 44 recalls, via the anticipations in mm. 42–43, m. 39, and m. 35, motivically *(x)* and in terms of instrumentation the first violin entry in mm. 19–21, and this curve goes on arching back to m. 1. For as a compound thematic structure (compare the commentary to Example 8) and in its formal function, the fresh start in m. 44 seems a heightening, an intensification of the beginning of the symphony. Motivic elements *m* and *x*, which at that stage were in separate configurations, are now combined in varied form, and the quarter-pulse of the start is shortened to eighths. After the low point represented by the trombone measures, activity in the texture begins afresh, and it does so in a simplified meter (without the stratifications of groups of beats), the eighth-notes making it sprightlier, freer, as though taking new breath.

– This is the time, in parentheses, to avert a misunderstanding. When the opening of the movement is described in these pages as an active process, using such words as "slowing down," "halting," or "livelier," "sprightlier," this does not mean the tempo and not, therefore, a ritardando or accelerando. Instead one is dealing with decelerations that are caused by textural patterns, and that are already written out, as also with accelerations that are similarly written out. The kettledrum-trombone episode, for instance, does not call for a slower tempo, since by dint of the one beat per measure instead of a quarter-pulse it is already "slower" in itself; the reverse applies to the eighth-notes from m. 44 onward. The basic tempo is unchanged; the nuances have been written into this tempo, and the interpretation has only to make them graphic, not to create them. –

– And similarly in parentheses, although this is important to the conscious realization of the analysis, a word about the method seems appropriate. The categories used in the analysis—polarity, intensification, mirroring, metamorphosis, pregnant moment, unity in diversity, and so forth—are derived from the aesthetics of German classicism around 1800, or, to be more precise, the conceptual framework of Goethe's writings on art and the natural sciences. This does not happen arbitrarily, nor is it a mere whim on the author's part (although he by no means denies an affinity with these categories and their form-theoretical hypotheses as tools in the analysis of Viennese "classical" music from Beethoven to Schoenberg). There is an objective reason for it. For a study of Brahms's musical thinking in general, and also analyses of his works when seen in the light of their aesthetic premises, will show that he remained particularly committed, in principle, to the work-concepts of German idealism and German (literary and musical) classicism respectively.[16] Brahms consciously placed his art within that tradition; in that sense he was a classicist. Now for the analyzing interpreter, Goethe's organicism seems to be particularly close to Brahms. Brahms's poetics do not recognize the dialectical leap as a formal category, or the radical reversal, or unmediated irruptions or outbursts. With him it was a matter of joining opposites through progressive, quasi-logical changes, universal mediation of even the most extreme contrast. Brahms's symphonic music opens up no abyss in the way Schubert's "Unfinished" does with that tremendous general rest in m. 62 of the opening movement, after the strings have abruptly broken off their lyrical singing, or in the way Schubert's "Great" C major Symphony does with the irruption in m. 250 of its second movement. Instead it conceals the unfathomable as the subterranean dimension of a seemingly secure composition, shaping it cryptically as a structural shift or disruption, camouflaging the breaks through all-around construction. –

Precisely the opening of the Second Symphony is an example of this. On the one hand the seemingly clear surface layout of the main theme is challenged, at a deeper level, by the aforesaid metrical and harmonic ambiguity. On the other, the music moves via a series of steps from the initial setting to the opposite pole (mm. 32ff.) in terms of emotion and

16. Brahms owned a copy of Georg Brandes's *Die Literatur des neunzehnten Jahrhunderts in ihren Hauptströmungen*, vol. 1 (Leipzig, 1882). He marked the following sentence: "Considered aesthetically, a book as a work of art is a totality, existing for itself, detached from all relations to the exterior world; it has its center within itself" (see Hofmann, p. 15).

musical language, and then the pendulum swings back to the starting-point (mm. 44ff.), now varied and intensified. The idea of polarity and heightening, the formal figure of the spiral are patent. And to go with the ostensibly organic joining of opposites there is the intricate mirror-relationship of prominent moments. The horn color at the beginning and the brass sound in mm. 32ff., for example, connect opposite poles, while the string tone in m. 44 and high violins in mm. 19–21 enter into a relation reinforcing motivic similarities; thematic material in mm. 1ff. and 44ff. is similar, but the texture and color (winds in the one case, strings in the other) are different. The opening section up to m. 44 traces a falling, renunciatory formal curve, the animation peters out, the construction strings phrases together; whereas after m. 44—the goal of the cadencing (Schachter 56) and parallel fresh start at, so to speak, a higher stage—the writing opens up, animation starts pulling, the construction develops the material. It will prove to be the case that such techniques of varying mirroring on different levels and the idea of a spiral tendency in the form, discernible at salient moments, apply to the whole first movement.

Exposition (mm. 1–183)

The unfolding of a movement in several stages, with the animation ebbing away right after the start, is not unusual for Brahms. Late Brahms in particular offers this kind of restrained opening. A good comparative example is the first movement of the Clarinet Quintet in B minor, op. 115, of 1891. There the layout is basically similar, albeit more constricted and small-scale than in the symphony on the one hand, and going farther on the other. The movement begins with a twofold motivic constellation in the strings, constantly descending, which after only four measures trails off in low register. Then the piece starts off afresh in m. 5 with the flowering of the clarinet sound, the new color that changes everything: an effect very like measure 44 in the symphony. But, unlike what happens in the symphony, this impulse too ebbs away, subsiding after just nine measures into the low clarinet register. In m. 14 there is a third beginning with the initial motif, which now manages to develop into a thematic contour, but again loses its forward impulse after only four measures. And the same thing happens, after an extended fading-away, to the repeat of the four-measure phrase from m. 18 onward, with its heightened density and register: here the writing at last seems developed thematically and in sonority, and yet it comes to a standstill in m. 24, where it peters out. A movement-opening made up of the taking back of short upswings, characterized both by the falling gestus of the motifs themselves and by the descending successions of them. Related to different stages of this opening split by caesuras, through the aforementioned technique of reciprocal mirroring, are some central points of articulation in the first movement, as well as the conclusion of the final movement. Thus the repeat of the exposition begins not with m. 1 but with the big clarinet moment in m. 5, whereas the recapitulation takes up measures 1 and 14 again. And finally, the end of the last movement, the close of the entire quintet quotes the motivic constellation from the beginning of the work and concentrates on that passage's falling gestures. This is what characterizes the formal attitude of the quintet overall—the idea of finishing, subsiding, as the gestus from the outset, the leading idea. Not so in the Second Symphony. There the taking back is only one side of the polar starting situation, not a principle of the whole. (It is tempting at this point to examine in some detail the subsiding close of the Third Symphony as it fades away, and its relation to the main theme of the first movement, but this is beyond the scope of the present study.)

The way the exposition opens, which is altogether remarkable for a symphonic work, has been repeatedly interpreted as an introduction in the literature on Brahms's Second Symphony; the "actual" beginning of the movement and indeed the main theme are then put at m. 44. And this argument has some structural and formal-gestural points in its favor. Particularly to be commended is Schachter's insight (see the Bibliography), derived primarily from an analysis of the harmonic disposition, that the measures prior to m. 44 should be regarded as one great upbeat up to the animated, animating D major entry of the violin theme. But from the standpoint of the analysis put forth in these pages, that one-sided view ignores the overriding formal idea. For in the first place, the initial measures state the basic material of the complete symphony, both motivically and structurally. Second, the formal meaning of mm. 44ff. is only comprehensible as a heightening in relation to mm. 1ff., taking these as the first setting. Third, the recapitulation and coda are, within the whole movement's mirror disposition, related on the large scale to mm. 1ff. as the starting-point (the recapitulation combines m. 44 with m. 1, thus confirming the analogy between them). And fourth, the symphony's central polarity—the idyll and its antithesis—is already introduced in the first forty-three measures. The opening is not something that precedes the "actual" events of the symphony but a distillation of the symphonic meaning; it is a first "exposition." Thus the traditional repeat of the exposition section also begins with m. 1 and not, as would correspond to the Clarinet Quintet, with m. 44. What we are experiencing musically is, as so often with Brahms, the deliberate dual function or, indeed, the ambiguity of formal sections: a wealth of perspectives realized with compositional sophistication. (A similar symphonic opening, apparently starting off rather slowly, was composed by Dvořák in his Symphony No. 8, in G major; the formal idea has all the signs of being influenced by Brahms, although it is simpler and consistently direct. For that reason the compositional model of the hesitant symphonic beginning can, in Dvořák's case, also become the fortissimo climax in the recapitulation.)

Internal caesuras of varying weight divide this exposition. In terms of musical content, and against the background of traditional sonata procedures, five main paragraphs can be discerned, each of which has its own secondary caesuras. The opening section has been described in detail because it sets the basic pattern for the work and its analysis. The four additional paragraphs will now be explained more briskly, as concisely as possible and yet in the detail that is needed to understand their character and their function.[17] The methods and categories developed so far can now be applied without further ado.

17. The temptation to examine all the subtleties and refinements of Brahms's compositional technique is especially strong with the Second Symphony, where the construction is particularly sophisticated. But the purpose and scope of this book prevent it. After being introduced to the principal compositional ideas and techniques, the reader eager to know more must be left to his own further thoughts and discoveries in the case of

Mm. 44–81(82): Fresh Beginning, Transition

The entry of an intensifying variant of the main theme with its D major tonic (Example 10)—the first outright D major in the movement—indicates a reopening on a new level (compare the commentary to Example 9). Technically, however, the paragraph more and more acquires the

character, to be expected at this point, of a transition in the normal sense of a sonata exposition. The abbreviation of phrases, splittings-off, metrical shifts, imitation and stretto, dynamic intensification with harmonic sharpening and broadening, along with the expansion of the orchestral

---

many passages. It always takes patience to follow a written analysis, and here the reader's patience will probably be taxed enough already.

apparatus and tonal scope, are the technical features of this. Yet there is no real modulation to the key of the dominant, for the A major at mm. 52ff. only tends to the dominant, and what emerges as the goal of the developing process is not a second theme but, in m. 66, a scherzando episode in F-sharp minor (see Example 13), which is inserted into the process and here seems rather incidental. (Its meaning and significance will only be revealed right at the end of the movement, when it is taken up again in the coda.) Finally, at m. 78, a chromatically sliding chord sequence in the orchestral string quartet ushers in the paragraph that can be described as the second subject. It is, like the scherzando, in F-sharp minor.

Some points of detail. The new old theme in mm. 44ff. is, in the terminology of musical syntax, a *Satz* ("sentence"). The work's initial "period" uses four-measure units to build four-square, so to speak, while the "sentence" here develops, qualitatively and quantitatively. At first the parallels with the construction of the main theme are obvious, and they go beyond the motivic relation already demonstrated. In both cases there is the opening toward the A major dominant, now quicker (end of the counter-phrase, m. 52) than in the main theme (end of the consequent, m. 17); in the analogous place in m. 52, the first violins play the first motif of the e''' (as a fifth) on which, significantly, they first entered the music in mm. 17–19. But after m. 52 the difference in the "sentence" becomes apparent.

This concise paragraph amounts to a model of a Brahmsian design for intensification and will therefore be described in more detail. It begins with five-measure phrases that, by interlocking, produce four-measure units (mm. 44–48/48–52). After m. 52, which is the pivotal point of the evolution, the phrases are shortened to three-measure units that—overlapping once again—follow one another two measures apart (mm. 52–54/54–56). Both times, the phrase and counter-phrase are distinguished instrumentally (strings/woodwinds). Imitational entries (second violins at m. 53, basses m. 55) give rise, within the double-measure organization, to one-measure series of impulses. In m. 56 the phrase-lengths shrink to 2/4 units that disrupt the beat with a hemiola. In the end there remain, at mm. 57–58, figures of only one quarter in length.

The background to this development is a process of motivic splitting-
off and compression. In mm. 52–54 (first violins) the front part of the
theme is isolated and compressed into three quarters immediately after-
ward (the dotting is omitted) (Example 11). This produces the irregular

three-measure unit. In m. 56 (violins, basses) the front of the theme
shrinks once again; motif *x* is omitted, and only the falling 4/8 figure
remains. And at the end of the motivic shortening (mm. 57–58), nothing
but the simple third moving downward is left; the five-measure phrase
has turned into a 2/8 figure, a motivic remnant that is scarcely perceptible
as such any longer. Together, the two features of the music's evolution—
the principles of shortening and condensation—produce a written-in
acceleration (five-measure phrases that are four measures apart, then
three-measure phrases coming every two measures, with imitations inserted one measure apart, finally two quarters and one quarter), and also
a stronger and stronger motivic penetration of the texture (the filler-
parts so characteristic of the initial sound of this paragraph either dis-
appear or, from m. 54, set accents that are sharpened by syncopation).

Condensation is followed by strong-arm methods. The complete process has already been helped along by a heightening of the apparatus and
dynamics. Now at the point where the motivic contours vanish as a result
of the splittings-off, the writing changes in character. Nearly all the parts
are combined in a vigorously summational unison—to be more precise,
in octave passages (a compositional device which Handel and Beethoven
had already used to captivating effect), descending via three fifth-
intervals in the end (mm. 57–58, b–e–a–d). At the same time the dynamics have swelled to *forte*. This leaves its mark on the next segment,
which is given the appearance of a firm new platform within the transition by the clear-cut two-measure units and the taut rhythms. It is

permeated by the strongly assertive motif *x*, which is heard here complete (with fourth) in the manner of a developmental model and dominates the scene for the first time. A characteristic touch is the dissonant intensifying of each second measure (m. 60, m. 62) with sharply accentuated diminished seventh chords; here the chromatic continuation of the E minor after m. 61, and the unexpected conversion of the motivic bass note b in m. 62 into the seventh of an incomplete ninth chord over c-sharp, are particularly crucial to the harmonic construction.

So after condensation, acceleration, and drastic simplification, one now has harmonic tension, which is followed eventually (m. 64) by overt metrical complication. This affects the division of the triple meter. The configuration of the main theme has brought about a metrically ambiguous compositional structure, and the transition's motivic shortening in m. 56 has resulted in the hemiolic modifying of the measure with its range of accents (which, from the entry of motif *x* on the border between mm. 58–59, has to be offset by lengthening to restore the balance); now for two measures (mm. 64–65), the 3/4 pulse turns into a 6/8 pulse. Motif *x* is halved rhythmically in direct succession (Example 12), basses and subsidiary parts articulate the motivic unit of three eighths, and sforzati support this. In this way the 3/4-time is "irregularly" divided into two, the metrical pulse changed. (It is a formal function of this passage briefly to anticipate, in the exposition, principles of the development.) Of course this seems a speeding-up in relation to m. 63, but with the brakes applied. And the relation of meter to measure is also affected. The tendency toward a weak-strong sequence of measures (mm. 59–64) becomes a distinct upbeat tendency in the individual measures (mm. 65–66).

The result of this purposeful procedure in several stages from m. 44 onward might have been the appearance, at this point, of a second theme, perhaps a melody giving vent to lyrical song after the tersely dissonant intensification from m. 59 onward. A contrast does in fact appear at m. 66, but one of the scherzando type (Example 13), characterized by light staccati (see the commentary to Example 7 on the derivation). Basically this is the same procedure as in the opening of the movement. There, it was the somber contrast that was interpolated, whereas here it is a bright contrast. (This is "interpolation" in relation to conventional sonata form.)

– A note on polarity, in parentheses. The scherzando episode is, from the viewpoint of motivic content, identical with the two 6/8 measures that precede it; in character it is their opposite, so that overall it is like the other side of the coin—the same thing, but seen from a different angle. –

To satisfy the turn to the interdominant region of C-sharp major (m. 62), the scherzando starts off in F-sharp minor and is thus more restrained than it could be. An interesting detail (and typical of Brahms) is his fresh variant on the metrical gradation of measures. The first measure of the scherzando (m. 66) is, in the motivic upper part, identical with mm. 64 and 65. But since the 3/8 phrasing and the half-measure accent are absent, the 3/4 gradation comes back stealthily into its own.

And at least by the time of the characteristic, quasi-upbeat grace-note figure in m. 67 (top note = metrically heavy), three beats to the measure are restored. Hence the twofold motif *x* in measures 66, 68, and 70 (especially the last two) is stressed in the face of the motivic structure. The beat is placed counter to the repeated motif. Syntactically the scherzando paragraph is a transitory episode, part of the bridge passage. Two-measure "setting-up" phrases without answering counter-phrases are strung together in a downward sequence (mm. 66–71), all of them being opening theses without closing antitheses. Then at m. 72 there follow splittings-off of the second measure, again duplicated thrice to form two-measure units, with a darkening of the sonority in the low register from the last phrase onward, before the full string texture takes this up (mm. 78–81) and leads hemiolically to the next formal segment, inserted like a large colon.

Two afterthoughts about the transition. The first concerns measures 46–52 and the way in which the horn color is emphatically recalled here as an expressive subsidiary part under the string melody. The horn will assert itself anew at the end of the first exposition and fulfill these approaches in the coda. (Not every recording pays sufficient attention to this subsidiary part. Such things are touchstones of a conductor's grasp of compositional processes, and some conductors are found wanting.) The second afterthought, too, concerns a subsidiary feature, its origin, unfolding, and continuation, and is part of the rich store of Brahmsian mediation techniques. It begins at m. 59 in the basses. This sees the first appearance of an accompaniment figure consisting of a falling third, a to f-sharp with a quasi-upbeat and octaves suffixed. It ensues from the unison thirds in m. 58 (Example 14) and goes back, as a motivic cell, to

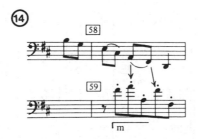

the nucleus of the main theme, *m1* (compare the derivation in Example 7). This accompaniment figure proceeds to expand, appearing in m. 61, m. 63, lengthened in the 6/8 bass of mm. 64–65, filling every other measure of the scherzando from m. 67, then omnipresent from m. 71 onward. From m. 82 onward (see Example 15) this figure will envelop the second theme—background continuity in diversity beyond the caesura.

Mm. 82–117(118): The Second Subject

This paragraph is the "second subject" *(Seitensatz)* first of all in terms of formal position. For in spite of the two starts made by the main theme (mm. 1ff., 44ff.) and the delay which the scherzando episode causes (mm. 66ff.), the new theme appears at that point where the sonata convention leads one to expect the second subject—which is to say, as the exposition's second large, independent portion after a more loosely structured, modulating bridge passage (although here it has a considerable formal weight of its own and is, furthermore, combined with the main subject).

The paragraph is also the "second subject" *(Seitensatz)* in terms of musical character. This new tone of animated string sound has already begun earlier, in the bridging "string quartet" passage of mm. 78–81. And it is reminiscent instrumentally of the main theme's start in m. 44, with the florescent violins. Now, however, it is the low strings that determine the sound, and they are brought in differently from the time before (Example 15).

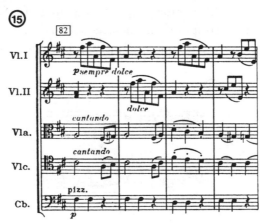

The 3/4 rhythm acquires a dance-like animation from the upbeat plus long end-note over the pizzicato bass, with its resting third quarter. In legato song the parallel thirds of violas and cellos vibrate euphoniously within themselves, the sonorous cellos leading the melody above the violas, with a slight melodic emphasis in the third measure after the repeated first measure (in m. 95 this is increased toward the interval of the fifth in confirmation); and everything is embedded in an initially unchanging ribbon of motifs and timbres (whose thematic derivation was shown earlier—see Examples 7 and 14 with the accompanying commentaries). The tone of restrained adoration recalls some of the Brahms *Liebeslieder* Waltzes, while the melodic contour with its third and its upbeat gesture is reminiscent of the cradle song "Guten Abend, gut Nacht" from Brahms's Opus 49 (Kunze 112). Another, indeed the principal reason for this restraint in the lyrical utterance, for the muted emphasis, is the darkening of the subject through the minor. This is unusual in this particular place, contradicting the classical norm: here the second subject is heard not in the dominant, not in the radiant key of A major, but in the murkier relative key of F-sharp minor, and in addition there are characteristic injections of the minor subdominant g in measures 88 and 97 (where the e that is a potential dominant-of-the-dominant—see the bass step c–a in mm. 88–89—appears in a different interpretation). Of course just such a toying with the element of darkness can, for Brahms, be significant, and it throws special light on this work: the serene symphony that has a minor-key second subject. To evoke a German saying: *Bei Brahms dürfen die Bäume nicht in den Himmel wachsen* (Brahms always keeps his feet on the ground). It is highly revealing that later on, at the end of the exposition, precisely this second-subject theme, now enriched and formally changed by a playful subsidiary part, is used as an epilogue, lends itself to such use. At that point it is an *Abgesang*, a valediction, and it already has valedictory features in this passage.

But the theme has some other notable features as well. The strongly plagal cadences at mm. 89 and 98 are aiming at a return to D major (and later on, the passage leading back to the recapitulation will exactly reproduce the harmonic model b–G–g–D 6/4 from mm. 86–89), as though the harmonic movement now indicated away from D major were to be avoided or at least suspended and delayed until it eventually appears at mm. 108ff., powerful but belated. The F-sharp minor of the seccond theme appears, from this angle, the third degree of D rather than a tonal plane in its own right. This cuts across the "second subject" viewpoint and gives the paragraph something of the character of a leading on, and over, that a "bridge" would possess. The main subject's ambiguity is followed by an ambiguous shadow over the second subject. (David Lewin regards the harmonic sequence from D to F-sharp [m. 82], back to D [mm. 89/98], and finally to A [half-cadence in m. 108] as an unfolding of the central d–c-sharp–d–a motif. Carl Schachter, on the other hand, would regard the dominant-tending C-sharp as being already stable at m. 82 and not only after m. 98. A decisive nuance is the importance attached to the aiming at D major in m. 89 and m. 98.)

The paragraph is a second subject *(Seitensatz),* finally, in terms of its firmer, homophonic compositional structure. From the viewpoint of syntax it is organized symmetrically, the motivic contents of the measures evolving so as to correspond; they alternate first as two-measure phrases (mm. 82–89) and then as four-measure phrases (mm. 90–97). In terms of formal theory the whole paragraph is a tripartite "song"— schematically an A-B-A'form (mm. 82–89 / 90–101 / 102ff.), with that typically Brahmsian hemiolic phrase-variant toward the end of the middle section (mm. 96–97), and finishing with an intervening four-measure phrase (mm. 98–101) before the repeat of section A. This repeat—naturally—shows instrumental changes (woodwinds begin the *Hauptstimme,* the principal voice) and is enriched by expressively sonorous subsidiary parts that open up the writing in quasi-dialogic fashion. There are inherent reasons for this. The "song" as lyrical form corresponds to the second-subject character. But as a pure tripartite formation it is a closed, self-supporting unit and would therefore be at odds with this sonata movement's evolving tendency. Brahms has allowed for this. The repeat of section A (mm. 102–107) remains incomplete and then gives way—over, at first, the same bass—to a processual motivic motion. So the song-form is used for lyrical characterization and yet opened up at the end, being tied in with the changing course of the movement.

Mm. 118–155: Tutti, Ben Marcato, and the Great Espressivo

The flow of song is succeeded by strong rhythmic accents. In the arrested forward movement there appears a percussively assertive motif, in two portions, in the full orchestra with the strings predominant, *forte*, sforzati, syncopation. In the first portion of the motif the tutti is contracted in a "unison"; the single note e is sharply dotted across two octaves, the musical space wrenched open. The continuation replies with concise cadencing, motivic constriction, and chordal writing. The fourth paragraph of the exposition, the big tutti tableau, begins with a vigorous grabbing motion (Example 16).

But once again the contrasting characters are mediated. The built-in symmetry of the preceding second subject has already been breached by the end of m. 107. The upbeat eighth-note motif is exploited recurrently, while harmonically the dominant's region of A/F-sharp is departed from, and via C major and A minor the music reaches F major, which finally appears with a quasi-Neapolitan inflection to E. The motivic insistence is accompanied by an orchestral expansion. There is also harmonic intensification by means of upward-moving chromatic alterations (first violins, mm. 114–117) and hemiolic straining against the measure (mm. 116/117), the upbeat motif being abridged. Timpani strokes underpin the sound. The augmented sixth-chord f–a–d-sharp (mm. 116/117) marks the termination of this divergence from the second-subject character and produces the music's gesture forward. Against the background of classical sonata dispositions it defines the following E as the area of a dominant, and as an accentuated dominant-of-the-dominant within the overall plan of the movement. And even the apparently new motif, as already goes almost without saying, is in diastematic terms a variant of the motif provided at the beginning (compare Example 7).

Once again, too, Brahms "plays about" with the metrical meanings. The prominent octave motif's changing position in the measure is indicative of this: first it appears on a downbeat (m. 118), then on an upbeat (mm. 119/120). Being a 5/4 unit, it cannot be fitted smoothly into the 3/4-time. But even when it has been lengthened and "fits in" on the downbeat (mm. 131ff.), there remains a contradiction between the notated time and the real accent. For intrinsically the octave motif has an upbeat character. The ostensibly forceful gestures are complicated by manifold metrical ambiguities.

[In the global design of the exposition, the fourth paragraph attains a new degree of rhythmic diminution. The ratio at the beginning of the movement was half:quarter, and this became quarter:eighth at m. 44. Now, sixteenths are introduced as the smallest note values.] At m. 118 they appear at first within the old relation, as the division of the quarter "upbeat." From mm. 120/121, and then continuously, these dottings become prevalent. Measure 127 sees the sixteenth-pulse spreading through the complete texture (Example 17). The eighth/sixteenth figure is linked motivically. It figures the semitonal turn of x (compare the commentary to Example 7; on the Beethoven reminiscence, see Example 3). At the fresh start in mm. 130/131 the broadened second-subject motif is connected up to the phrase (first violins, f-sharp–g-sharp–a, bass reverberation from the beat before).

But the diminution of x only decorates a series of quarters in a "unison" framework. There are three steps of a third, which can best be seen in the accentuated bass, and whose final g-sharp–b is repeated in

mm. 129/130 and filled up to form two secundal steps. On the violins and violas this "unison" is enriched motivically (I am putting "unison" in quotation marks because one is dealing, *de facto*, with octaves). The high strings further confuse the position with a spreading of chains of thirds. And over and beyond this, the entire nucleus constitutes a spreading of a secondary order which is answered, in mm. 129/130, by a contraction in contrary motion (seconds) (Example 18). Also in measures 129/130, the "unison" layout (moved up by syncopation) is succeeded by a chordal writing, the motivic step-decoration by a syncopated sixteenth-pulse. In essence, there is a change of facture similar to that in mm. 118/119.

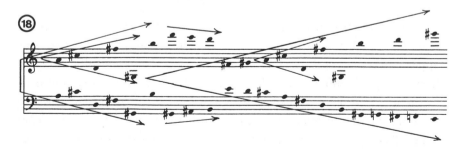

At the repeat of the four-measure phrase (mm. 131ff.) the wedging of the intervallic steps is intensified. The thirds in the bass are inverted in each instance (with c-sharp–a replacing a–c-sharp, and so forth), and the vigorous downward movement is continued chromatically after m. 133. In the upper parts, the upward swing to the high g-sharp‴ is pursued twice over, without any further contraction of the writing in response. The *ff* dynamics support the creation of a great syntactical colon.

This gestural opening-up goes side by side with a metrical displacement. The chains of thirds in mm. 127–128 had been already marking a 2/4-pulse, but 3/4-time is restored with the upbeat secundal progression in m. 130. From m. 131 onward a similar metrical ambiguity leads to a contradiction between the musical content and the beat, as is manifest with the repeated (to some extent upbeat) syncopes in mm. 133/134. This produces the metrically "crooked" layout of the entire subsequent paragraph, where the doubly "irregular" (2 + 3 =)5/4-length of the fortissimo chord in mm. 134–136 brings about yet another kind of metrical displacement.

One is tempted to offer a more far-reaching interpretation of Example 18. The upper voice in the two lines of thirds articulates, two quarters apart, a twofold series of fourths moving upward, while the lower voice articulates a twofold series of fifths moving downward:

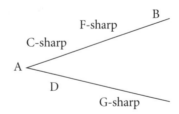

This overlaid structure is made clear by rhythmic means, through the hemiola. The E that is no longer reached by the upper line of fourths appears in m. 130 and subsequently in m. 134 as the powerfully exploited harmonic goal after the varied repeat. The hemiola of the rising fourths in the upper voice recalls the scherzando episode at mm. 66/67, where the same chain appears at the same pitch in hemiolic eighth-notes. That which takes place successively in the exposition—the dual relation of small and large hemiola against the same metrical background—is then presented in the first movement's development section as a complementary layering (see mm. 248/249 in Example 20). The theorist Moritz Hauptmann would regard this as a rhythmic analogy to the relationship of subdominant and dominant (Lewin 264; see the Bibliography).

Proceeding from the colon upon the E, the unfolding of the exposition after m. 136 presses toward its climax. The technique featured in mm. 129/130 is taken up and extended. Around the ribbon of sound flowing in syncopated sixteenths, two contrapuntally related voices of low and high strings move in great arching lines. Four times there occurs the ostinato bass figure whose rhythm and step of a fourth are derived from *x*, which is also the source of phrase *m*'s chain of seconds across m. 6 (compare the intermediate stage in mm. 130/131). This is answered by the violins with an emphatically delivered line, at first in imitation, then developing and heightening in contrary motion. Two abridged sequences of the bass ostinato follow (m. 144, m. 148). Here the high and low strings combine in "unison" octaves (the woodwinds take over the filling of the gap in mm. 149/150): once again, simplification has a potent effect. The passage has grandeur. The cessation of the ostinato in the bass of m. 151, in favor of the continuation of the secundal motif, then leads directly to the climax of the exposition (m. 152) with its cascading eighth-notes (reminiscent of m. 56).

This climax following the great espressivo, like the whole paragraph from m. 136 onward, shows a displacement by one quarter in the measure. And, as with the prototype of such techniques, the trio in the second movement of Beethoven's late String Quartet in A minor, op. 132 (mm. 142ff.), the ear has meanwhile adjusted to this displacement as "normal" because of its length. Hence the return to the old basic rhythm with the approach of the beginning of the epilogue, at the end of m. 155, comes as a jolt and seems an irritating discrepancy. The flow of the music is channeled back into the time that is notated.

Mm. 156–183: Epilogue, Return, Transition

As an epilogue the second subject enters, bipartite now, brightened toward A major and decorated with bright flute figuration—decoration which, with its semitone turn and leap of a fifth, is derived from *x* (compare the commentary to Example 7). The repeat changes around the instrumental colors in the old familiar way and carries through the tendency to the C-sharp major mediant (m. 159/mm. 167ff.)—perhaps a reference to the second subject's F-sharp minor? It comes to a halt upon a turn of two chords that will become very important later on (m. 178a and then, via 436, mm. 455ff.) in connection with the emergent solo horn. After the orchestral evolution the exposition closes with exceptional restraint. At the end comes an expansion of the descending chain of seconds from the second subject's third and fourth measures. Starting out six times, they traverse the musical space from top to bottom, tending after m. 178b toward motif *x*, which at m. 178f. is finally anticipated in its original register as a semitonal turn, before the exposition repeat commences.

Two elements of this ebbing away and subsiding of the exposition remain to be considered. One is the turn to the minor subdominant G in m. 178f. directly before the main theme re-enters—again, an explicitly darkening signpost (compare the second subject, mm. 88 and 97), here at a prominent formal point of intersection. It is the same harmonic turn, the so-called semi-diminished seventh chord upon e, with which the return to the recapitulation will be carried out (mm. 298ff.), much broader use then being made of it. (And G minor will then, to a significant extent, pervade the closing measures of the movement.) The other element to be considered is the horn color emerging only for a moment, but memorably, in the *prima volta* passage (not the *seconda volta!*), with the inversion of the semitonal turn which, widened to a major second on exactly the same pitch e from m. 455 at the beginning of the coda, proceeds to usher in the great, fully realized string melody. This is the third time the horn is given particular significance, following the opening of the movement and the expressive subsidiary part in mm. 46–52. It belongs to a chain of further prominent moments and constitutes a persuasive argument for repeating the exposition as a matter of necessity. Only a few conductors (even among the so-called maestros) perceive this.

Our analysis is mentally allowing for the exposition repeat. The *seconda volta* then has the development following on from a somewhat abridged downward climb (without harmonic darkening through the minor subdominant). After the appearance (m. 182), accelerated by syncopation, of bass motif *x* in the position it had at the beginning of the movement, the dominant's change of sonority is led over the A of the basses toward a false close in F major. This harmonic "punch line" inaugurates the new formal paragraph. The solo horn is entrusted with the thematic beginning.

Development (mm. 183–301)

A clear-cut, textbook separation of exposition and development, where the one consists solely of a thematic/harmonic statement or proposition and the other of its "working-up," is basically impossible with Brahms. (Even where Viennese classicism is concerned, the abstract doctrine of forms fails, in its purism, to match the musical reality.) The exposition of this symphony movement has been shown to have its basis in a manifold transformation of the initial material, giving it in part the character of a development, and this poses the question of the definitory distinction between the two sections. Two essential differences are the following.

First, the exposition is a historically molded paragraph, functionally articulated as such, with the broadly fixed structural and characteristic features of main subject, transition, second subject, and epilogue—here specifically modified by Brahms through the graduated beginning, the scherzando episode before the second subject and the tutti tableau after it, as well as the harking back to the second subject in the epilogue, all these subdivisions being related in a unificatory way to the initial material. A basically premeditated organization of this kind is not possessed by the development. (Which is not to say that it lacks any organizing principle at all, but the principle is an individual one to suit the particular case. Nor does it mean that the development is not, in specific instances, oriented to a model: this does indeed occur in Brahms.) A similar situation obtains for the harmonic disposition. The exposition is generally obedient to a limited scale degree scheme, and even the divergences from it (for example, the substitution we have noted in the second subject of the mediant for the dominant) remain within its bounds. The development is free to open up wider spaces. The F major with which it suddenly begins in this case confirms the point like a signal. (But of course in mm. 114ff. it was already there for a moment.)

Second, there is a qualitative difference between exposition and development with regard to the working-up of the basic material. The exposition is aiming generally, within its pre-arranged framework, at the formulation of new characters, new shapes *(Gestalten),* whereas the development aims at new constellations of those shapes, at different divisions and combinations, at confrontations, and at new interrelationships of the elements: thematic-motivic, harmonic-modulatory, rhythmic-metrical, and structural. A completely new theme within the development would, in the evolved classical conception of form, add up to an extraordinary event with important consequences. (That is why the few symphonies that illustrate this are famous models for formal exegesis.) Brahms's Second Symphony contains no new theme of this type. The thorough exploration of the possibilities of the material stated is a central principle of the developmental discourse. But technical procedures, textural models, and metrical patterns can be "developed" as well.

The Change: Argument and Discussion

This symphony's development begins with the harmonic signpost of m. 183. It opens thematically with argument and discussion. The solo horn plays the complete first phrase of main theme *m.* This is a backward glance, an emphatic return to the beginning of the movement, which marked the theme's only previous occurrence in this guise; and it is also a glance forward to the start of the recapitulation, the only place where the theme will reappear thus. In this central position it reflects a changed situation in the functional gradating of the form and itself initiates changes to the compositional structure.

The changed situation is indicated by the texture. No longer is there the pure horn sound that was heard at the beginning; instead, the solo horn (followed by the oboe with second violins, and then by the flutes) plays against a darkly agitated background which is first provided with hemiolas, then interwoven with chromatic lines. A rising arpeggio de-

rived from the eighth-note figuration in m. 44 appears on different instruments from one measure to the next. The theme is isolated in terms
of sonority.

And, just as at the beginning, we have the sixteen-measure thematic
configuration of x and m. Basically the same metrical divergence obtains;
x again appears with the drone notes a and d as well as the change of
the third degree (now the minor third) before the d. But the F major
turn in the midst of the preparatory x (mm. 182/183) already causes a
shift in the nuances of meaning. The upper voice and the fabric of subsidiary voices become central. The drone a is not now the root of the
chords but a third (of F major) and subsequently a fifth (of D minor),
while similarly the ensuing d is converted into a bass third (of B-flat
major). And x is lengthened both times—from four to eight measures
in the one case and from four to seven measures in the other. It is now
like a distant backdrop, no longer the counterpart to m. This is not,
primarily, another instance of an ambiguous toying with the meter and
blurred harmonies. The thematic idea m itself constitutes the subject of
a discussion.

Here again, m is a sixteen-measure period with a similar syntax and
rendered open-ended, but by different means and for a different purpose. The wavering tendency toward the subdominant area that was
latent in the start of the movement now becomes firm with the B-flat
major (related to the F major of m. 183). And the instrumental variation
of horns/flutes is—in a parallel way to the lengthening of x—transferred
from a relation of phrase and counter-phrase to that of antecedent and
consequent. A complete change is seen in the motivic content of the
counter-phrases. This is what becomes the driving force behind the thematic process, which goes into action from the period. Here there is no
to-ing and fro-ing, no muddying of the waters, no stagnation. The motive impulse is aimed firmly forward. This is fundamentally different
from the beginning of the movement.

The metaphor of speech and counter-statement may illustrate the process. The first phrase's argument, as it were, is answered by the counter-
phrase with its well-turned, four-measure periodicity (mm. 187ff.). This
is changed by comparison to m. 6 and takes up the third measure of the

argument, the quarter-note figure, sequencing twice over, before ending with the fourth measure of the argument. (Phrase and counter-phrase did not "rhyme" in mm. 5/9, but they do here.) The consequent transposed by a fifth (mm. 191ff.) renews the argument with an unchanged third measure (compare the contrast with m. 12) with varied instrumentation, so that it is the same in substance but with a slight nuance to the expression. The answer comes from the same counter-phrase (mm. 195ff.). It turns toward G minor, and its reply is more vigorous, given out by three woodwinds. Caustically echoing string figures support it, and the basses join in. In this way the discourse picks out and discusses part of the argument, the fragmentary idea of the first phrase's third and fourth measures. All this occurs in orderly four-measure units, with intensity arising through enrichment and layering. When the thematic instrumental partners begin to speak simultaneously, the result is a first fugato (m. 197). This twice combines pairs of counter-phrases in high and low register, starting from c and then f. Thus the consequent is actively opened, its second four-measure unit forming the first term of the fugato. Its last term has a vigorous cadential formula attached to it (mm. 204/205). This seems to conclude the discussion as regards this round, this thesis. Full stop.

At once there begins a second discussion. Over the cadential formula in the bass (m. 204), without preamble, a different idea is stated by the first violins. An even livelier debate is sparked off, and a richer, more intensive fugato commences, with two stubbornly fixed partners (meaning counterpoints) and many free, quasi-spontaneous interjections. One could pursue the metaphor, using the speech-like character of Brahms's music to describe the specific discourse of the development. For this music seems literally to speak, to act a speaking part: structurally it is an unfolding of ideas, human speech in a different medium and with purely musical means. This, however, may suffice for the time being as a conception of one possible form of comprehension—and, of course, one possibility of understanding by listening. The stages of the development will next be briefly characterized according to their chief musical ideas and techniques.

Stages

After growing from the periodic-symmetrical design of its beginning, a start whose syntax is like that of an exposition, the development as a compositional principle seems to come into its own at the second fugato. The subject of this fugato, a pregnant so-called development "model," eminently suited to thematic discussion, derives once more from the principal subject. Whereas the first fugato started out from the new counter-phrase in mm. 187ff., this minor-oriented model goes back to the original one in mm. 6ff. Through a rhythmically pointed, purposefully stretching, leading-note close, it now modulates and expands into a five-measure phrase. The nucleus of the fugato is in three-part "strict" writing with two firmly sustained counterpoints *(Cp1, Cp2).* Formulaic additions are thrown in—the cadential motif four measures apart, furthermore a striding motif deriving from *m* and filled up with syncopation. The contrapuntal outer parts sometimes leap between the real ones. In Example 19 the three-part nucleus and the additions are distinguished from one another.

   Again the heightening by structural-technical means is followed by an orchestral-dynamic heightening. The additions become more concentrated, while motivic splittings-off, in the compositional nucleus, and hemiolic abbreviations reinforce the expansion. Before the full orchestra's great fortissimo outburst there then comes a particularly salient moment, a focus of attraction which has only been matched so far in mm. 32ff. Just as he did then, Brahms entrusts it to the trombones, but it has the opposite character. Over a variant of thematic head *m1* in the bass, the three trombones intone in E minor a hemiolic stretto version of *x* (mm. 224ff.). In terms of sound this is an extremely bold passage, emerging from the tutti with their isolated *forte,* ultimately with harsh clashes of seconds (mm. 225–226): an openly rough and almost coarse sound, surprising and unexpected within the bounds of this symphony. It is an instant of enormous tension, a dramatic pointing of the course of the development. And now things happen one after another. The stretto is answered by the full orchestra, fortissimo, vivified by the string

tremolo, successions of *x* with layering and spinning-out. After m. 230 the process is repeated, with the stretto in the partitioned sound-mix of the winds, and the tutti reinforced. What follows in no way reduces the tension. The thematic-contrapuntal discussion begins to include meter as well. The meter itself (and the hypermeter) becomes a subject for development.

Divisions in the triple time: over and above the hemiolic "acceleration" of double-bars, this device is foreshadowed in the passages that precede the exposition's scherzando episode (compare mm. 63ff.). And it is surely no accident that the thematic design of each of the initial tutti measures in this development section (mm. 226–227, 232–233) recalls measures 59ff., ahead of the scherzando. The development is expressly taking up an element of the exposition afresh and evolving it in a quasi-systematic way.

At first there is, as in the exposition, simple division. In mm. 236–237 all the parts are united in halving the 3/4 time in a metrically "irregular" way into two 3/8 units. As in mm. 64–65, x is manifested four times as an eighth-note motif (with lower fourth). The quarter-note answer (mm. 238–239) places the normal triple time against this. In the process the syntax of the preceding tutti is retained: mm. 236–237 correspond to mm. 232–233, and mm. 238–239 correspond to mm. 234–235. But one can also, starting out from the procedures, relate the metrical complication of mm. 236–237 to the hemiolic stretto complication of trombone measures 224–225 (and mm. 230–231 respectively) and regard the answering groups of measures as counter-phrases of varying length. Successive metrical confrontation is followed in m. 246 by simultaneous confrontation: un-doubtedly the structural heart of the development. The timpani roll, the first since m. 32, throws this into outward relief as well. On close scrutiny it is a repeatedly simultaneous and doubly successive confrontation. In mm. 246–247 there is a division by three from measure to measure in the winds, together with a division by two in all the strings. In mm. 248–249 there follows the opposition, from measure to measure, of a division by two in the high strings and a division by three in the low strings. At

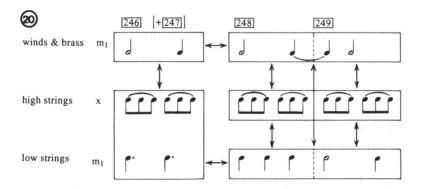

the same time, there appears as a double-bar in mm. 248–249 a hemiolic division in the winds, as opposed to a normal division in the low strings (*de facto*, therefore, duple time versus triple time), while the continuous 3/8 meter cuts across both of these (Example 20).

This is a kind of focal point for the varieties of metrical organization used in this music. Translating it into sounds involves making these different levels audible. (The majority of conductors, contrary to the compositional meaning, opt for an unequivocal statement and bring out the upper level.)

This point of conflict in the G major subdominant is answered, subsiding by degrees, by two four-measure phrases coming from G minor, with a downward-tending melodic motion over sustained sounds. The first of these phrases takes up—as a new element in the development—the violins' eighth-note theme in m. 44, and this, as it splits off, now legitimizes thematically the accompanimental figure in mm. 184ff. In its expressive character it does not have the vigorously opening-up influence it had in the exposition; here it has a palliative, calming effect. The second of these phrases brings the important counter-phrase from mm. 187ff., but with sharpened chromaticism and with inversions of the secundal turn (thereby creating a link with the secundal descent in m. 298). While the timpani strokes, two at a time, recall the rhythm accompanying the second theme, the third trombone emerges from the sound of the low brass and adds a particular coloring—a kind of echo of the trombone stretto passage. It is altogether striking that precisely these winding-up passages are underlaid by low trombone sounds.

In m. 258 the passage containing the great conflict recurs, this time in B-flat major and with a very slight difference in the instrumental distribution, the volume being slightly increased. Again there is an answer from the analogous four-measure phrases. Now the winding-up, the *Auslauf*, is expanded—m. 262 has the violin theme from m. 44 plus the counter-phrase, m. 270 the theme from m. 44 once more, plus counter-phrase, while m. 278 brings the counter-phrase again: a regular arrangement of clearly defined units. The twofold extension of this backtracking by degrees seems to signify that the development is ebbing away. But with the timpani roll from m. 270 onward, the long pedal-point a of the dominant, reinforced by the pulsing eighth-notes and the doubled trombones from m. 278, the opposite tendency toward a fresh upswing commences. At the same time a contraction occurs in the harmonic contrast between the sounds of F-sharp/A, on the one hand, and B-flat/F, on the other. The last counter-phrase (mm. 278ff.) evinces this in the direct sequence of F-sharp minor, A major, B-flat major, and F major.

The result is the outward climax of the events of the development (mm. 282ff.). It comes as the third tutti in the series of analogous conflict passages (mm. 246, 258, 282)—again the situation is one of mirrorings. This is a dramatic climax, not a structural one. The principle behind it is structural reduction combined with orchestral expansion. Here again, as at two points in the exposition, a qualitative heightening is succeeded by a quantitative heightening. Once more Brahms uses, for the last climax, a drastic effect and not a refining process—a feature that is quite irritating in view of the subtle motivic and metrical techniques used in the symphony. Metrically, this passage dispenses with a simultaneous opposition and contents itself with a succession of hemiolas, which makes the conflict two grades simpler than in mm. 258ff. A radical simplification in the texture, a "unison" in the full orchestra with the insistent repetition of the one third-motif m_1, and extreme dynamics are combined with one another. It is the greatest feat of strength in the symphony. The utmost dramatic pointing, however, is effected within this actual passage through the chromatic switch from f to f-sharp (m. 286). This is the formal turning-point. From the way it is introduced, this last climax in the development seems clearly in F major. Going by the main theme, to be sure, the f–a would have to be interpreted as a third-fifth. And the chromatic shift from f to f-sharp, with D major to follow, is a confirmation of this after the event. The end of the climax of the development is already a motivic anticipation of the start of the recapitulation.

Developmental turning-points, or peripeteias, often lead in nineteenth-century sonata movements to emphatic entries of the recapitulation, decidedly surpassing the corresponding start of the movement. From Beethoven (the Fifth Symphony, for example) and Liszt (as in his symphonic poem *Die Ideale*) up to Schoenberg (the Second String

Quartet), such "consequential" recapitulations are part of a dramatic sonata concept. With his initial material, and after the drastic dramatic pointing of this symphonic sonata movement, Brahms would have been perfectly capable of designing a similar recapitulation. He chose not to do so; his Second Symphony reflects a different approach to form. The unison tutti passage with its chromatic switch is, although marking the extreme climax, still not the last word in the development. From the way it evolves after measures 250 and 262 respectively, with the increasingly prevalent downswings, and in view of the continuation, it seems to be almost extraterritorial or at least labored. The second part of the development is governed by a dual strategy. There is, on the one hand, the extreme culmination in the conspicuous sequence of three tutti confrontations. And there is, on the other, the soothing arrangement of running-down four-measure phrases to counteract that tendency. The two tendencies criss-cross. The recapitulation, finally, is seen as a component part of the retrogression, not as the goal or result of the dramatic pointing.

The recapitulation might conceivably be heard at m. 290, directly after the apparent peripeteia. And there, in the main key of D major, the chordal writing of the beginning does in fact appear, with the first two measures of main theme m in the horns. This seems to be the recapitulation; in fact it is a four-measure phrase analogous to the three tuttis, with metrical oppositions of m and x, only with an altogether soft dynamic and also incorporating the eighth-note theme from m. 44 (mm. 292–293). And again the eighth-note theme from m. 44 answers to sustained wind chords underlaid by the timpani roll. The apparent recapitulation is just the reverse side of the conflict passages. But by superimposing the themes from the beginning of the movement and from m. 44, this passage anticipates an important element in the real recapitulation.

The latter enters, quite undramatically, at m. 302. It is approached via the scale calmly descending through two octaves that has already occurred at the end of the exposition and that later on will lead to the coda as well. It is a lead-back figure which marks the conclusion of the three big formal paragraphs and at the same time tells one something about the manner of their association—a measured advance, not an inexorably driven process.

Bound up with this is the strong presence of subdominant harmony on the border of the recapitulation. The stratified harmonic layout of the start of the recapitulation—it matches the beginning of the movement—is treated, within the network of Brahmsian structural safeguards, to a careful preparation. Measures 294–295 are based on the minor six-five chord over b, the minor subdominant of f-sharp, which played its part as the second subject's key, and within the development (just as the harmonic series b–G–g–D 6/4 first appears in mm. 86–89 and hence within the "second theme"). Measures 296–297 provide, with a stress in the bass on the adjacent chromatic step, the major six-five chord over g, the subdominant of the main key of D major. In line with the descending scale (in harmony lessons at the conservatory we would have described it as "minor-major"), this subdominant's minor-key variant follows at m. 298, again as a six-five chord. In m. 300 the dominant follows on in A major, and it would be possible to cadence in a limpid D major to the start of the recapitulation in m. 302. But first, the minor subdominant g–b-flat–d–e appears with the e in the bass, and thus as a so-called semi-diminished seventh chord of the second degree in the minor. Second, this e as a pedal-point remains stationary at the turn to the dominant and then produces, with the fourth ascending to the a in m. 302, a strong "dominant" step (from, as it were, the dominant-of-the-dominant to the dominant). And third, the dominant in m. 300 is followed by the minor subdominant once more directly before the recapitulation. So when, in m. 302, the movement's opening configuration with the six-four chord in d appears (with the arrangement of dominant foundation and tonic theme), we have both the basic step II–V and also II–I. The transition "reacts," at first, on several levels, like the thematic constellation itself. Contemplative calm has taken the place of drama. (And the aforesaid lead-back passage to the recapitulation with the series B minor–G major–G minor–D major 6/4 also first appears in mm. 86–89, within the lyrically singing second subject to which valedictory fea-

tures were attributed earlier.) Seen from this perspective, the events of
the development after m. 250 give the impression of a downswing preparing the way long beforehand.

Recapitulation (mm. 302–446): Connection and Reaction

A recapitulation is basically a repeat of the exposition. It is the same and
yet different, being not quite the same thing. It sounds the same, but in
a different place, and it is heard with variants—which are connected to,
and react to, past events. The changes compared to the exposition will
come to the fore.

The very beginning provides a signpost. Absent is the preliminary
measure with motif x, which was one element in the metrical ambiguity;
the start is more direct than at the beginning of the movement. (Unless,
like Toch [175ff.], one assumes that the augmented anticipations of x at
the end of the development—especially in the trombones in mm. 299–
301, directly before the recapitulation—represent this preparatory Vortakt. But the metrical aspect of the "preliminary measure" is eliminated.)
The end of the motif appears, however, as a pedal-point, and after m.
305 the full configuration of the displaced four-measure groups also recurs unchanged. On the other hand, two important elements of the
opening of the movement are combined with the inwardly swaying principal theme m and its active variant from m. 44. The recapitulation
begins as an emphatic formal concentration-point. The abridged eighth-
note theme figures lower, more darkly in the violas (with a complementary figure in the violins); m is heard in the bright oboes, an important
instrumental change. In the relative distribution of color the theme
emerges in the woodwinds, although the horn color heard at the beginning is not entirely absent. The horns, which, quasi-recapitulating, had
already suggested the main theme in m. 290, are given a different task.
They complement the two-measure phrase hemiolically as a metrical
opposition, thus carrying a central development principle into the varied
repeat of the beginning. The changed recapitulation is, in its facture,
clearly a result of the development's textural complexities, not of the
orchestral strong-arm tactics.

The tightening-up of the quondam opening passage, the bringing together of m. 1 and m. 44, creates a problem for the continuation. Since
the eighth-note theme of m. 44 occurs as an addition to the primary
main-subject configuration, Brahms carries on with this main subject,
in a similar way to mm. 20ff., without attaching the bridge passage from
mm. 52ff. This eliminates the entire intermediate area from m. 52 to m.
81, including the scherzando episode. One of the scherzando's functions
was to prepare metrical constellations in the development. This has been
done, so its omission at this stage makes sense. In the coda the scherzando episode will reappear in a new light. But also affected by the
thematic synthesis is the timpani/trombone passage in mm. 32ff. For this
was part of a carefully designed polarity and can hardly be made to make
sense without its antithesis from m. 44. The general point—over and
above the element of concentration—of putting together m. 1 and m.
44 could be the avoidance of the opening in its old form here. It is, in
fact, only conceivable as the opening of the movement, as the repeatedly
interrupted start of this symphony; simply to reiterate it after the development, at a point where there is nothing left to open, would, within
such a well-thought-out formal plan, be a contradiction of shape and
function. There remains the question of how, under these conditions,
the main subject is to lead directly to the second subject, and what is to
happen to the trombone chords.

In the counter-phrases from m. 306 onward, the thematic voice is
decorated with a parallel string figuration derived from the eighth-note
theme in m. 44. This gives rise to a continuous ribbon of eighths which
twirls around the principal line like a garland. With regard to the basic
rhythmic units of the main theme (half/quarter) and the eighth-note
variant (quarter/eighth), this paragraph is "combinatorial" throughout,
beyond m. 320. At this point, the continuation of the main subject at
first proceeds entirely along the lines of mm. 20ff., starting off with the
semitonal turn in the upper strings and with the eighth-note motion
made to match. But this descent over a period of eight measures now
occurs not only once but three times, starting out from e, f, and f-sharp
(mm. 319, 327, 335), an extension from twelve measures to twenty-six.
This not only puts the necessary distance between main subject and

second subject, compensating for the cut a little, gaining breadth; not only recalls the downswings recurring in the second half of the development; it also creates scope for a momentary revival, with F major/B-flat major and F-sharp major/B major, of central key-areas, and for suggesting the chromatic turn f–f-sharp from mm. 285–286—an allusion typical of a recapitulation. At the end only the eighth-note motion, now made to match chordally, is left, *sich verlierend* ("dying away"), again with the subdominant G minor. Two timpani rolls on d, pianissimo (mm. 342, 344), refer to what is about to be heard: the isolated kettledrum, the trombone sounds (mm. 346ff.; compare mm. 32ff.). But compared to the low point at the start of the movement, these are completely transformed. The context does this on its own, by incorporating these features in an even formal downswing where the flow is never checked. The eighth-note pulse, which transfers itself smoothly to the kettledrum and trombones, suffices to indicate the difference from the first, halting version. The radical clouding-over is avoided, yet the big moment in the exposition is recalled, as color and chordal writing. So here there are no diminished seventh-chords repeatedly circling. The trombones appear only once, blending with the horns (with the first horn playing the upper part), and they are simplified harmonically to a smooth cadence, striding ahead, ending with an open gesture in respect of the dominant. After the kettledrum's d, the incomplete dominant ninth-chord leads from a to pure D major, and this is followed (interpreting the D major as the relative key) by the dominant seventh-chord over f-sharp. The position and function of the "trombone sounds" are changed, and so their shape is also affected. The agreement with mm. 32ff. is now only partial, leaving the listener with the impression of a mirror relationship that brings out the difference. Here it is a matter of proceeding smoothly to the second subject. This can follow on directly in B minor, the way it ought to: a fifth lower than in the exposition.

(The instrumental revision of the passage between mm. 347–349 on page 35 of the autograph cancels the original use of the cellos, replaces the bassoons, matching them *ante correcturam* with horns, and keeps the low brass only. But the same revision transfers the melody-leading, which has been changed into something more emphatic compared to m. 33,

from the trombones to the horns. Thus directly before the second subject, with its pure deep string sound, there comes the pure wind tone,
uncompromised by an admixture of cellos, which subsequently emerge
in mm. 350ff. At the same time the expressive character is, by dint of the
melodic high note and dominating horns, adapted to the advanced
formal process. Those trombone sounds heard just after the beginning
of the movement cannot be repeated.)

From the second subject onward, the recapitulation reproduces the
corresponding passages of the exposition essentially unchanged. Naturally we notice little variants: the accompaniment to the second subject
now reacts to the evaporating main subject's eighth-note figuration, the
instrumentation is varied in the middle section, and so forth. But these
are just nuances compared to the main subject's fundamental revision.
After the completion of the reprise, the end of the movement then has
to be considered. The coda it presents is highly important to the whole.

Coda (mm. 447–523): A Summing-Up

Like the development section, the coda enters with a false close, that
tried and tested device for signaling, in sonata movements, the formal
expansion, the stretching of the train of thought beyond the recapitulation. Once again Beethoven's *Eroica* Symphony would offer a possible
point of comparison. Brahms, to be sure, is here (again) less dramatic
and aggressive in his harmonic and orchestral methods than his prede-
cessor was. There is, heard in B minor (with subdominant sixth), a four-
measure phrase that harks back to the hemiolic metrical conflict of the
development tutti. Without the motivic layering this four-measure
phrase is plainly more relaxed than its obvious datum point in mm.
290ff. It starts out softly, makes a crescendo with an expansive gesture
over the timpani roll, and in m. 451 it aims at a situation which in facture
and impulse is analogous to m. 298. But in contrast to that passage—
and this indicates the change of position in a coda designed to finish
things off—the motion on the dominant pedal-point, still accentuated
in mm. 451–452, rocks to a close diminuendo with a smooth change of
chords.

And now comes the solo horn's big moment, already mentioned in the first chapter with reference to Beethoven. For a long time it has been carefully prepared through the significance of thematic horn color at central articulating points in the form (the horn choir in m. 1 and the repeat, the solo horn in m. 183, the choir again in m. 290), and through the gradual, momentary emergence of one horn part (mm. 46, 178a, 347, 430, 438). Interestingly, a direct anticipation is the addition of the horn to the end of the epilogue in the recapitulation (not in the exposition!); and both motivically and functionally (as a bridge), the coda passage is naturally related to the horn in the *prima volta* of the exposition repeat. The solo horn now takes up this secundal turn, mediated via its expansion in the previous measures between mm. 451–454, in a syncopated form, and it grows as a characteristic color out of the brass writing. The major second provides the figuration instead of the minor second of m. 178a. And the secundal turn may again remind one of an important horn passage in Beethoven, at mm. 116–120 in the Adagio of the Ninth Symphony, shortly before the first fanfares, which resemble a caesura in the way they cut across the course of the movement. Or of the echo of the horns, leading one back, in the second movement of Schubert's "Great" C major Symphony, at mm. 148ff., subsequently to be adopted by the clarinets before the end of the movement (mm. 322ff.). With Brahms, however, the horn has a different task and significance. And its long drawn-out solo connotes more than simply a synopsis of the anticipations. In character it is a summons. Yet it is not about to issue a challenge. Instead the horn is sounding a farewell, gathering the movement together, conducting it to its fulfillment.

The familiar final version is, like the first major point of attraction of the trombones in mm. 33ff., the result of a second thought. Although the first version can hardly be deciphered amid the superscriptions and the heavy deletions on page 45 of the autograph, the upper strings were evidently mere inert sound, stationary in the background. An attempted reconstruction of the measures, while having to leave some details open, especially in mm. 465–468, produces a picture of the score as shown in Example 21; for all the uncertainty, this can nonetheless convey a general impression.

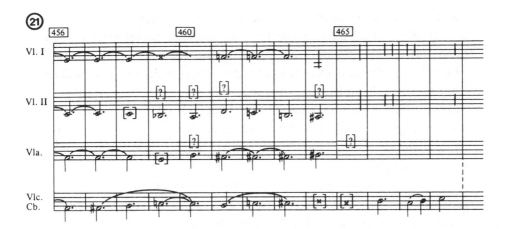

Brahms initially revised this first version within the original systems for the three upper string parts; erasures and superscriptions from this stage are still discernible. Probably for reasons of legibility, he then copied out the new version in the three systems above the strings, which were empty in this passage because of the rest for the brass. The original three systems for the upper strings were subsequently deleted completely and heavily.

The new version animates the background through motivic intensification, to which the horn responds. In preparation for the great string melody, the solo horn's monologue gradually turns into a dialogue. Logically, page 46 of the autograph sees the deletion of the horn, which originally extended into the string melody of mm. 477ff., joining in with it up to m. 481. In the new version the horn has been already drawn into events before the entry of the string melody. And it is no accident that this passage comes after the four-measure quotation of the conflict-torn climactic point of the development and reconciles it with the "peaceful solution" (Vincenz Lachner) of m. 477—a relaxing of the structural tension would not do justice to this formal objective.

Thus over the quiet, deep underlay of string sound, the solo now begins in m. 454 with the syncopated call-motif e–f-sharp(–e), like a challenge, to some extent setting the orchestra in motion. Chromatic step progressions in the bass from m. 457, which intensify as they grow shorter (two four-measure units, one of two measures, two consisting of one measure), form a counterpart to this, and the vagrant motivic head of the eighth-note theme from m. 44 fills up the space in the strings. The volume of sound increases, and the tempo picks up slightly. The horn reacts to the intensification and soars, exclaiming emphatically, to the top b-flat in m. 469. Here all the strings are combined, under the dominating horn, in a long and assuaging descent, diminuendo and ritardando. The diminished seventh-chords are resolved on the dominant into limpid triads. The writing, which at first remains so organized as to complement the syncopation, leads via the simple cadence with the fourth-suspension in the horn (m. 475) to a chordal unisonance. The expressive character and formal gestural language of this eventful moment are aiming at a fulfillment.

This fulfillment comes with m. 477. It is the one extraordinary moment in the movement and stands out from everything preceding it.[18] (In Brahms's working copy of the first edition of the score, which he used for conducting, the handwritten entries show particular underlinings for this passage. Brahms the composer wanted to draw attention to it even if he was himself to conduct.) Three factors, which have to do with shape and with context, make this passage appear so remarkable: first the aforesaid manner of its introduction, whereby all the interest is concentrated on this point; then the singular espressivo of its rich, flowing string melody; and finally its position as the third appearance of the main thematic configuration, now with the metrical, harmonic, and thematic ambiguity resolved, or rather, with the configuration so changed as to bring about unity.

Heard in a low register, the rich, warm, animated sound of the orchestral string section begins. The big motivic gestures of the two leading thematic outer parts have a complementary relation to one another rhythmically, while the chords of the middle parts fill the texture, pressing behind with syncopation. Compared to the differences between the recapitulation and the beginning of the movement, there is a com-

18. On this point, compare Steinbeck and Brinkmann in *Brahms-Analysen* (see the Bibliography).

plete change here. And two further devices are crucial. The motivic series *x*, in the bass, is fitted into the tonic-dominant scheme (see especially mm. 479–480) and compressed into two-measure units to achieve a firm periodic structure. And main theme *m* on the first violins is simplified with regard to rhythmic symmetry, reduced to the head-motif, but above all lengthened at the front by one measure with the tonic keynote d. This produces the amicable concurrence of *x* and *m*.

Harmony and meter, strong and weak measures are identical in the two components, and the urgently intensified repeat with the chromatic version of *m* (mm. 485ff.) removes any remaining metrical fluctuations. (Incidentally, it is very revealing that in the proof copy for the first edition of his piano reduction for four hands, Brahms divided up the violin melody from m. 467 onward, which was all assigned originally to the upper, right hand: the first d in m. 477 is meant to be played by the left hand, the continuation by the right. The separation points back to the problem that has now been concealed. In the autograph of the piano reduction, the division of the parts was there from the outset.) The chromaticism, already beginning with the horn tints in m. 483, is derived in its motivic eighth-note form (mm. 486–488) from *x*, so that after the connective new formation in m. 44, the layering at the start of the recapitulation, and the concurrence in m. 477, a further reconcilement now follows, a direct integration of *x* into *m*.

The consequence of the three important "points of attraction" (an epithet neatly coined by Franz Brenn) in this sonata movement can be seen anew in "repeated mirroring." At the start of the recapitulation, the metrical configuration from the beginning of the movement was already simplified by removing the "preparatory measure" *(Vortakt)* *x*, and through the impact made by the eighth-note theme from m. 44. Here, it is transcended. Thus the coda not only sheds new light on the insertion in the recapitulation, its formal intermediate position; it is in this coda that the form-process of the whole movement is first fulfilled, and the meaning of the ambiguity present throughout and the metrical confrontations is revealed. Harmonization as summing-up?

No, for this does not then prove to be the case after all. In spite of the strong and singular emphasis on this one pregnant point, in spite of all its expressive and structural weight, there remains a nagging doubt about pure harmony, about the possibility of undisrupted serenity, at least in this movement. When the woodwinds are added in m. 491, the expressive flow is checked by secundal turns, and the actual strings (with the oboes) see the musical activity evaporating, fading away hemiolically—in G minor, a key that had been already recalled at mm. 490–491. So again there is a decided clouding-over, again the minor subdominant is added in a prominent place. The incandescent melodic espressivo is taken back, a question mark placed over its connotations.

And once again there begins the play of polarities. Proceeding from the finished downswing, a chromatic turn leads to a recurrence of the scherzando episode in D major (m. 497). The formal purpose of its appearing here is a balancing recapitulatory function. In the recapitulation itself this scherzando was omitted, but now, right at the end in the coda, it intervenes, and the omission is repaired. Of course, it "signifies" here, representing a brightening that is in contrast to the previous minor tonality, whose tied eighth-notes it turns into lightly uttered staccati. It is lighter in a special way. With its somewhat plangently articulated after-phrase in the exposed high woodwinds and the pizzicati with delayed accompanying chords, it seems an almost ironic reversal after the great espressivo of the string tone. It is as though Brahms's distrust of anything too openly emphatic called for an activity that would counter it. The scherzando provides this interruption. And naturally it is changed to conform to the coda, in exactly the same way as the string melody. And now there is a clear periodic syntax. True, the answer given by the after-phrase is, in Brahmsian fashion, a little irregular, being delayed in the woodwinds by one measure, but it catches up in m. 505 by overlapping at the repeat. The new phrase in m. 502 begins with x inclusive of the following fourth (upward moving), and it cadences firmly, summarizing events.

But this conceals a further element which the composer has surreptitiously introduced. In his working copy of the first edition of the score, Brahms inscribed a text underneath the woodwinds: "Es liebt sich so lieblich im Lenze" (see the illustration in Floros, 206). This is the title and repeated line of a song (op. 71, no. 1) which Brahms composed in the early part of 1877, during the breathing space between symphonies described at the start. The song is in D major, and its strophic endings are completely identical with this after-phrase in their harmony and almost identical in their melody. Doubtless the symphony's passage here is a quotation. As such, it points beyond the song to the complex of "nature" as the compositional intent and, through the element of playful humor, to the topic of the idyll.[19] And Brahms's reference to *das liebliche Ungeheuer,* his "lovely monstrosity" *(G),* quite permits of an allusion to the song's "lovely" love in the springtime. Yet this word was, at the very least, equivocal, and our quotation also needs to be examined more closely. The text of the song, by Heinrich Heine, speaks in a typically light tone of a spring-like amorous mood, the desire for fulfillment, and a missed opportunity with the ensuing deep disappointment. And the last two lines with the repeated words of the title are, if not an ironic commentary, then one that is sadly resigned. This mental figure is also conducive to a grasp of the ending of the movement as signified by Brahms through the quotation. In the song, corresponding to the dis-appointment in the last stanza, there is a first and quite fleeting reference to G minor. And the little lyric piece closes with the plagal cadence g–b-flat–d–e, a six-five chord of the minor subdominant before the final D major chord. This is exactly the harmonic constellation for the ending of the movement in the symphony. The string espressivo finishes in a resigned G minor, the scherzando song-episode harks back to it in its varied repeat (m. 512), again only in passing, and the final cadence is quite expressly "minor-key," on the subdominant. Here one may again apply, now in the narrowed-down context of the specific work, that historically sweeping idea which Thomas Mann propounded in his novel *Doctor Faustus:* at the end of this symphony's first movement comes the

19. Mahler's Rückert song "Ich atmet' einen linden Duft"—another song in D major—comes very close to this Brahms self-quotation in its melodic gestures. Possibly this is by no means a coincidence in view of the idyllic nature/love themes, especially in light of the Brahmsian allusion at the beginning of Mahler's First Symphony, in D major, which (as will be shown below) clearly refers to an episode in the finale of Brahms's Second Symphony.

"taking back," the doubt regarding the great espressivo, regarding serenity, harmony in the world of the symphony. (We will return to this
idea later, at the very end of this book.)

The repeat of the scherzando period brings the horns into the thematic
activity at m. 505 once more, and for the last time; the after-phrase with
its rhythmic delay breaks up the melodic contour. In mm. 513–514 the
head-motif of *m* appears on horns and trumpets, with harmonic coloring
toward G minor on the part of the strings, pizzicato in a low register, to
the bass note d. In the process the sustained a of the head-motif's ending
on the dominant clashes with the plagal G minor. This is repeated,
starting off one octave lower, in mm. 515–516. The movement's last main
thematic statement is, like the first, entrusted to the horns. The G minor
appears in this constellation with subtle arpeggiation (Example 22).

Horns and trumpets sustain the dominant pedal-point a. The string
basses unequivocally present the G minor triad in pulsating quarter-
notes (in contrast to m. 514, the double basses are now involved as well).
Violins and violas confirm the g chordally as G minor, interpreting the
delayed b-flat as the ninth of an incomplete dominant ninth-chord and
the d as a D minor root. But the plagal character of the bass arpeggiation
continues to predominate, and it produces, together with the dominant
pedal-point, a dark sound-mixture that is very idiosyncratic, very
Brahmsian. And the insistent a in the horns and trumpets (mm. 516–
520) leaves a strong dominant component affecting even the achieved
tonic. (With his belated insertion of the penultimate measure in the
autograph, moreover, Brahms transformed the originally weak metrical
position of the concluding measure into a strong one. The change occurred before the piano reduction was made, and thus before the premiere.) A significant feature of the dying close is that held tones and

sounds appear only in the wind instruments, while the potentially expressive strings play pizzicato. After the expansive development, after the big orchestral tableaux in the exposition and recapitulation, and above all after the special moment of expressive fulfillment in the coda, this amounts to a very remarkable close. It is obviously related to the ending of the development, and it is quite definitely dictated by that formal thinking which caused the exposition to commence so brokenly. The trombone writing in those opening measures was conceived in the same spirit.[20] Skepticism is its hallmark.

Melancholy

Melancholy is a very fine state. I succumb to it very easily and willingly. Less so or not at all in the country, where I work, but at once in the city . . . For me there is no finer place than Vienna and the melancholy which I feel in the city, and always have felt . . . It is the people I have known there for two decades who yield the melancholy . . . It is the streets of Vienna. It is the atmosphere of this city, which is *the city of study quite naturally*. It is always the same sentences that people there speak to me, probably the same ones that *I* speak to these people, a marvelous prerequisite for melancholy. One sits somewhere in a park, hour after hour, in a café, hour after hour—melancholy. It is the young writers of yesteryear, now no longer young. One sees suddenly that somebody is no longer a young man, he just *acts* like a young man—probably in the same way as *I* act like a young man, *but am no longer a young man*. And that grows stronger with time, but it becomes very agreeable. I like going very much to the cemeteries in Vienna, to the Döbling Cemetery right in my vicinity or to the cemetery in Neustift am Walde, and I look forward to seeing the inscriptions I know from earlier years, seeing the names. The melancholy when one goes into a shop: the same woman behind the counter who twenty years ago moved with such *incredible speed* is *now very slow*. She fills up the bag with sugar *slowly*. It is a quite different movement that she takes the money with, and closes the drawer of the till . . . It is the same bell jingling at the door,

---

20. Peter Gülke has vividly described the trombone passage's "memento," and it is surprising that he was so mistaken about this movement-ending in his reference to the "relaxed first movement," compared to the "unredeemed melody" of the ensuing Adagio (*Brahms Bruckner*, p. 29).

but it is melancholy. And this state can last for weeks. And I think to myself that melancholy is perhaps the ideal or the only practical resort for me, the continual taking of melancholy in tablet form.

THOMAS BERNHARD, *Der Italiener*

Ay, in the very temple of Delight
Veil'd Melancholy has her sovran shrine

JOHN KEATS, *Ode on Melancholy*

Between August 7 and 9, 1879, Brahms wrote a letter from his summer vacation—again spent at Pörtschach—to Vincenz Lachner, the former court kapellmeister at Mannheim and younger brother of Franz and Ignaz Lachner. The letter relates to the Second Symphony, which Vincenz Lachner had first heard in Karlsruhe in the fall of 1878 and then himself conducted in Mannheim in the summer of 1879. Lachner, who was a cultivated musician of classicistic principles, had, in the letter which prompted Brahms's response, criticized certain aspects of the symphony's first movement, or at any rate confessed his uneasiness about it, out of a profound and sympathetic admiration for the masterly construction of the whole.[21]

Here, the trombones play a special role. Lachner wrote of them:

Why do you throw into the idyllically serene atmosphere with which the first movement begins the rumbling kettledrum, the gloomy lugubrious tones of the trombones and tuba? Would not that seriousness which comes later, or, rather, that assertion of vigorous youthful manliness, have had its own motivation without these tones proclaiming bad news? Must grace be reconciled with strength through something unnerving? . . . In all, I would prefer the trombones and tuba to be excluded from this movement, because they don't seem to me to be

21. The full text of both letters in the original orthography was first published, with commentary, in Brinkmann 1989 (see the Bibliography). Lachner's letter is to be found in the archives of the Gesellschaft der Musikfreunde in Vienna, Brahms's reply in the Library of Congress, Washington, D.C., Whittall Collection.

necessary to the basic atmosphere and they add nothing essential to the abundance of strength displayed in the concentration of all the orchestral resources. That would also eliminate the passages where these particular instruments take up the bass motif (1st measure) in imitation in a disconcerting way, suddenly exhibiting a tone quality that contrasts with the surrounding nobility, and proceeding in the intensified repeat to a garish outburst of rage and pain which offends my ear, although my eye may admire the thematic use of the motif. The intonation of these instruments is never quite pure, and to go so far in putting one dissonantly on top of another seems audacious to me, gravely affecting the euphony.

Lachner also expressed his failure to comprehend the first movement's conclusion with its superimposing of the dominant sustained note a on the minor subdominant g–b-flat–d. Of this he wrote:

But a whole day spent talking would not persuade me that the a on the trumpets and horns at the close with the G minor triad underneath is necessary, useful, or even beautiful. Even if, with some effort, a theoretical explanation could be offered for the simultaneous occurrence of the dominant and plagal close, the ear will never be reconciled to it. Everything before it is designed to convey us to the natural, unspoilt dominant close, to carry us peacefully into the tonic. The whole coda section beginning with the passage quoted in my letter [Lachner had appraised the significance of mm. 477ff.] forms a true transfiguration, after the strife and conflict, of marvelous beauty, of ravishing euphony. Then, at the moment of supreme satisfaction, in the middle of the celebrating, there comes this confounded nuisance, this interfering G minor triad. When, without previous sight of the score, I came to this passage in Karlsruhe, I heard besides the sustained a something that was disconcerting, not immediately understood, and I pricked up my ears to listen with the utmost acuity. "Get away from me, you uninvited ear-blowers," I said to myself, "don't disturb me when I'm thoroughly enjoying the purest of harmonies in a conclusion to make one happy!" –The a is so rich in tone, lodging in the ear as it continues and commanding attention, that the nagging G minor triad in its brief appearances, divided by rests, proceeds alongside it like a mere shadow; which alleviates matters.– Maybe people will tolerate this kind of thing in future, perhaps finding pleasure in it, but my ear is too old for such things.

Brahms's reply reads as follows:

Aug[ust]. [18]79

Dear Friend,

My letter will hardly tell you what great, sincere pleasure your letters are giving me. They leave nothing to be desired except the promised continuation. I shall say nothing of your heaping too much praise on me, but it is so good to know that what one has created with love and hard work is also being studied lovingly and carefully by another person. Your perceptive and understanding words are the first of the sort, printed or written, that I have heard about that work. They would merit my pondering a reply—but I'm unable to and can only ponder a first movement!

Only, in the knowledge that you are spending this period with your brother, I must at least send a brief word of thanks!

I will also say briefly that I very much wanted to manage in that first movement without using trombones, and tried to. (The E minor passage I would gladly have sacrificed, and so I now sacrifice it to you.) But their first entrance, that's mine, and I can't get along without it and thus the trombones. Were I to defend the passage, I would have to be long-winded.

I would have to confess that I am, by the by, a severely melancholic person, that black wings are constantly flapping above us, and that in my output—perhaps not entirely by chance—that symphony is followed by a little essay about the great "Why." If you don't know this (motet) I will send it to you. It casts the necessary shadow on the serene symphony and perhaps accounts for those timpani and trombones.

– All this, and especially that one passage, I ask you not to take altogether too seriously and tragically!

But as for the note a that goes with the G minor in the coda, I'd like to defend that! For me it is a gorgeously beautiful *(wollüstig-*

schöner) sound, and I think it occurs in the most logical way possible— quite of its own accord.

After this, dear friend, you will think it strange if I ask you to let me know above all—what you *don't* like. But remember: whether your objection has some effect or whether I won't admit it for the individual passage in question, I shall have heard the objection, which will hold good and be of help some other time.

As for being "effusive," that's something *you* don't need to beware of. When one is reading a letter, one instinctively pictures the writer's face. In yours, life has etched lines that are handsome and grave, and so one listens to what you say.

But now to conclude, all best wishes and cordial regards to you and your brother.

Until we get in touch again, I hope!

Yours most sincerely
J. Brahms

This letter amounts to a great confession. And it is a particularly remarkable letter for Brahms, who was always so taciturn and reserved. The quite extraordinary thing about it, however, is the way it combines a very personal, private message with work-interpretation. The interpretation put forth in the present book finds excellent support in Brahms's attempt to reveal the "serene" symphony's deceptiveness, to explain its hidden depths. Two elements of the work are expressly mentioned in this connection, two elements of the first movement which also have a special place in the foregoing analysis. The fact that Brahms addresses these points with an emotion unusual in him makes them stand out all the more.

First and foremost Brahms is concerned with the need for trombones. For the disposition and character of the first movement in particular, he was unable to "get along without them." The Second Symphony's special position in Brahms's symphonic music, with its individual quartet of low brass instruments, and the marked employment of these in the first two movements are thus determined by the content as announced in the specific tone of the work. Here the "E minor passage" (mm. 224ff., the stretto treatment of *x* by the trombones in the development) is not so crucial. But the vastly significant moment of their "first entrance" in mm. 33ff. is strongly defended: "that's mine"—here Brahms regards himself as being completely at home, and it is something profoundly personal to him. The composer's own commentary provides a welcome validation of the foregoing analysis of these measures and their function, and also of the conclusions drawn from the corrections in the autograph.

As an argument in support of the need for "timpani and trombones," the letter mentions a compositional "essay about the great 'Why.'" Brahms is referring to the a cappella piece *Warum ist das Licht gegeben dem Mühseligen?*, the first motet of his Opus 74, seen here as being not only close in time but also inwardly in contraposition to the "serene" symphony. Brahms's cryptic expression "pious" in his letter to Billroth at the beginning of September 1877 *(C)*—"Whether I have a pretty symphony I don't know; I must ask clever people some time. But pious I was, at times, in the summer"—presumably refers to this work on the motet (as well as the second piece of Opus 74) side by side with the symphony, work that was probably not finished completely until a year later. Now this interrelationship of the motet and the symphony might suggest some quite concrete musical parallels. But that, as a comparison of the scores will show, is evidently not the case. That "shadow" which the "pious" adjacent piece is said to be casting on the professedly so continuously "serene symphony" is not identical musically, either in the form of a quotation or as a more covert correspondence. (Such features as the juxtaposing of D major and G minor for the *Warum* at the start of the motet are too normal in a Brahms work in D minor to guarantee any links—with, for instance, the harmonic situation at the end of the first movement. Even the chords proceeding in contrary motion in mm. 32ff. of the motet are not enough to evoke the trombone sounds in m. 33 of the symphony's opening movement.) But certain of the symphony's expressive features and formal ideas are probably identical in origin and in spirit to that which the motet is directly stating, and this evidently reflected Brahms's perception of life and creative ethic: the "great 'Why'" that the "master struggler" *(der meisterhaft Mühselige)* is skillfully articulating, the "abyss" lurking beneath the very closed surface

structure of his works, the "black border" *(N)* that secretly surrounds a whole work. Brahms's letter suggests that by working on the two pieces side by side he was deliberately controlling his creative activity and providing a chronological contrast in order to keep doubts alive about the friendliness of the world, just when the pastoral idyll could become the theme of a symphony. Thus the motet's verbal component, the text taken partly from Job, and the confirming of the constant raising of doubts, renders it, as an adjacent work, so important psychologically for the composer.

Second, and with the same emphasis, Brahms "defends" his ambiguous movement-ending, with its mixture of the dominant sustained a and plagal G minor. For this he advances two arguments. The mixed sound itself he calls "gorgeously beautiful" *(wollüstig-schön)*, thus explicitly underlining the sensuous element in this mildly melting dissonance. And he suggests how the sound is derived in a fairly natural and "logical" way from the formal process of the movement-ending.

The letter puts these compositional strategies into perspectives that are of altogether far-reaching importance for an understanding of Brahms. In his argumentation, the compositional features are projected back upon a personal state of mind and spirit. Although this deeply private confession is surprising in Brahms, it does manifest itself in a typical way. And if one takes the form of expression literally, his statement goes beyond the realm of the merely private and personal; it offers a metaphorical diagnosis of the times—in just a brief image, but memorably phrased. The theme of melancholy was also addressed by Brahms himself in other contexts, such as the Intermezzo in B minor, op. 119, no. 1, in the case of the later works, in his letter of May 1893 to Clara Schumann (Schumann/Brahms II, 513). Here, revealingly, fourteen years after the letter to Lachner, Brahms again describes the same association of "melancholy" and "voluptuous delight" *(Wollust)* as an aesthetic experience, which he relates to a similarly "veiled" (Keats's term) dissonance. In contrast to the Intermezzo, however, where melancholy is seen as a constituent factor in the actual piece, the letter to Lachner mentions a personal state of mind as providing the symphony with a definitory background, its compositional idea. First, the "I am . . . a severely mel-

ancholic person": a statement that sounds like the confession of an ill-
ness, accentuated by the adverb "severely." Then there is the extension
into a general statement with the plural, which expresses or at least seems
to indicate a wider, contemporary perspective: "black wings are constantly flapping above us." It was in this spirit that Brahms invented the
trombone chords, the movement-ending, and the "score . . . with a black
border."

Ernst Bloch's elegant formulation of the "melancholy of fulfillment"
as the "secret keyword of the age" offers itself here as a gloss on the
letter and passages in the symphony: every "Carpe diem" is, Bloch is
saying, profoundly touched by melancholy. "Moreover there is everywhere a fissure, indeed an abyss in the very realizing, the actuated-actual
arrival of that which was so beautifully foreseen and envisioned; and this
is the abyss of uncomprehended existence itself. Thus the surrounding
dark also provides the *ultimate basis for the melancholy of fulfillment:*
there is no earthly paradise which does not have, at its entrance, that
shadow which the entrance still casts" (*Das Prinzip Hoffnung* I, chapter
20). The "entrance" of trombones that "casts a shadow" in the opening
paragraph of the Second Symphony seems to make these words manifest
in musical sound.

Brahms, however, immediately partly retracts the confession in his
letter in typical fashion by removing it to that discreetly suggestive
halfway-house where—although there is more irony in them—the statements about the Second Symphony in his letters *(N, O, P, W)* also belong. Even the actual confession is hedged round with the conditional
subjunctive: "Were I to defend" / "I would have to be long-winded" /
"I would have to confess." Then the strangely casual "by the by" further
lessens the weight of the statement even before it is uttered. Finally, the
confession is at least half retracted again later, with reference to both the
individual and the work: "All this, and especially that one passage,"
meaning the trombone measures, is not meant to be taken "too seriously" or even "tragically." And yet the subsequent description of the
ambiguous cadenza in the coda as sounding "gorgeously beautiful" ends
up by indirectly lifting, a little, the veil that has been thrown over the
symphony's melancholic dimension. As if it were a latent commentary

on the whole private game of disclosures and disguises, the letter ends with that beautiful paragraph which allows one to be "effusive" provided it has to do with life's serious side, the "lines" life has etched. (There will in any case be no real effusiveness from Brahms; we can be sure of that.)

The results of the first-movement analysis, taken in conjunction with the letter's central catchword of "melancholy," can be considered further, beyond the personal sphere. Brahms's plural ("that black wings are constantly flapping above us") confirms the rightness of Ernst Bloch's historical perspective of melancholy as the "secret keyword of the age." Through his work and his epistolary self-diagnosis, Brahms places himself within that "secret society" of a "company of melancholics" living at the end of the nineteenth century that is mentioned by one of the mournful characters in the novels of his Nordic contemporary Jens Peter Jacobsen. "Melancholy" as a pathological condition, as the symptom of a psychic state, is an age-old theme associated with the brilliant, creative individual as far back as late Antiquity but especially since the Renaissance. From Dürer's *Melencolia I* to Beethoven's string quartet movement *La Malinconia* from his Opus 18, No. 6, the allegorical depiction of the melancholic temperament finds important examples in all the arts. In the eighteenth century, the age of bourgeois sensibility, the theme acquired new artistic dimensions, and a veritable cult of melancholy came into being. During the German "Storm and Stress" period this was chiefly to be felt in literature, as in the characteristic novels of the second half of the century, Goethe's *Werther* and Moritz's *Anton Reiser*. The sentimental reception of James Macpherson's *Ossian* was also part of this phenomenon, which was carried on by Jean Paul, had in Kierkegaard its perplexed analyst of tedium, and culminated in Proust's great novelistic reflection on time. The middle and late nineteenth century appears, in its identification of melancholy with depression *(Schwermut)* (which Kant had regarded as a lower form of melancholy, and which came to the fore with Schelling's Romantic philosophy of nature), to be a continuation and heightening of the eighteenth century. This is linked with a historically significant change of estimation that was anticipated in the late eighteenth century (being already discernible in the critical configuration of *Werther,* where the main characters admire Klopstock in the first part but Ossian in the second). Melancholy as depression, as a pessimistic and deep-seated feeling of inadequacy and failure, is a negative condition and experience of the nineteenth century. Brahms's confession about the "black wings" that are "constantly flapping above us" belongs to this late period in history.

Melancholy is, as Wolf Lepenies has shown, one hallmark of the bourgeois age. Recent philosophers have seen in it one of the most important categories of the modern era as well. Melancholy is based on an awareness of the inadequate state of the world generally; the relevant definition by Diderot, in the *Encyclopédie* of 1778, can be taken as the great common denominator for the basic feeling producing melancholy up to this modern era. Melancholy is a "mourning for a lost possession" (Schelling). The causal connection between politico-economic power relations and bourgeois melancholy as the typical mood of the times has been demonstrated in regard to the eighteenth century by Lepenies. He has also proved the continuity of the social consciousness regarding the disposition to melancholy and depression in the nineteenth and early twentieth century. The social and cultural history of bourgeois melancholy, and its illustration in art and aesthetics up to the modern era, are broadly outlined and described in some detail.[22] If I have grasped their basic determinants correctly, then Brahms, as one of the nineteenth century's "great melancholic lone wolves" (Lepenies 71), belongs to the penultimate phase of this bourgeois history. With him the actual and immediate social causation seems less tangible than the artistic causes and those rooted in music history. The creative doubts, melancholy resignation, taking back of oneself, and the introversion are no doubt reactions to a feeling of inadequacy regarding the actual praxis of life as well, but they seem more dictated by an artistic self-questioning, by a skepticism about the historical worthiness of his own artistic existence. In

22. Background material to the above summary will be found in the writings of Lepenies, Szilasi, Landmann, Rehm, Benjamin, Sontag, Klibansky/Panofsky/Saxl, Bandmann, and Dahlhaus 1983 (see the Bibliography).

my view there are seven essential determinants concerning Brahms's diagnosis of melancholy.

1. Melancholy as an individual, albeit historically mediated state of mind and spirit. "I would have to confess that I am, by the by, a severely melancholic person"—the word Brahms uses in his letter, the frequency of the references to "melancholic" qualities in his works or their simulation in the aesthetic experience, the similar interpretation of sounds from nature (see Kalbeck III 81)—this is seen as evidence of that lasting psychic condition which can be called melancholy because "resignation takes on the character of being 'finitely' valid" (Lepenies 164). But for the artist, depressed isolation and the solitary life can be claimed as a mark of distinction. Brahms's fear of contact resembles this melancholy form of artistic legitimation.

This explains the intensity and character of melancholic self-understanding. The awareness of one's own ability to portray melancholy, to present an anthropological component as an artistic fiction and thereby to exorcise it, produces that exceptionally sensual feeling of pleasure which is always in evidence when Brahms is addressing melancholy. In particular his letter of May 1893 to Clara Schumann (Schumann/Brahms II, 513), about the Intermezzo in B minor of Opus 119, confirms the association of melancholic states and experience with a sensual feeling of pleasure, describing this as "voluptuous delight" *(Wollust):* "a little piano piece . . . It's teeming with dissonances! . . . The little piece is exceedingly melancholy, and to say 'play very slowly' is not specific enough. Every measure and every note must sound like a ritardando, as though you wanted to suck melancholy out of every single one with delight and pleasure [*mit Wollust und Behagen*] from the said dissonances! Lord above, the description will amuse you!" The letter to Lachner also uses this sensual image and the same term for the ending of the Second Symphony's first movement—a term that Brahms had already chosen a year earlier, in his letter to Joseph Joachim, for "this piece especially, or a number of things in it" *(Z)*. Melancholy resignation as the self-enjoyment of one who has the artistic talent for, the privilege of, portraying it: this may have been the intimate Brahmsian experience.

The word *Wollust* used in this context is not an exclusively Brahmsian term. It is one of the common aspects of melancholic experience. Grimm's Lexicon notes the following (vol. 14, 2, col. 1394): "*Wollust* . . . , especially marked as part of an oxymoron, used of the sense of pleasure associated with depression, with tears, with mental pain, and the like."

2. Melancholy and mourning. In Brahms's letter to Simrock (*N;* see also *X*) he juxtaposes the two ideas in an ironic manner: "The new symphony is so melancholy that you won't stand it. I have never written anything so sad, so *mollig* ["minor-key"]: the score must appear with a black border." And in the letter he wrote Elisabet von Herzogenberg the same day (*O;* see also *W*), the "minor key" is concretized as F minor, to be struck on the piano "alternately in the bass and the treble, *ff* and *pp.*"

Sigmund Freud's essay of 1916 takes as its theme the relationship of "mourning and melancholy" (and David Lewin prompted me to elaborate on that aspect here). Mourning, according to Freud, is "the normal reaction to the loss of a loved one or an abstraction put in that person's place, such as the fatherland, freedom, an ideal, and so forth" (p. 429). Melancholy is the pathological equivalent of mourning, and by comparison with the latter's features ("pained resentment," "loss of interest in the outside world," and so on), an additional feature of melancholy is a "disturbance of one's self-esteem" which is expressed by "reproaching and cursing oneself." Those "diminutives" which Brahms bestowed on his symphony as a seemingly jocular disguise (*K:* "It will at all events be a proper flop, and people will say that this time I took it easy"; *O:* "The new one, though, is really no *Symphonie* but merely a *Sinfonie*") acquire a hidden significance in light of Freud's interpretation, which brings out the melancholic's "littleness mania." Here we indeed see "how one part of the ego is opposed to the other, appraising it critically, taking it for its object, so to speak" (Freud 433). To be sure, self-examination and self-criticism are, in principle, an essential element in the planning of a work of art. What stands out in Brahms is the "melancholic's enjoyable self-torment" (Freud 429; compare Brahms's *wollüstig* ["voluptuous"]), as voiced in statements about the works themselves and their relative importance. But here an additional perspective seems called for.

Brahms's "melancholic" readiness to communicate, his willingness and, indeed, determination to depict himself as a melancholic (and hence as ill in fact, as he does in his letter to Lachner), drawing the works too within this definition, make it seem likely that the melancholy was a pretense, a defensive act, a stage-managed self-deception—perhaps even, paradoxically, a conscious one. Klibansky, Saxl, and Panofsky in their classic study *Saturn and Melancholy* have investigated this "attitude of artistic self-portrayal" in the interests of inspiration as a centuries-old phenomenon in European intellectual history. They conclude with the "new melancholy" of the nineteenth century, with Keats, Hölderlin, and—right at the end—Verlaine and Jacobsen, identifying the looking-back, the historical perspective of the artistic "latecomer" as the determining feature of this "Weltschmerz" pose. Here they could have mentioned the name of Brahms.

What might the concrete background be to Brahms's melancholic invocation of F minor and the particular texture (in the broader sense) of this kind of music (see *O, S, V*)? This is worth a conjecture, although it must remain no more than that—assuming that Brahms was specifically alluding to a real piece, or the idea of one, at all. Of works close in time to the Second Symphony, the ballade "Edward" was mentioned earlier in this context, purely on account of the F-minor key; nowhere, however, does its texture resemble that alternation of fortissimo/piano chords in the treble and the bass which Brahms describes in his letter. As a symphonic work the Third Symphony would come into consideration, but of course this was composed much later and would only be possible, at the outside, as the "idea" associated with F minor. In discussions with David Lewin we identified a "family" of such pieces containing references to the aforementioned chordal texture: the Intermezzo, op. 118, no. 4 (which the ear would then similarly anticipate as being a variety of F-minor melancholy); the end of the first movement of the Piano Quintet, op. 34 of 1862–1864; and, by other composers, Schumann's "Concert sans Orchestre pour le Piano-Forte," op. 14 (with its variations on the "Andantino" by Clara Wieck; here I shall refrain from making the biographical and psychological connection which interpreters more interested in such things have apparently overlooked so far), as well as Beethoven's *Appassionata* Sonata, first movement, measures 16–23. For the purposes of our primary D-major connection, this sketchy excursion may suffice.

To return to my main argument, there seems little hope at this stage of tracking down the concrete object that might have sparked off Brahms's invocations of melancholy—a concrete person least of all. But Freud may well have hit the nail on the head by suggesting that one has, as a rule, "to relate melancholy somehow to an object-loss removed from consciousness, as distinct from mourning, where there is nothing un-conscious about the loss" (p. 431). This can be directly applied to Brahms's artistic self-understanding, and it leads to the next feature.

3. Melancholy as a latecomer's reaction. Within the context of the prevalent idea of the German bourgeoisie's "permanent belatedness" (Lepenies 55), Brahms's insight into the Viennese tradition cultivates all the symptoms of a late position in music history. The "anxiety of influ-ence" depicted earlier with regard to Beethoven, as the "strong poet," is, as a feeling of inevitable artistic dependence, akin to melancholy (Bloom 7). Here the genre of the symphony, fraught with tradition, is particularly affected. Brahms's oft-quoted statement about his difficult relationship to Beethoven as a symphonist, passed on by the conductor Hermann Levi from the start of the 1870s, is eloquent proof of this (and many more proofs could be added to it). "I shall never compose a sym-phony! You have no idea how someone like me feels when he keeps hearing such a giant marching behind him" (Kalbeck I, 165). The rich-ness of meaning here ought to be recognized: the "someone like me" identifies the artistic latecomer, in the sense of our first definition of melancholy; "feels" refers to the melancholic state; "giant" evokes the burden of tradition; and the "anxiety" is that of being an epigone. On the other hand, the commitment to this tradition is productive. In order to assure himself of this, to subsist in the face of it, the musical latecomer will pursue the traditional procedures with their formal ethos to ex-tremes. Every creative detail, as it were, each note of the symphony has to be justified by the construction of the whole. That aspect of the Second Symphony which could be described as extreme unity in diversity, the integral through-construction from the elements to the whole, the ele-

ments themselves evolving from the idea of the whole—form, organization through constructive work: all this seems, from the angle of melancholic awareness, like a collection of anti-strategies. And this yields a further heading.

4. Melancholy and "incessant labor." "What one actually calls invention, meaning a real idea, is, so to speak, a higher perception, inspiration—that's to say I can't help it. From then onward I cannot disdain this 'gift' enough, and through incessant labor I have to make it my legitimate, well-earned property" (Kalbeck II, 181–182). Brahms's words transpose into an artistic maxim, almost literally, the epitome of the Protestant work ethic as it used to be hung up in bourgeois living-rooms (with the image of a ploughman embossed in silver), in the form of a Goethean saying about one's patrimony, which one must earn in order to have it. The work of art is not serene but demands labor and effort, unremitting and "incessant," to be capable of becoming something "good" in the end. The "lasting music" (Jenner 74) Brahms strove for was the product of that kind of painstaking craftsmanship, a "skeptical substitute for the emphatic idea of art" (Brinkmann 1984, p. 116). But masterly craftsmanship—and this is a Brahmsian, historically conditioned inner experience—"mastery" does not free one from melancholy and resignation. "All winter I have been doing contrapuntal studies quite energetically. What for? Not so as to pull these fine things of mine to pieces the better, for that wouldn't be necessary. Nor so as to become a professor at the conservatory. To learn how to write notes better?—no, I'm not hoping for that, either. But it's a tragic thing if one ends up being smarter than one needs to" (to Clara Schumann, April 1, 1872; see Schumann/Brahms II, 9). Too much skill and too much knowledge as the root of inadequacy: the *Warum* motet, which asks why it is for the "struggler" that the light shines, is part of the portrayal of this very experience. Elmar Budde (p. 335) has related it to a knowledge of the historically inevitable loss of some basic artistic assumptions.

The historical latecomer's excess skill and knowledge beget reflection; late periods are always "ages of reflection" (Kierkegaard; see Lepenies 89) and, as such, extremely open to melancholic states. The enjoyment of sorrow, the voluptuous "delight" of depressed contemplation of one's

own toil, can then become productive in the artistic deed. Lepenies
(p. 154) quotes from Georg Lukács's *Theory of the Novel* the following
pertinent sentence: "Having to reflect is the deepest form of melancholy
of any genuine and great novel." This could also be applied to the large-
scale symphony of the late nineteenth century. Considered from this
angle, it seems by no means an accident that in the symphony of the
Gründerzeit, the age of commercial expansion, expansive symphonic
components and lyrical chamber-music components criss-cross: "The
element of reflection in bourgeois melancholy . . . represented a return
of disempowered subjectivity to itself" (Lepenies 153). This gives rise to
the following.

5. Melancholy as introversion. In the art of music, the internalized
spaces are taken up by chamber music or musical lyricism. And it seems
worth remarking in this connection that the late Viennese symphony at
the turn of the century tends toward lyricism, toward an inwardly directed concentration both in Mahler (with his striking combination of
large-scale symphony and intimate song) and also in Brahms (with his
symphonic texture's "chamber music" aspect, as it is often called). Musical lyricism born of the melancholic spirit came to dominate the late
works of Brahms—the works for clarinet with their somber tints, the
Four Serious Songs, the lyrical piano pieces. (Hanslick [1896, pp. 258–
259] calls the late pieces of Opus 116 and Opus 117 "a breviary of pessimism," while the piano pieces op. 118 and op. 119 are, to his mind, "mon-
ologues that Brahms is holding with and by himself during solitary eve-
nings, in pessimistic yet defiant rebellion, in brooding cogitation, or in
romantic reminiscing, and sometimes in dreamy mournfulness.") The
later Brahms wrote no more monumental orchestral works. This constitutes both a retreat from the broad-based, "global" dimension (the
sign of a flight in this perspective) and immersion in a concentrated act
of "thinking matters over and further"[23] (a gathering view both inward
and ahead, in this perspective). And the specific attributes of internali-

---

23. A conception of chamber music which has been expressed by Hans Werner
Henze, and which I am glad to borrow. I have applied it in particular to Schoenberg's
"musical lyric" on the threshold of Viennese atonality (see Brinkmann 1992).

zation appear in another relation, one which in regard to Brahms the symphonist was discussed earlier, in the self-determining reaction to Beethoven. *An alternative (like Schafer) to society, etc.*

  6. Melancholy and nature. "Nature" as the antithesis of "history" was the given reception-setting through which Brahms drew up his symphonic credo in support of Beethoven and also (as shown earlier) against him. From the viewpoint of the "anxiety of influence," the "misreading" in the First Symphony and Brahms's self-discovery in the Second are signs of an act of liberation. The melancholic perspective again observes an escape from the world and an internalization, even in the monumental form of the symphony, and this explains the "black border" surrounding the works as permanently marking the liberation. The psychic disposition to melancholy, and its historically mediated form, are still potent, and as witnesses to this, the symphony's trombones are "indispensable."

  For the late nineteenth-century composer, the musical portrayal of nature as an artistic principle has a real social external side. Getting away from the city is seen as a prerequisite of artistically productive work. Living in the metropolis that was Vienna, Brahms especially was one of those artists who preferred a summer dwelling (if only a rented one) for composing in, whether on the isle of Rügen, in the Black Forest, or up in the Alps, seeming to need this for themselves as a "natural" refuge. It is here, in the "freedom" and apparent immediacy of open tracts of nature and what were felt to be "natural" living conditions, that the great conceptions were planned and executed. And in principle they could have originated nowhere else. Brahms's first two symphonies as well as the Violin Concerto are direct evidence of this practice (see also document *B* with its ironically formulated truth: "the Wörther See [is] virgin soil, with so many melodies flying about that you must be careful not to tread on any"). Like Brahms, Dvořák too was famous for needing to get away from the city in the summer in order to compose. Mahler was subsequently to ideologize, as it were, the split between conducting operas and orchestral concerts in the city during the winter, which he regarded as a professional obligation, and his creative ecstasy in the natural ambiance of the summer cottage where he used to compose. Ob-

Isolation is implicit –

viously these habits are the privileged bourgeoisie's continuation of aristocratic modes of life, divided between a country summer residence and a town house in winter. The middle-class artist set free from the ties of a menial position in society will experience nature as an analogue to the freedom and immediacy of creative activity. Urban civilization represents the professional daily round, the freezing of inspiration. Thus since the Romantic era, if not before, "nature" (as the spatial equivalent of historical distance, which is to say distance in time) has contained a store of longing which directly affects the creative process and guides it, entering into the works themselves as both ideological program and compositional structure. This leads to the final topic.

7. Melancholy and idyll. The process of civilization defines the flight into nature as an idyll, at the same time relativizing and questioning the promise of happiness. It is true that the idyll presents the *form* in which the "dream of the great unity" is perceived, and where "social harmony and nature's immediate presence" might come together in a higher synthesis—in a nutshell, the imagined promise of a harmony between man and life, prefigured in the work of art. "But it will prove to be the case that this idyllic fulfillment can only be achieved at the cost of a separation: one must turn one's back on cities and city-dwellers" (Starobinski 159–160). At the onset of the modern age the compensatory dream of the idyll is seen through as such; the idyllic and utopian plan, on the one hand, and the thought of its unreality, on the other, will together generate that "melancholy enthusiasm" which blends idyll and elegy. "So the mind gives itself up to contemplating an asset which it lacks, which exists no longer or does not exist as yet. It gives itself up to the passion of absence, to thinking continually about a desire that will no longer find a commensurate object" (Starobinski 160). This is where the voluptuous "delight" and "mourning" of the "latecomer" have their melancholy place. The late idyll of the nineteenth and early twentieth century is always purchased through an act of renunciation with regard to the totality of life, as Renate Böschenstein-Schäfer has shown in poems by Mörike and Trakl. The crucial point is "that the idyllic state is one which has been battled for, where the banished demons can still be traced" (Böschenstein-Schäfer 94).

Such brokenness is, in the perspective of my interpretation, precisely the hallmark of Brahms's Second Symphony, or at least its first movement for the time being. But in contrast to this, the work's reception right from the first remarks by a friend of Brahms *(M)* up to our own day has, unanimously and one-sidedly, underlined the unbroken "serenity" of its expressive character, and seen a calmly idyllic quality as its hallmark. (See Manfred Wagner, 218ff., with the reviews of the premiere.) And only in a very few, exceptional cases (such as Gülke 1989, 52ff.) has a writer perceived the significance of those passages which disturbed Vincenz Lachner, and which Brahms sought to justify in his reply. Brahms's letter seems a spontaneous attempt (with Brahmsian reservations) to make a sympathetic friend and interpreter aware of the demonic undercurrents to the work. Its object was to correct the reception, to identify the interrupted idyll as the shaping idea. So from an interpretive angle, the letter can serve to support the musical analysis, although the analysis must, of course, prove its soundness independently through the score. Using this double starting-point, the ironically broken toying with "melancholic" meanings in Brahms's correspondence with friends before the premiere which I have documented will also have to be viewed afresh—and that means taken seriously.

Right at the end of this book, after analyzing the finale of the symphony, I shall return to discussing the subject of the idyll.

One postscript, however. (Peter Palmer suggested it.) There is a further dimension to Brahms's predisposition to melancholy; here it will only be touched upon, although the letter to Lachner provides the means for a more detailed discussion. I refer to the biographical or social aspect. In her portrait of Walter Benjamin, "Under the Sign of Saturn," Susan Sontag has rightly stressed the correlation of different factors in the melancholic experience of life: work, solitude, bitterness, fear of contact, and irony form a kind of chain. First there is the melancholic's work ethic, making him feel "condemned to work" (Sontag 126); and this "immersion" and "total concentration" (Sontag 128) produce the inner compulsion to be solitary, an inability to open oneself up to others, to socialize. But the self-isolation also produces, as its permanent reflection, bitterness, the sense of the injustice of this deliberately solitary life. "The need to be solitary—along with bitterness over one's loneliness—is characteristic of the melancholic. To get work done, one must be solitary—or, at least, not bound to any permanent relationship" (Sontag 127–128). Thus in the intercourse with others, defensive strategies are developed, and a permanent taking back of oneself, an irony become the solitary's way of protecting himself. "Irony is the positive name which the melancholic gives to his solitude" (Sontag 133). How directly the complex network of such experiences and reactions applies precisely to Brahms and his social behavior will be evident. And, of course, Brahms's curious, quixotic relationship to the women who mattered to him also comes within this context. His manifest shyness, or inability to enter into a lasting personal bond, is partly explicable from the disposition to melancholy, just as this reinforced the melancholic state itself. But this book is not a biography; and we can leave it at that.

The Middle Movements

In Romantic symphonic music the inner movements are, as mentioned, usually character pieces of "medium" dimensions and weight, or they tend in that direction (even when headed "Scherzo," as for instance with Schumann). This is already evident from the tempo markings: Andante or Larghetto, not a large-scale Adagio; Allegretto or Moderato, not a demonic Scherzo-Allegro or Scherzo-Presto. Of course there are the exceptions like Schumann's Second with its symphonic pretensions, like Tchaikovsky's *Pathétique* with its weighty Adagio, like the whole of Bruckner. And, in part, like Brahms's Second. In his First, Third, and also his Fourth Symphony (where the burlesque third movement is a borderline case in terms of genre), the inner movements speak that lyrically restrained, lighter language "on a medium level of feeling" (Hanslick 1886, 363–364). And Hanslick found fault with this from the standpoint of balanced proportions: "For all the fundamental difference between them, the first and third symphonies of Brahms are nonetheless alike in one respect: their two middle movements appear, in their content and breadth, somewhat too little compared to the mighty pieces of music surrounding them." Whether this reproach and the assumptions behind it are justified is certainly debatable, but Hanslick has estimated correctly the relative proportions of the individual movements. The course of ideas in Brahms's First Symphony, say, is realized primarily in the outer movements.[24]

In the Second Symphony the problem is more complicated. It features, after its important first movement, the demanding, expansive Adagio with its expressive cantilena, its imposing tone, and its adherence to sonata form. But then comes a particularly light, uncomplicated, and, in spite of its five sections, relatively short third movement. And finally there is the "last dance" *(Kehraus),* con brio. These relative proportions in terms of tone and character are matched by the lengths of the movements. Let us take the statistics for the premiere—19: 11: 5: 8 minutes. The first movement alone is nearly one and a half times the length of the last two put together, while the first added to the second is over twice the length of the third added to the fourth. And in contrast to the First, Third, and Fourth Symphonies, the finale does not counterbalance the first movement. It can scarcely be termed a "finale" in the emphatically symphonic meaning of the (late) nineteenth century; it recalls closing movements of the Haydnesque type. From the viewpoint of formal proportioning, the third and fourth movements together, at the outside, provide a counterpart to the opening movement or to the Adagio. The movements in this symphony are not evenly balanced. It is decidedly top-heavy.

The movements are connected in a similar way by the disposition of keys. Movements I and II are the more closely linked on the one hand, movements III and IV on the other. There are also cross-connections between all four movements. The submediant B major Adagio, with its dominant beginning, expands corresponding harmonic zones from the first movement (such as the F-sharp minor/B minor of the second subjects) so as to give them independent status, extending the tonal framework. It substantially adopts the realm of G minor internally, in its de-

---

24. The correspondence with Clara Schumann also discusses the format of the middle movements. And we can now reconstruct Brahms's tussles with the form (and length) of the second movement of the First Symphony. On this subject see Brodbeck, pp. 424ff.

velopment-like middle section. The third movement, with its G major key, is pitched another third lower in relation to the Adagio; within the overall framework it is subdominant, leading back to the tonic D of the closing movement. Internal B major/F-sharp major episodes inhabit tonal spheres from the first two movements. And the injections of G minor are by no means surprising if one considers the minor subdominant's role in the opening movement. The subtlety of this movement's tonal layout applies to the whole. (The last movement adopts the two realms afresh.) In the way that the harmony opens up in the Adagio and leads back in the third movement, the overall tonal plan refers to the formal turning-point in the symphony. The caesura occurs after the second movement.

Second Movement: Adagio non troppo, 4/4 – L'istesso tempo, ma grazioso, 12/8 – B major

The great Adagio song at the start of the movement—the cello cantilena so typical of late-Romantic symphonic espressivo—determines the artistic level. And the movement is formally demanding. The change of key, meter, and character between the lyrical passion of the opening paragraph (mm. 1–32) and the graceful animation of a contrasting passage (mm. 33ff.) is not envisaged as the inner articulation of a song-form, or as the initial provision for a set of double variations (as was possible after the way Beethoven handled the Adagio of his Ninth Symphony, and was later realized in Mahler's Fourth); the change is governed by the sonata principle. Although a song-like contrast between paragraphs seems to outweigh the developmental principle at first, the first paragraph is to be read as the main subject and the second as the second theme. At m. 45 there follows an epilogue whose five-note motif subsequently serves as the model for a brief but intensive development (mm. 49ff.). To be sure, only the first subject appears in the return of the first section (mm. 62ff.), the recapitulation. The contrasting paragraph—the sonata-form second subject—is omitted. A coda (mm. 97ff.) containing the principal idea concludes the movement. Tripartite song-form has been expanded into a sonata. But in its internal tripartite structure (with the partial return of the principal idea after m. 28 and m. 87 respectively), the main subject retains, in the modulating transition, an element of song-form.

Surveyed schematically, the events of the movement are as follows:

mm. 1–48	A	*"exposition"*
1–32	*a*	main subject 4/4
	a1	1–17
	a2	17–27
	a1	28–32 (m. 28 = m. 3)
33–44	*b*	second subject 12/8
45–48	*c*	epilogue 12/8
49–61	B	*"development"* 12/8
		primary material: *c*
		reverse course after m. 57 with *a1*
62–96	A	*"recapitulation"* (changed)
62–91	*a*	main subject 4/4
	a1	62–80
	a2	81–86
	a1	87–91
92–96	*c*	epilogue 12/8
97–104	C	*coda* 4/4
		primary material: *a1*

The Sections: Song-Form, or Sonata

A, or the Exposition

Before soaring freely, from the upbeat to m. 3 onward, in a more and more vivifying way, the cello cantilena is fitted into a compact texture of narrow compass which it serves to frame (Example 23). Everything proceeds from the one f-sharp, through several octaves, and everything

hangs, as though between stakes, on the framework of this dominant drone, which will not submit to any shading of the other parts in the texture. A scalic descent begins (m. 1) in the cellos with measured strides, in a double start leading from dominant f-sharp to b, differentiated in melodic-harmonic terms as an opening-up first phrase and a tonically closing counter-phrase. A counterpoint in contrary motion in the bassoons completes the texture; its second phrase is intensified rhythmically and harmonically, and it is longer by one quarter, stretching as far as the upbeat to the third cello phrase.

As though from a distance, this counterpoint of cellos and bassoons seems to recall and elaborate on the voice-leading, in contrary motion, of the trombone chords in mm. 33ff. of the first movement. Max Kalbeck dealt with this reference long ago (and, as pointed out earlier, even made a connection with the slow introduction to the First Symphony), and once the reference has been pointed out, the ear will be able to follow it.

Quasi-strict writing, then, in the opening Adagio measures, and a sonority that is distinctively fixed in a low register. Only at mm. 3–4 is there a gradual change: fourth upbeats to provide animation, eighth-notes twirling around the scalic descent, and then the upswing gesture. A motivic, gestural, harmonic, and orchestral unfolding begins. But, as so often with Brahms, this blossoming is subject to small-scale organization, controlled, and somewhat arrested emotionally. The third cello phrase (m. 3) is still clearly a variant of the scalic descent; it is followed by a twofold upswing, intensified in itself (mm. 4–5). This alternation of a scaled and regular downward motion with rhythmically accentuated upward swings is continued until m. 10, after which these upswing motifs incorporate the secundal step of the gliding eighth-notes augmented, and finish swaying with splitting-off; and at the end of m. 12 the initial model returns within an orchestral space that has now been enlarged. Thus even here, within the smaller compass of a paragraph, the initial setting (mm. 1–2), development (mm. 3–12), and intensified repeat (mm. 12–17) present the symmetry of the return as a formal principle. Hence the "song-like" ABA articulation, raised to a higher power, operates on three levels: within a_1, in the larger main subject a, and finally in the way the recapitulation is organized in the entire movement.

But this essentially very clear, solid framework is not only broken up, or overlaid, by principles of sonata writing, it is also rendered more complex internally, as it were. Right at the start of the movement—and basically in the same way as the first movement, although the realization is now completely different—the motivic articulation, metrical grouping of measures, and the cadential rhythms enter into a musically productive conflict. That which, at the start, sounds completely normal in the time is, in reality, already a metrical displacement as far as the graded-accent measure is concerned. The notation does not reproduce what the ear perceives and shows this discrepancy by one quarter. Until nearly the end of m. 2, however, the ear perceives two phrases which are clearly downbeat and no upbeat or syncopated components (although the melodic lines in themselves could also have been realized as upbeats). It is only with the fourth-upbeat ahead of m. 3 that the ear registers a metrical irregularity. Here the melody is locked within the time as it is notated.

But even now, the notated mensural framework has not yet been established with regard to the cadencing. The upbeat f-sharp–b on the borderline of mm. 3–4 is the first occasion when the notated mensural scheme and the melody's cadential rhythms are in agreement. At the same time, however, steps are being taken to counter this. The melodic top note of the fourth cello phrase, f-sharp, accentuates the "2" of the measure, and furthermore the "1" stays vacant in the accompanimental and filler parts. The tendency toward the 3/8 upbeat and melodic center of gravity f-sharp' in m. 4 is quite distinct, and is increased in the following measure.

The equivocation between a cadential rhythm that confirms the time and a melodic *habitus* that confuses the time goes on, and specifically in mm. 6–8, as indicated by the phrasing. Also to be considered are the various positions and valuations of identical and analogous elements such as the fourth-interval b–e in mm. 2–3 and m. 4, or the model of the descending diatonic scale inherent in all the components. Brahms's art of melodic differentiation is immense. A good part of it depends on the metrically controlling power of the measure, with its hierarchy of accents, and the deliberate play of nuances between suspension and ful-

fillment.[25] And, of course, the whole thing is furthermore open to interpretation: different interpreters will choose different ways of placing the
accents, some tending to ambiguity and others more to the unequivocal.
Here again, Brahms's music is composed with these options in mind.
Walter Frisch (p. 123) has rightly drawn on Schoenberg's concept of musical prose to characterize this paragraph of the second movement.

Paragraph *a2* (mm. 17ff.) employs, growing out of *a1*, the fourth-
element as its head motif and develops it, with chromatic continuation,
into the subject of a little fugato. First the motif is heard in the solo
horn, that important instrumental color in the first movement, soon to
be reinforced by the bassoon, with oboes to follow; the flutes and, eventually, the basses form a second imitational pair with a different position
in the measure—in contrast to the dominance of strings in *a1*, the sonority relies chiefly on woodwinds.

Technically speaking the passage represents an intensification, having
the effect of a small developmental area, in which capacity it points ahead
to mm. 51ff. and main paragraph *B* (both are middle paragraphs!). Since,
however, the subject remains formulaic, no contrapuntal part-writing
evolves; it is more of a static oscillating and rotating, even in the layering
of the subject's chromatic continuations. Just as *a2* arose from *a1*, so it
leads back to *a1*—via the fourth. From this angle it appears consistent
for the return of *a1* to begin in an abridged form with what was originally
the third phrase, that of the fourth-upbeat. This appears, in the modulatory continuation, on the dominant-of-the-dominant, as a conclusion
to *a* which has been intensified compared to m. 3 and m. 15, and also as
a bridge to the contrasting *b* portion. The latter is on the F-sharp major
dominant (Example 24).

b contrasts with *a*, and especially with *a1*, on several levels:

- as 12/8-time which, given the unchanging basic pulse, is like an in-
  vigorating dose of triplets after the 4/4-time;

25. Peter Gülke (*Brahms Bruckner*, pp. 29ff.) has described this "conjunctive tense"
of the melody.

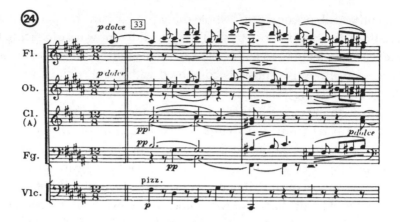

- the notated time and the filling of the measure are metrically no longer at odds, the forward eighth being continuously syncopated, the melody floating over the firm background of the beats;
- as metrically clear-cut, "four-square" two-measure grouping, thus constituting "verse" after the "prose" of the start;
- as high woodwind writing (prepared by *a2*!) after the dominance of strings in *a1*;
- as a lighter, dance-like type of motion after the great adagio tone of the beginning.

This range of contrasts points, in the sonata context, to the second subject. And the definition is supported by the obvious affinity with the second theme of the opening movement: a composed analogy. Both complexes have a dance-like character—the individual stamp of a 3/4 rhythm in the earlier instance, and the 3/8 filling of the beat in the latter; the tempo difference results in the same rhythmic relations. Moreover, both themes are heard above typical pizzicato basses. Both are based melodically upon the same intervallic nucleus, related to F-sharp minor in the one and to F-sharp major in the other (Example 25), and neither of them disdains parallel thirds—sound pure and simple, and this is the right place for it. (In the case of the opening movement's second theme, the tone is—as mentioned above—reminiscent of some of the *Liebes-lieder-Walzer,* but also of the cradle song "Guten Abend, gut Nacht.")

The paragraph is, as usual with a second subject, divided into very clear-cut periods. Three inwardly symmetrical four-measure units succeed one another, the first unit (mm. 33–36) being an antecedent/consequent each with a one-measure first phrase featuring wide intervals, and each with two counter-phrases of half a measure falling diatonically; the following two units (mm. 33ff., 41ff.) are similar but with more forward movement, evolving through a directly repeated first phrase and counter-phrases. As with *a1* on a smaller scale, an upswing on the high violins with the same emphatic octave upbeat (end of m. 42; compare m. 29) concludes the paragraph—strongly highlighted here as the climax of the complete A section or, in sonata terms, the exposition. There follows a brief epilogue *c*. This has the effect of an echo at first, its motif *c* being derived from the counterpoint of *a1* and taken up via mm. 39–40. But the epilogue itself mediates ahead at the same time. And this marks the first unequivocal break with the principles of song-form. Proceeding from an intensification that starts off in the epilogue, motif *c* becomes the thematic model for a developmental passage. The main subject and second subject could be interpreted as the bipartite A section of a song-form, despite the sonata relations; but what follows can only be accounted for in terms of the sonata principle.

B, or the Development

Section B (mm. 49–61) is first, because of its fabric, the concise working-up of initial material, no longer to be viewed as simply a song-form middle section. Structurally and functionally it is a development section—admittedly very short and, as it were, one-dimensional in regard to the types and characters of the working-up, yet altogether commensurate with the length of the movement. And, as with the second subject earlier, Brahms supports this view with composed references to the analogous formal situation in the first movement. There, the development and coda were prefaced by quasi-restraining melodic oscillations stemming the flow, motions that went back to the central motif *x;* here, figures revolving similarly are heard before the development (mm. 45–47) and the reprise (mm. 55–56 and 60–61 in the brass). But the direct parallels affect the beginnings of the two developments themselves. Both are governed by fugati. The idea that the first movement's great development section came into its own at the second fugato as a compositional principle was put forward in the earlier analysis. The Adagio's development begins without ado as just such a fugato, and in so doing it unmistakably adopts and transforms the subject of that second fugato in the opening movement, with its characteristic three-step/four-step beginning. The details of a complicated affinity could be pursued further (three-step plus third plus fall of a fifth in the subject on violas and cellos, four-step plus a swaying second in the varied consecutive subject on flutes and oboes; the second fugato's motivic elements are divided between two subjects). But here the earlier indication may suffice. Furthermore, there is no overlooking the fact that the complementary, oscillating semitone motifs heard in the trombones and other bass instruments after the winding-down of this Adagio development's fugato (mm. 55–57, also mm. 60–61) go back to the first movement's motto *x*—though more loosely packed within one another than they were at the end of the earlier fugato (mm. 224–226, similarly with trombones). And, of course, the development is consistently two-part in texture, with cadential chordal interjections on the brass (something else that occurred in the opening movement). The two contrapuntal parts, which are an octave apart and with a 3/8 gap between entries, are identical and yet dissimilar. Identical aspects include the motivic nucleus, particularly the progression at the beginning of the subject, and also the syncopations. What is different is the way the motion continues: runs of sixteenths in the low initial voice, swaying eighth-motifs in the high subsequent voice. The textural compression is matched by dynamic and, to an increasing extent, gestural sharpening. With the third pair of voices (the first pair is from the b in m. 49, the second pair from the g in m. 51, in quasi-double counterpoint, with the bridge in G minor to the first movement's important harmonic area), the consecutive voice is adapted to the leading one in terms of movement and responds a fifth apart; at the same time there is splitting-off and shortening of the entry (m. 53: a–e and b–f-sharp), which are typical devices for constructing a climax. This is followed by a reversal in the shape of a two-measure phrase (mm. 55–56) with Wagnerianly "brooding" retardation: over restless string tremoli and the aforementioned oscillating motifs on the bass instruments (it is pertinent to recall the harsh trombone imitation in E minor in the first movement's development section), chromaticized head-motifs of the fugato theme are related back to the contrapuntal voice of *a1*. In the superimposing of flutes and oboes combined with the bassoon part in m. 57, this derivation is audibly evident. Measures 57–58 bring with them, over a pedal-point d but related to g as the harmonic center, a two-measure anticipation of the reprise of *a1*. The time-placing changes, and furthermore 12/8 and 4/4 time are expressly combined. After an interruption caused by an upsurge similar to mm. 54–56, the reprise just invoked really does enter at m. 62—more complicated after all than was perhaps expected.

A Changed, or the Recapitulation

First, the recapitulation features a half-measure dislocation of the time, brought forward like *a1* in m. 57 earlier. Second, *a1* is played not as a sonorous cello cantilena with a low bassoon counterpoint but as a descant on the first oboe and with a counterpoint of violins. Third, the 12/8 division is still present in the bassoon triplets, the reprise being, beyond m. 57, a union of previously separate elements: a tendency that will increase from m. 67 onward. And fourth, the reprise enters in the subdominant. In the simpler classical sonata movements in the major (such as Mozart's Piano Sonata in C major, K. 545, first movement), this is, among other things, the easiest way to avoid a change in the transition; with a subdominant reprise the second subject is automatically in the tonic. But that is not a consideration here: as I have mentioned, the second theme *b* is left untouched anyway in the reprise. The purpose of the device in this Adagio is to differentiate the return of the main subject. For the "head" of *a1* appears twice more, which it did not do in the exposition; the thematic, harmonic, and metrical recapitulations become separate.

On the first occasion, then, the main theme is heard with rhythmic dislocation, and in the subdominant. The end of its second phrase (m. 64), however, does not confirm the subdominant E as its goal but turns instead to the tonic B. Two interlocking thematic fragments lead to the second entry (m. 65). Now the theme does appear in the tonic, thus recalling the harmony of the opening, but it is still displaced by half a measure. Moreover, the added timpani roll makes the dominant f-sharp drone seem a typical preparation for an entry, and even the thematic two-measure phrase itself is still open in the dominant at the end (m. 67; note the contrast with m. 2!). Only with the third entry (end of m. 67) is the harmonic and metrical situation obtaining at the start of the movement arrived at (and now the continuation of *a1* also proceeds along the lines of mm. 3ff.). But at this stage the thematic variation in progress has already moved away from the prototype of *a1*. Recapitulation as a fluid process in three stages, therefore (four stages with the anticipation in m. 57). The first goal (m. 62) is still incomplete, whereas with the third and last (m. 67) the music has already evolved beyond this actual goal.

This thematic development of the reprise is rooted in a constant orchestral restructuring; a fanning-out and enrichment of texture go hand in hand with the figurative dissolution of thematic contours. Transforming and transcending the expository material—aesthetic riches, that is—as well as combining material within the texture—the element of unity again—are the main ideas behind the changes. Compared to the first term of the recapitulation (mm. 62–64), which adopts the strict part-writing of the opening, albeit more brightly and with a scattering of triplets, the second is already less ascetic. This appears (mm. 65–67) across the full sound-spectrum with a kettledrum underlay and descant triplets. At the third approach (mm. 67ff.), pizzicati (an important factor in second theme *b*!) in the fanned-out accompaniments replenish the sound. And to an increasing extent the violin part with the triplets has assumed control. The starting-point is the triplet motif from *c*; as described, this is returned to the counterpoint of *a1* at the end of the development (see mm. 55ff.). Still hidden in the bassoons at the start of the reprise, the motif shifts to the violins at m. 65, overgrows the phrase-end in m. 67, and becomes the figurative element in the thematic variation, running through the entire *a1*-reprise. Thus thematic aspects of *c* (and with it, of B, the development) and rhythmic aspects of *b* come together with *a1* in the recapitulation. This may be the reason why, in a reprise involving so much development and combination, the contrasting second subject *b* is left out.

The triplet figuration hides the fact that at m. 67 the initially complete return of *a1* has commenced. Measure 70 corresponds to m. 3; m. 72 modulates, hence the contents of mm. 66ff. appear a fifth lower in mm. 73ff. There is no longer a return to the thematic head of *a1* on the lines of m. 15 as a result of the graduated reprise with its restructurings; the preferred modulatory procedure makes possible, via further changes (in mm. 78–80), the immediate addition of *a2*, in the register of the exposition.

This *a2* is drastically changed. Not only is the horn that opens it now covered by the flute (mm. 81ff.); the chromatic continuation of the part is omitted, and there is no longer a growth and superimposing of lines to form a fugato. Two sound-areas of contrasting color (winds in one, strings in the other) succeed each other, and in the second of them the fourth-upbeat already repressed in the reprise of *a1* is converted, for modulatory purposes, into a major third. Via the F major and C major thus created, *a1* returns after only six measures (instead of the exposition's ten)—in m. 87 on the lines of m. 28 with its third phrase, but in the minor subdominant E, and substantially varied. The sixteenth-note sextuplets in the leading violins surrounding the thematic nucleus are a clear reminiscence of the development. The five-measure paragraph's grabbing motion, with the timpani blows that recall the development, lends it a character which is forward-directed, more than that of a return. It can be said that in A' the fugued middle passages of sections A and B are brought together in principle. Again the impetus of the changing and evolving gains the ascendancy over the formal sense of a mere return.

The working-up element continues to dominate beyond the development: the reprise is governed by processual forms, is more and more something akin to a second development. Sonata thinking outweighs the song-form architecture. So the reflective and dance-like second subject is now also omitted. This "development" leads, after a vigorous cadence, into the epilogue, which starts off at m. 92 with a deceptive cadence, thus avoiding a closure. In a changed form, it is drawn into this process.

C Coda, or the Kettledrum Echo

With the minor-key coloration and the sharpening of the motion after m. 87, the tone has become more effortful, more somber. This expressive turnaround gives the movement its final direction. Its fulfillment is—after the last climax in the chordally saturated string sonority toward the end of the epilogue (m. 94)—the conclusion: a restrained coda that restates *a1* in the strictly composed form of the tonic starting position (mm. 97ff.). What determines this coda's tone and meaning, with its switch from the woodwinds to the strings, is first the splitting-off retention of the half-measure motif ♩♩♫ ; then the insistence, underlined by bass pizzicati and the only sforzati to occur outside the development, on the thirty-second figure played by the cellos, which was hitherto used rather casually; also the ninth-chords; and—the renewed importance of the kettledrum. This instrument, which in the first movement was reserved for a number of outstanding moments, comes to the fore at the end of the Adagio, even though—paradoxically—it stays in the background. It had helped to determine the impact of the E minor passage in mm. 87–89, had established the impetuous, restless character of the epilogue (mm. 92–93) as a roll forming its own crescendo. Now, with m. 99, the kettledrum takes over from the horn the triplet motif reduced to a single pitch, leading it via a mixed rhythmic pattern back to quarter-repetitions. The kettledrum literally provides the dark undertone to this shaded conclusion.

And this could also be the underlying reason for leaving out the second theme with its ethereal animation: the dramaturgy of the symphony is aiming for a problematic close to the first two movements, not a smoothly serene one. The second movement began sonorously, disporting itself freely, and striking a light dance-like note in the second theme, but it too finally ends in underlying skepticism. Here a further perspective presents itself. In Max Kalbeck's view (III, 173), the rhythmic form and contrapuntal layout of the principal idea of *a1*, and especially the thirty-second figure, relate back beyond the first movement's trombone measures to the First Symphony's slow introduction, with its tragically insistent tone. If there is any part of the Adagio of the Second where such an affinity can be heard quite indubitably, then it is this coda. And the kettledrum would be the distant, introverted echo of that symphonic world now being summoned up once more.

The coda was originally one measure longer and thus had the outward appearance of an orthodox eight-measure period. (Measure 97 is part of the epilogue in terms of its content and function.) In the autograph, on page 18 of the manuscript now in the Pierpont Morgan Library, Brahms deleted what was formerly the penultimate measure (103a), which in essence merely repeated what became the definitive penultimate measure (103). Thus the coda in its seven-measure form appears to be "irregular." But this is reflected in the metrical dislocation of *a1*, which, as at the beginning of the movement, enters virtually as a downbeat on the last quarter of m. 97. From the middle of m. 100 onward, this dislocation is set right by the motivic splitting-off, and with m. 101 the metrical organization is regulated according to the written time. The movement ends with a perfectly normal four-measure phrase that finishes in B major, reassured—or rather, it sets the ending to rights in regard to the relation of meter to measure. For the kettledrum "echo" lingers on in the ear.

Third Movement: Allegretto grazioso (Quasi Andantino), 3/4 – Presto ma non assai, 2/4 – Tempo I, 3/4 – Presto ma non assai, 3/8 – Tempo I, 3/4 – G major

In this work's symphonic dramaturgy, the third movement—this was mentioned earlier—comes after the central caesura. It executes overall the imagined step from an interrupted idyll to the tone of one rocking peacefully to and fro. It is the shortest, most lightweight movement in the symphony. The real brass instruments (trumpets, trombones, tuba) are excluded, and in light of the reason Brahms gave in his letter for introducing trombones, this may already be a pointer to the movement's intention, or at least the absence or omission of certain types of expression. Analytically it seems to pose no problems on account of its clear articulation and unequivocal characterization. Let us approach it from five perspectives.[26] (The terminology used will distinguish between sections and their individual paragraphs.)

Character

The perspectives that have been particularly discussed in the existing literature are *character* and *form*. For this much is patent: here we have dances, dance-types which for all the obvious stylization are clearly defined and have concrete names—something by no means unexpected with Brahms, and at this point in a Romantic symphony, yet taking remarkable and singular shapes. So early a writer as Kalbeck stated (III, 170–171) that this third movement presented a scherzo "in an idiosyncratic manner": the basic melody, he observed, twice changes shape and tempo, appearing first "as a minuet-like Ländler . . . , then as a *Galopp* . . . , then as a pungent quick-waltz." The dance sequence has been regarded as being like a suite (Floros 211–212), and even as harking back directly to the Baroque orchestral suite (Kahl, *Die Musik in Geschichte und Gegenwart*, XI, col. 1686). This view is certainly not entirely wrongheaded. And yet the whole is more artificially broken, and carried in different directions, than these statements imply (and this, too, is by no means unexpected in Brahms).

Three pairs of woodwinds over a pizzicato bass, an eminently realistic ensemble, begin by playing a Ländler, but one with a rather refined and elegant accent (Example 26). A dance, yes, but a highly stylized one. (Kalbeck's reference to a minuet-like quality endeavors to capture this

26. On this movement, see in particular the studies by Komma, Toch (pp. 187ff.), and Floros.

stylization.) One conspicuous feature is the tendency to *Satzform* (to use A. B. Marx's distinction) instead of the "four-square" period as a phrase-structure, the melody being designed to evolve. The eight-measure theme, as already described, goes back to the central motif *x* as an inversion. It acquires its particular, gently floating character from the metrically "irregular," pointed gesture in the third beat of the measure, with its grace-note to the accentuated melodic top note after the repetition (Komma's "upswing accent"), and from the "Lombard," unlocking final flourish prefigured in the suspension in m. 6. This Lombard secundal step e–d in m. 8 becomes, as it repeatedly falls in with the swaying motion, the moving spirit of the second paragraph with its Brahmsian proliferation of sixths. Here the texture becomes more complex, and the dance turns into more and more of a character piece—in the G minor shading of m. 26 in the reiterating closing paragraph (prepared in the D minor of mm. 14 and 20), in the very typical submediant extension to E-flat major in m. 29 and the echoing major-minor alternation at the end with its almost Schubertian accent, that nonviolent force of darker and lighter nuances which Mahler, too, was capable of evoking in his songs with such eloquence.

The B section oscillates even more between dance and scherzo. At the start the quick form of the Ländler theme is heard in regular staccato eighth-notes (Kalbeck was quite right to refer to a *Galopp*), and the internally contrasting, dotted, *forte* tutti passage in mm. 51ff. can be converted perfectly well into the concrete motion of a rapid "sprung after-dance" (Komma 450) (Example 27). But the "durchbrochene Satz," the

melodically fragmented writing in mm. 41–50, and especially the staccato eighth-notes in the strings from m. 63 onward are already typical scherzo passages—and the section retains this character until the music returns to the A section. The closeness of the passages in mm. 63ff. to the string motions in the third movement of Beethoven's *Eroica* (mentioned ear-lier) is too obvious: the paragraph becomes, in part, a veritable scherzo. One could enlarge on this in the form of a question. Ländler/minuet and dance/scherzo—a minuet that turns into a quick-step, and then into a scherzo: was Brahms also composing one aspect of the history of the symphonic third movement in general? In a way that is quite similar, and in an analogous place from a formal standpoint, the second quick dance comes around in m. 156 to the character of a scherzo. And in the third A section, the closing section, the extension into a character piece is even greater than at the beginning. The intermediate areas, the places where the separate characters, seemingly so clearly defined, brush to-gether and change—these are what interest Brahms.

Before raising the question of tradition once more with reference to the "form" perspective, it seems a good idea at this point to look at Brahms's contemporaries. The links between themes and dance char-acters in the third movements of Brahms's Second and Dvořák's Eighth Symphony, in G major, are well known and have been addressed a number of times.[27] The Dvořák symphony dates from 1889, so the chron-

27. Petersen (see the Bibliography) has recently examined this subject in detail. Gerald Abraham, in his preface to the Eulenburg pocket score 525 of Dvořák's Eighth Symphony, has proposed a similarity between this symphonic Trio and the trio-like middle section of Tomík's song "Pantáta Lenku" from Dvořák's comic opera "Tvrdé Palice" ("The Diehards"). The one-act opera was composed fifteen years before the symphony. But

ological order of the two is not in doubt. Dvořák's third movement, like Brahms's, is an "Allegretto grazioso" in G major. Its middle section actually quotes Brahms's initial theme, transformed, and the binary Presto form (in this case, Allegro vivace) also appears—as with Brahms, first *piano,* then in the full orchestra. Dvořák was able to adapt Brahms's style to his own idiom because here, Brahms himself was making use of "Bohemian" folk-music elements. This applies not only to the (afore-mentioned) parallel thirds-sixths, or to such melodic-harmonic gestures as those in mm. 225–226, which—as David Epstein has observed orally—could occur in Dvořák's Slavonic Dances. What is especially striking is the similarity to the furiant with its changing time and its openness to the hemiola, or—and this is taken up directly in the Brahms theme—to the polka-mazurka in 3/4-time, with the so-called "whiplash step" on the "3." But unlike Brahms's middle section, Dvořák's is the genuine "trio" of a dance movement, and the quick form with its contrasting even time serves as a stretta-like coda. Moreover, as Peter Petersen has shown, Brahms's dance characters are far more stylized. To a certain extent Dvořák was restoring to its native "Bohemian" province of music-making the artificially used *Zwiefache* (to quote the South German term), whose changes of rhythm were so well matched to Brahms's liking for hemiolas and metrical playfulness in general. And the formal function of the dance characters is different as well. Dvořák's symphonic move-ment is clearly tripartite (with a supplement). Not so with Brahms. This leads to the second perspective:

Form

The movement is clearly in five sections, with a double repetition of the initial section, symmetrically arranged so as to form the centerpiece and frame. This organization is outwardly reminiscent of the extended scherzo form and its tradition from Beethoven's Seventh, which

---

the thematic similarities between Dvořák's symphonic Trio and his opera song are less distinct than the thematic relationship, and the formal "inversion," between the two symphonic movements of Brahms and Dvořák.

Schumann carried on (with two not wholly identical trios), but imbues it with a quite different spirit. Applying the standard categories, it is already not a triple scherzo with two trio sections but the opposite: a primary, twice repeated trio-like movement with two (non-identical) scherzo-like contrasting sections.[28] A back-to-front scherzo and trio, so to speak, dressed with the artificial dance characters and their various guises.

The formal principles that are most obvious to the ear have now been stated: contrast and repetition, realized on different levels—the time, tempo, sonority, textural patterns. Roughly speaking, A-B-A-C-A''.

A: base section in G major (mm. 1–32). 3/4-time and Allegretto/Andantino with quarter-motion. Internally tripartite: eight-measure theme, developmental paragraph between mm. 9–22, fermata followed by varied repetition of theme. Prevalent woodwind sonority of two oboes, clarinets, and bassoons, hence a "trio" worthy of the name; plus a string bass pizzicato on the cellos. Homophonic writing, leading melody-voice (first oboe), and accompaniment divided in terms of sonority and texture, with strong drone elements. In all, a guarantee of the pastoral tone.

Then B: first contrasting section (mm. 33–106), again in G major. But 2/4 and Presto with eighth-note figuration, thus breaking down the time and tempo from triple to duple, as well as shortening the motion. The strings dominate, the woodwinds being used mostly as doubling instru-

28. Compare Floros, p. 211, and Komma, pp. 448–449. Floros's reference to an analogous construction in the case of the Brahms String Quintet No. 1, in F major, while correct, is not quite differentiated enough. The quintet has only three movements, the middle movement being, therefore, a combination of slow movement and dance movement in tempo. The three appearances of the main section, which is a sarabande-like "Grave ed appassionato" in 3/4-time, varied on each occasion, are interspersed with a section that does contrast like a trio but is quicker. The first insert is an "Allegretto vivace" in lightly tripping 6/8-time, the second a binary-measure, alla breve version of the first, marked Presto. This variational relationship distinguishes the quintet from the symphony movement. – Brahms adopted a different approach in his String Quartet No. 2, in A minor, constructing the five sections of the third movement as a varied interlacing of minuet and scherzo, although here the middle minuet section on the dominant is rudimentary.

ments in tuttis, occasionally more independently *im durchbrochenen Satz,* in melodic filigree, amounting in one instance (mm. 83ff.) to a thematic four-measure unit. Soft beginning, change of character, and loud dynamics from m. 51 (Example 28). This marcato tutti with its stressed quarter-notes, the rhythmically taut dotting, and the scherzo-staccato presents a relative contrast again within the section. The return after m. 101 mixes B with elements of A.

A': first repeat section, now in itself bipartite. At the beginning (mm. 107ff.), reappearance of the Allegretto melody at the same pitch but with revised harmony tending toward (an initially dominant) E major in slightly varied woodwinds, with pizzicato bass. Then, however, a completely changed continuation as the second paragraph (mm. 114ff.), now insistently stressing the B major like a pedal-point.

C: the second contrasting section, analogous to B in construction, but with varied musical contents (Example 29). Beginning on unison strings,

at first apparently in G major, but soon pointing toward C major; 3/8-time and Presto, thus again breaking up and speeding up; strings and woodwinds alternate from paragraph to paragraph. As in section B, the strings enter *piano,* followed by a variant of the tutti section played *forte* and over the pedal-point c (mm. 144ff.; compare mm. 51ff.). The extended leading-back (mm. 188–193) "mixes" elements of the two even more strongly, at the same time submitting them to significant harmonic development and arriving eventually at a dominant C-sharp major.

A″: the concluding and expanded base section, when it is varied beyond A, above all instrumentally, can thus branch out harmonically, beginning in F-sharp major (mm. 194ff.). It starts off (an important variant, this!) on expressive strings, attaining at m. 210 an analogous situation to m. 14 (but still with the mixed sounds of strings and woodwinds), and only at the closing paragraph, in m. 219 (analogous to m. 23), does it return via the pizzicato but reinforced by the horn, to the basic key of G major and to the "trio" layout of the beginning. It is then considerably extended (mm. 225ff.) in orchestral scope and expression once more, especially in the strings, and eventually it has the movement finishing with a thematic closing flourish, again in the strings, sostenuto.

But this is no more than a truly "rough," superficial description of the formal principles of contrast and repetition. Their interplay is subtler, and also more mysterious; as with the symphony's dance characters, contrast is mediated toward the identical, and repetition toward the change that brings contrast. Like and unlike, unlike and like –

Mirrorings

The third perspective. Section B (mm. 33ff.) indeed begins as described by strongly contrasting with the A section that is ending. Thematically, however, the scurrying staccato sequence in the first violins is simply a version of theme A itself with the same notes, but changed in rhythm and character; it even preserves the "irregular" accents on the last part of the measure. And the step-wise downward motion of the "ben marcato" motif in the tutti paragraph of B (mm. 51ff.) is prepared in the formally analogous place in A. There the note-sequence e–d extending, as it oscillated, from the closing flourish of the melody in m. 8 achieves independence and initiates the turn toward complicating the structure. The dotted marcato figure in m. 51, however, proceeds (via mm. 10–11 and 40–41) from this closing flourish e–d. Then in the second contrasting section, C, the dotted tutti motif of section B is again carried back (mm. 130ff., and especially mm. 144ff.) to the Lombard form of mm. 8ff. in section A. The analogy of the ternary measure makes this changing-back possible—in different ways, measure 144 is analogous to, while at the same time contrasting with, both m. 51 and mm. 8ff.

The initial unison idea of this section C is, similarly, only partly new. It obviously derives from the third-filling, with triplet figure, in m. 4, the taking up and extending of this in m. 21 (oboe), and its broad spinning-out from m. 114, directly before the "contrasting" section C. And section C *in toto* with its quick 3/8-time is, as a three, analogous to the similarly ternary section A and contrasts with the binary section B. With regard to the tempo, conversely, section C is related to the eighth-note Presto B, and it contrasts sharply here with the quarter-Allegretto of the A passages.

Conversely, the beginnings of the three A sections are identical with one another, and yet not quite identical. A' begins the theme in the same form but with slightly different instrumentation, without the clarinets, switching to the flutes in the second four-measure phrase, while the oboes—which had the melody throughout in A—change to an accompaniment of eighth-note figures that takes up the earlier horn entry from m. 110. The second paragraph (mm. 114ff.), however, does not, as in A, exploit the Lombard flourish e–d but restates the figural pattern of the fourth measure of theme A (the repeated b and surrounding triplet) over and over again, leveling the texture down to a plane of sound layered around the (dominant) pedal-point b, and cadencing as it turns on its own axis. This is prepared in the first four-measure phrase of A, in its differences from the beginning of the movement. At first this takes place harmonically in the aforementioned new interpretation, with medial cadencing from one measure to the next, of the beginning of the melody (E seventh-chord and ninth-chord respectively). The B major "answers" by making this allusion secure *post festum:* A' finishes in E major. Moreover, the triplet figuration of the fourth measure of the theme in A' (m. 110) is recessed by superimposing a repeat of the antecedent, which now begins in the flutes, as an upbeat, and strangely askew. It is only after this second four-measure phrase, which comes between antecedent and consequent, that the one-measure pattern appears, set apart as an independent motif (m. 114), and is developed. Such a textural pattern— and moreover for the strings—did not occur in base section A. But the pedal-point-like layout of these measures, and the expansion of the dynamics and sonority into a tutti in precisely this second passage in the section, connects A' with the pedal-point tuttis in B and C. The second repeat section, A″ (mm. 194ff.), in contrast, makes its way back to A in this respect. Yet on the other hand, while continuing the harmonic expansion of A′ (and thus diverging from A), it begins a further fifth "higher" in F-sharp major and leads with the figure from the fourth measure of the theme—that now well-established point of interchange—toward B major. And here (mm. 201ff.), the manipulation of the Lombard secundal step starts up anew (and is, of course, varied anew compared to model A).

The "surface" clarity of the formal articulation, the aurally striking realization of contrast and identity becomes, in this view, simply the conditioning framework for a rich play of shadings. That which ostensibly is being articulated simply and clearly makes the subtle variant a possibility: is that what the clarity of form means? At all events it is the relations, the mirrorings, the "undertones" that give the movement an extra dimension. But this exceeds the bounds of the movement itself. To look backward and forward, to listen out for . . .

Undertones

This is the fourth perspective. More strongly than the second movement did, the beginning of the Allegretto goes back to ideas stated at the start of the symphony (see Example 7 with commentary), but the metrical-harmonic disruptions of the pastoral tone do not occur here. Nonetheless, the movement is not altogether without reminders of those darkenings of the idyllic world which underlie movements I and II. This is audible in cross-connections, in the adoption of harmonic planes which have acquired particular meaning in the opening movements. The G minor at the end of section A (mm. 26ff.) and its variant with the complementary use of expressive strings in the closing paragraph of A″ (mm. 222ff.) are such moments, impressive in themselves and thus capable of guiding the retentive ear and mind back to the first movement's skeptical ending with its minor subdominant—that G minor which, blended with the dominant pedal-point a, so disconcerted Vincenz Lachner. The fugato episode in the second movement (mm. 51–52) has already sounded this G minor again, and it will be heard again even in the finale's "last dance" (mm. 32–33), although less weight is given to it there than in the third movement. If this third movement's subdominant G major still suggests a G minor (which must therefore be specially stated to make a special effect), the B major/F-sharp major passages (mm. 114ff., 194ff.) are already striking as such. They are, of course, harking back to the second movement's main key of B major and to its second theme in F-sharp major (m. 33), whose explicitly grazioso character is probably no accident in this relation to the Allegretto grazioso. But one can proceed a step further. The striking F-sharp major in the strings, with the pizzicato bass, in the third movement's closing section is plainly analogous to the opening movement's second theme in F-sharp major (mm. 74ff.), whose elegiac dance character recalls Brahms's *Liebeslieder-Walzer*, and which also is played over a pizzicato bass. And the characteristic accompaniment to the aforementioned F-sharp major second theme in the second movement is also a cello pizzicato. (Let me just add in passing that the second theme of the finale, in its specific form, takes up in two ways the third-movement Ländler theme.) Now it seems by no means a coincidence that F-sharp major strikes up again in the D-major finale as well—in the "trio"-like Tranquillo paragraph in the middle of the development section (mm. 206ff.). This passage, in turn, refers through its motivic construction to another F-sharp minor passage in the first movement, the "Scherzando" episode in mm. 66ff., which subsequently reappears (in D major) in the coda, widened and "tranquillo." The harmonic extension to F-sharp major—which is surprising in a G-major movement—and the pure string sonority at A″, the second return in the third movement, are thus supported, perhaps even explained by such parallels extending over different movements. And the entire third movement is repeatedly incorporated in the overall context in this subtle way—albeit with obvious restraint, compared to the first two movements, regarding what we, like Brahms himself, may call the symphony's melancholic dimension.

Now there are a number of outstanding compositional moments or pregnant points which the interpreter (whether performer or one who is realizing the music in his imagination) usually suppresses or overlooks, but which the eye—or rather, the ear—needs reminding of for the movement to be represented accurately. Fifth perspective, then:

Moments

So far the horn has not been mentioned. But as in movements I and II, it serves as a pointer here. It enters in m. 12 seemingly hidden, but the specific color changes the overall sound immediately and acts as a signpost to the point of interchange for the whole movement's formal development: the emancipation of the secundal step e–d at the start of the second portion of A. The same applies to A: the horn enters with a flourish that covers the curious phrase-structure of mm. 110–111 and initiates the counter-figure which then appears rather often in both A′and A″ (straight afterwards in mm. 112–113 in the oboe, for instance) and which later on, ending as a low passing voice in the cellos and violas, will stamp the close of the movement (mm. 233ff.). The special function of the horn's subsidiary melody in the upswinging middle section of A and A″, which to some extent frames the aforementioned horn entry in A, is not to be ignored either.

Next, once again, the measures 9–12 that have been described earlier as a point of interchange, and their consequences (which Toch, pp. 187ff., examines in particular detail). How the secundal step e–d from the end of the theme in m. 8, animated by the Lombard rhythm, comes in and rises through repetitions to initiate the second paragraph of A, and how the change of texture is heralded by parallel sixths (only now does the second oboe appear) and the additional horn color—this was described earlier. But something which is of importance to the formal relations is that now, inside section B, the second paragraph contrasting internally as an "after-dance," with its marked secundal step in a similar formal position, reacts to this development in A and continues it via the intermediate stage of m. 41 until it becomes an independent motif. Then the Lombard seconds (which do not occur in A) pervade the beginning of C, combining from m. 132 onward with the B motif from mm. 51ff., which gains the ascendancy in its tutti form, after m. 144, note for note, but now—the triple time makes this combination possible—in the Lombard instead of the dotted version.

Finally, closing section A″ (whose beginning in F-sharp major in the strings is extraordinary in itself in a dance context) features a change to the "point of interchange" from m. 8 designed with a view to closure, and expressively extended. The change is prepared, almost concealed in minimal variants, in the particular form of the preceding phrase-endings. The second four-measure phrase of theme A (mm. 198ff.) no longer has the turns with the active upward fourth (m. 6) and with the secundal step downward to the opening dominant (m. 8), and has instead the third step f-sharp–d-sharp on the paragraph's tonic B (m. 199), and formulaic leading-note resolution in the upward secundal step a-sharp–b (m. 201)—hence clearly a self-contained, eight-measure period. The Lombard rhythm, to be sure, is preserved. And this is now used in the alternation of leading-note and gliding-note steps between the strings and answering woodwind trio to provide the bridge to the second paragraph. In m. 204 the oboes "lift by a third" the e″ to g″, and at this point there commences a circling figure in the violins with repeated semitonal turns. This is a new element for this movement, but one that—especially in the form e–d-sharp–e–d–e—fleetingly recalls an exposed moment in the first movement: the high violin passage in mm. 20–21, which in that opening paragraph first ushered in the curious downswing and then provided the melodic model for the transitional phrase as it blossomed again. Also quite clearly related to those measures of the first movement, in the structural constellation of a high unison string melody over long-held woodwind chords, is the parallel passage in the closing paragraph of the third movement, that restrained lyrical gesture in mm. 225–228 which, being "molto dolce," is in the context of the movement so emphatic nonetheless. It goes beyond the lyrical restraint of the quasi-Schubertian major-minor change in mm. 29ff.; and both in its individual expressive character and as a reference back to the first movement, it gives this final harmonic darkening particular weight.

Then the transitions have yet to be discussed. The return from B to A′(mm. 101–106) mediates between the binary and ternary measure through a grouping of twice three two-measure units; in addition the cellos are already anticipating their pizzicato on the quarters from m. 101 onward, while the oboes four times anticipate the interval d–b, with which they subsequently begin the Ländler repeat. (Can one see a similar anticipation of the unison 3/8-motif d–c–b at the start of section C on the oboes in mm. 124–125?) The return from C to A″ is analogous formally, but not in regard to the relation of measure to meter. It begins by grouping twice three measures of the initial meter in a quite similar way and notates them as two 9/8 measures (mm. 188–189); after which, keeping the same musical contents at first, this constellation is transferred with four 3/4 measures (thus doubled in proportion) to the successive meter of the Ländler, with Lombard and hemiolic rhythms superimposed on the new basic time.

Ultimately, another aspect of the transitions is the art of drawing breath by setting fermatas. These occur as rests *extra metrum* in the two outer A sections before the repeats (between mm. 22–23 and mm. 218–219 respectively). There the movement holds its breath for a brief moment, prepared in each case by the syncopated subsidiary part for oboe or first violin and by the anticipatory quotation of the theme on clarinet or oboe—a pause for breath capturing, as it were, the pointed accent on the "3"; then comes the complete theme. Compare the fermata in the small, coda-like final paragraph of the movement. The violins' far-reaching lyrical gesture at the end of A″ (mm. 225ff.) presses for a repetition in the high woodwinds (mm. 229ff.), which glides chromatically downward in quarter-notes and eventually reaches G major again (m. 233). Once more the head of the theme is played by the woodwind trio, but over the disappearing figure in the lower strings derived from the horn flourish in m. 110—and with the first quarter-notes recessed and a new harmonic interpretation in mm. 234 and 235. This weakens the "hypermeter" at the same time as the motion runs down, while the upswing accent now achieves prominence and finally keeps the motion going through a changeover to the seventh-chord (e–g–b–c-sharp) as well. Then, from the primary woodwind sound that is breaking off (in the woodwinds the fermatas occur on the eighth-note rests!), the sound being held in a fermata emerges in the medium strings through the technique of the overlapping instrumental rest. And the lightly dotted thematic closing flourish ends in the Lombard rhythm of the G-major chords, finally repeated by supporting brass and basses. Everything "poco sostenuto," in the context of this movement, of course.

A final reflection seems called for. Listening for the "undertones" fits in with the overall tendency of this interpretation of the symphony: the detecting of features that the work's reception has suppressed. And with the first movement at least, it can look to Brahms himself for support. But this specific interest cannot allow the contemplative elements to dominate the relative weight given to the third movement, in particular. The dances are stylized, as is quite natural in a symphony, but they are not so fictive that their realistic components can be ignored. The broken tones are sounded more softly and secretly anyway than in the first two movements, and also in a manner that is allusive, reminiscent of past clouds on the horizon, rather than introducing a new element, or any clouds of their own. And both the beginning and ending of the movement appear cloudless. The absence of trombones and of the tuba and kettledrum is really an indication of this. On the other hand, however, the exploiting of the G-minor region is greatly intensified, in the movement's final paragraph in particular, by the strings' lyrical gesture—and this conclusion does, then, belong to the strings after all.

Fourth Movement: Allegro con spirito, 4/4 alla breve – Tranquillo – In tempo – D major

Now, it seems, there is to be no more holding back. A finale with brio that—if taken at the right tempo—does not last even nine minutes, constantly wound up from the propulsive thematic beginning onward and hardly stopping to think, even including, right at the end (mm. 397ff.), fulminating, compactly blaring octave passages on the heavy bass instruments in the brass, which the first movement had once introduced for quite different reasons: a "last dance" using all the resources available rounds off the symphony. It races, with its motive impulse, through the formal framework of what is at first an obvious sonata layout:

Headlong culmination

- exposition (mm. 1–154) with double main subject (mm. 1–60), transition passage (mm. 60–77), second subject (mm. 78–113), and epilogue (mm. 114–148);

- then, after a brief transition, the development section (mm. 155–243), clearly articulated internally paragraph by paragraph, and with a more independent "Tranquillo" section at the end (mm. 206ff.), which the tempo modification already causes to stand out conspicuously;
- recapitulation (m. 244–circa m. 347), with changes compared to the exposition, and a fluid transition of the epilogue to a coda (m. 353–end) in three stages (mm.353, 375, 387).

There are, however, some formal peculiarities that lead one to reconsider this apparently clear-cut construction and to modify the view of the whole as being pure sonata form.

The movement pressing forward beyond the framework is mildly affected by just a few outstanding moments where the music partially pauses for breath:

- the clarinet's intermittent (as it were) exclamation in mm. 60ff., invoking the repeatedly mediated second subject with its initial "Lombard" gesture;
- the "Tranquillo" episode in F-sharp major (mm. 206ff.), which—being the one explicit reduction in tempo—in mid-movement makes a simple formal definition of the development more complicated, and which precedes that curious pianissimo passage (mm. 234ff.) that Mahler must have had in his mind's ear when composing the introduction to his First Symphony (similarly in D major!);
- and last, the beginning of the coda (mm. 353ff.) determined by trombones and tuba, which for one long moment darkens the sound appreciably with its alternation of D minor and G minor.

But even these stopping-moments are caught up in the drive of the willed forward movement, with the overriding intention of a euphoria let loose. (This movement seems, incidentally, to be Brahms's only "Allegro con spirito.") All this is already established by the main theme's outline and character and is perceptible therein.

Main Theme, Main Subject: A Collective "Go On!"

How this main theme (mm. 1–9; Example 30) is interwoven with the symphony's basic motivic material, *x* and *m*, has been shown in Example 8. Each element—

- the semitone turn *x* of the beginning, at the same pitch, or
- the figuration of the D-major triad analogous to *m* (and here, the diastematic relation to the main theme of the *Eroica* is almost more obvious than at the beginning of the opening movement), and finally
- the derived fourth-transformation with its secundal step downward, reminiscent of similar figures in other movements (such as the horn figure in mm. 17ff. of the second movement)

—each of the above can be related to something already stated, which is not, of course, difficult when the basic forms are so simple. Neither does the finale consciously present any fundamentally new motifs. That is why combination and character-transformation are the salient features here.

The theme's outward features are:

- the alla breve time,
- the bipartite thematic period with its rising antecedent and the small-scale element repetitions in the descending consequent modulating to the dominant, this consequent being made into a five-measure phrase by repeat measure 6,
- the "unison" beginning in all the strings (which is to say in octaves, the winds adding the sound of the open fifth), with the half-note d set in isolation, the subsequent 3/8 flourish, and the primary quarter-motion,[29]

---

29. Seldom does one find a unison theme of similar brio in a Brahms finale; the Third Symphony matches it in the symphonic field, although the progress is more restrained. In this respect, the Intermezzo for piano, op. 117, no. 3, comes closer to the Third Symphony's finale theme, although the tempo is more a moderate Andante. In their capacity as opening themes, the unison beginnings of first movements in Brahms's chamber music

- also the unfolding into three-part texture from m. 3, and
- the dynamics constantly kept at *piano* throughout the opening paragraph.

It is noticeable that this theme has no sharply drawn melodic figures, no marked characters. The motifs that have been quoted are used as flourishes (in, for instance, the stereotyped repetitions of mm. 5 and 6), rather than being pregnantly articulated rhythmically and melodically all the way along. The regular quarter-motion and the alla breve time in a

---

with piano have a different character (compare the Piano Quartet in G minor, op. 25, Piano Quintet in F minor, op. 34, and Clarinet Sonata in F minor, op. 120, no. 1).

very rapid tempo, flattening accents and aiming at larger measure-units, are the background that precludes the completion, here, of a thematic form with a weight of its own. This should be seen not as a compositional failing but as a set dominance of the general impulsive "drive" over a thematic and motivic individuation. The urgent forward movement, the willed brio of this finale's motive character do not permit an underlining of individual features, a dwelling on graphic detail. The resulting breathlessness with which the music advances is intended, and precisely the unwinding eighth-note figurations, which speed up the regular quarter-motion as they fill it out, rather than interrupt it (mm. 1, 7–8, 10–11, and so on), strengthen this tendency. Very typical of this is the way that, in the *forte* repeat of the beginning (mm. 24ff.), the third measure of the theme replaces the rising quarter-motion with the doubled rotating eighth-note figure from m. 1, which now compresses this four-note measure into a half-bar (Example 31). This figure of rejoicing with its eighth-

note impulse "winds up" the thematic motion even further, just as in the repeat section generally, the subsidiary parts with their regular runs of eighths give the impression of a further increase in tempo. And as early as m. 23, which anticipates the *forte* of the thematic repetition as a long upbeat, the eighth-note impulse after the previous retardation suddenly pushes the course of the music forward. Sforzati do more than their share.

The opening of the movement seems to have been constructed with this dynamic point in m. 24 in mind. First, the aforementioned breathless start, still keeping the dynamics down to *piano,* with the opening turn to the dominant (m. 9); the continuation—being a thematic derivation from m. 5—keeps the expressive character unchanged. The enlargement of the sound and space by woodwinds complements the reduced dynamics, and the activity of the revolving eighths is increased, as is the textural density when the lower part enters in counterpoint after m. 13 (similarly to m. 3). In measures 18–22 the low register, stopping of the motion, and breaking-off on the diminished seventh-chord produce a momentary retardation: as in classical drama, this is the dammed-up brink of the climax. Coming after a pause for breath resembling a general rest, the subsequent dynamic outburst is thus made stronger than ever.

From here until the second subject (m. 78) there is an unabating forward movement in the full orchestra playing *forte/fortissimo.* This hardly needs describing in detail, the stations being clearly marked: the dotting that is added to the store of figurations in m. 32, where the G minor remains an episode in the onward charge; then the instrumentally alternating texture from m. 44 on, soon to be heightened outwardly by integrating the dotting within the theme's fourth-note form and by breaking the eighths. The urge to complete the movement always takes precedence over the construction of its elements. And the climax of the main subject (m. 56), which is reached via repeated sequencing of the dotted model, reiterates the 4/8 flourish from m. 26 in the high strings with characteristic insistence, before changing to the diminished seventh-chord at m. 60 and making room for the clarinet entry—the first solo passage in this movement, which is otherwise wholly dependent on collective execution. One particular structural element must be considered here. For the main subject emphatically confirms the tonic D major as the goal of its formal process, and the *forte* repeat of the main theme does not entail a modulatory transition; in spite of the modulatory sequences of its bridge-like ending, the main subject remains static on the tonic D major, instead of reaching the dominant which formal convention leads one to expect here. To that extent it is reproducing in its formal curve—and here let us anticipate events—the curve of the whole finale, forecasting the close of the symphony with its D-major tableau, for which there is also figural evidence in the similarity, in regard to form and function, of the 4/8 flourishes at the two climaxes (mm. 55ff. and 421ff.). Naturally the orchestral expansion—especially in the brass section—for the close of the movement and the symphony exceeds the dynamics at the end of the main subject.

The Solo Clarinet

The clarinet entry is, indeed, a thoroughly important point in several respects, as was already noted by Tovey (p. 208).

– First, there is the form and tone of the actual passage, the specific clarinet color blossoming, as it were, from the tutti, the exclamatory character of the melodic gesture with its emphatic upswing to c‴, the filling up beneath the suspended note with the virtuosic flourish on the second clarinet, the taking up of the exclamation by the corresponding flute and the horn, and finally its third coloring on the oboe. This is complemented by the carpet of string sound with the vigorously loosening 4/8 figure from the tutti, which stretches into the second subject, and with the pedal notes on individual woodwinds and brass—another exceptional moment occurring at a formal turning-point, albeit less fraught than in some other passages.

timbre

texture

– Second, the solo gesture has the character of a call within the collectively determined movement, and the forward impulse is held back by consigning the eighth-note figuration to the accompaniment. The clarinet phrase thus takes on the character of a challenge, a pointer to a new orientation of the formal process, reinforced by repetitions of the phrase in the other woodwind instruments.

challenge to form

– Third, there is the connective association with other passages that seem to correspond to this one, above all in Brahms's own music. The function of the natural horn call in the finale of the First Symphony is based on very similar structural features and form-constellations. To be sure, compared to the First Symphony's horn call, which has an ideational dimension, the clarinet sound in the Second appears to be motivated more—or even exclusively—by the musical form, as a gesture that both continues and suspends a process, seeming to point a unified course of events in a new direction. Moreover—and this further limits the comparison—the clarinet call does not change the course of the music anything like as firmly and drastically as the e on the horn in the finale of the First Symphony. So drastic a harmonic turn to the entire movement and work is not intended here; nor would it correspond to the form and

like horn call

substance of this finale. Also, the clarinet phrase is a "two" in terms of the hypermeter, corresponding to the rhythmically analogous process in the string basses in mm. 56–60, although this is nearly masked by the instrumentation. (David Lewin criticizes Brahms for lack of enterprise here, seeing him as following in the footsteps of Schumann with his tutti instrumentation.) Thus in the context of the four overlapping five-measure groups (mm. 56ff., 60ff., 66ff., 70ff.), the clarinet color provides contrast, which is emphasized by its culmination and enrichment at m. 65.

– Finally, however (and this opens up a much broader field and may be a personal reaction that cannot be given without comment, which is why the statement is in the first person), I always experience this passage—in its formal placing as in its melodic *gestus*—as a conscious allusion to the intervention of the clarinet in Weber's opera *Der Freischütz,* that passage which is so distinctive in form, sound, and content. It comes in the overture before the great rejoicing and paves the way for it (as the "[Licht-]Strahl durch die Nächte," the nocturnal ray of light which Max invokes in his aria): one of the really great moments of fulfillment in nineteenth-century music. Another point of reference for Brahms's formal and timbral allusion could be the clarinet passage in the first movement of Schumann's *Overture, Scherzo, and Finale* of 1841. Here the clarinet tone is long-drawn, and at m. 59 a second idea blossoms out of it, unprepared as a quasi-antecedent but with a similar continuation in the woodwinds, in this case the oboe. Schumann's passage might be the intermediary between Weber's and Brahms's clarinet. (And something that may well have been affected by these predecessors is the thoroughly similar clarinet passage that supplies a contrasting theme in m. 66 of the finale of Dvořák's "New World" Symphony.)

These elements particularly distinguish the rerouting point in mm. 60ff. and make it significant. But in addition, it has a quite ordinary task which is connected with the peculiarity of the tonic-asserting end of the main subject. The function of the modulating bridge passage now falls to the passage determined by the clarinet continuation, which arrives at the level of the dominant in the usual manner, passing through the dominant-of-the-dominant, the final cadence being marked by string pizzicati.

The Second Subject: Warm Tone with Lombard Impulse

The subsequent theme in A major again presents something well known in a new guise. In terms of textural pattern, form, character, and cross-connections within the thematic weft of the symphony, this is a counter-subject, a softer second idea (Example 32). This theme is distinguished,

 expected

diastematically, by the third/root-of-the-chord figuration of the begin-ning, after which it swings itself up in the chord of A major; in sonority, by the full-toned parallel sixths in a relatively low string register of violins and violas; and rhythmically by the initial twofold Lombard impulse, followed by quarter-notes evenly spaced. The parallel sixths in the strings relate back to formally analogous passages in earlier movements, the second theme's chain of thirds in the opening movement (mm. 82ff.), and the sixths in the woodwinds and strings respectively in the devel-opmental passages of the third movement's A sections (mm. 1ff. and 205ff. respectively); and the Lombard rhythm, too, started on its impor-tant role in the third movement in precisely that developmental passage (mm. 8ff.). As a textural pattern, the finale's second idea is closely related to the second theme in the opening movement:

- the full-sounding parallel voice-leading of the main parts (sixths in the one instance, thirds in the other),
- the initial melodic gesture leading from the third to the root of the chord (c-sharp to a in the one instance, a to f-sharp in the other),
- the harmonic support of the basses (drone-like sustained note in

the one instance, pizzicati and turn from measure to measure in the other),

- and also eighth-note figuration as a quasi-ostinato subsidiary part, leaving out, in each instance, the "1" of the measure (motivically derived from *m1* in the one case, implicitly continuing the rotating 4/8 figure from the main subject, and its line of motion with it, in the other).

Yet at the same time the opening movement's second theme, which comes close to a waltz, seems both more expressive and more swayingly dance-like, the second theme of the finale being more even in rhythm (the quarter-notes), and also more sharply accentuated (the Lombard impulse with the note-repetition). In accordance with the whole finale's prevalent motive urge, the second idea, even though introduced "more softly" at first, has in these elements the potential to become overbearing; the brassily blaring conclusion of the symphony on trumpets and trombones will confirm this from m. 417 onward: significantly, it is the second theme that is used there, and not the first. As soon as the woodwinds first take up the theme (mm. 86ff.), with the resulting tutti upswing, this quality is outwardly adumbrated in the exposition. As a whole, the second thematic complex traces the same formal curve as the first complex. It also follows the tendency toward the final tutti-brio vigorously and unequivocally.

This leads to the paragraph which in sonata terms would be described as the epilogue to the exposition (mm. 114ff.). Here the dominant feature is the driving eighth-note figuration, which also assimilates the element of regular parallel voice-leading, with its adeptly chasing passages in thirds in the woodwinds (mm. 122ff.). Now the still warmly sensuous sound of the second idea's parallel sixths is lost in the sheer pull of the motion. (The word "still" in this sentence indicates that the sensuous element has diminished by comparison with the second theme in the opening movement.) Placed right at the end of the epilogue (mm. 138ff.), and marking the destination with the utmost effort, is a constellation that is interesting rhythmically and motivically (Example 33). Here the Lombard accentuation is transformed: the untreated "1" and the syn-

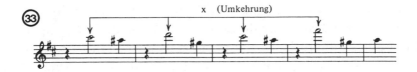

copated stress on the "2" produce a particularly vigorous display of en-
ergy, and the top notes of the four measures which are thus ejaculated
yield an inversion of the complete base motif *x*, that is to say along with
the following fourth. This is followed by the close of the epilogue (mm.
142–148), again sharpened rhythmically but in a different way, the Lombard principle being applied with curtailing effect to the quarter-note
articulation, leading to a bridge passage finishing on the achieved dominant. The new section commencing at m. 155 again begins with the
original main theme, played by strings in unison, and in D major, thus
on the tonic.

Development: Ambiguous Form

For a development section to begin on the tonic is anything but
"normal," at any rate where conventional sonata form is concerned.
What was already raising a few eyebrows at the end of the main subject
(mm. 56ff.) is now occurring in heightened form and obliges one to stop
and reflect. (There is, of course, no need or call to abide by historically
evolved norms of musical form. But with analysis it is a good policy to
regard striking departures from a norm as pointers, and to investigate
the reasons for them. Often, facts crucial to interpretation can be gleaned
from the interplay of a historical norm and the individual forming of a
work of art.) If the first section of this finale were entirely compatible
with the established sonata-form categories (main subject, second subject, epilogue—that is, an exposition) and their demands, their typical
manifestations and characterizations, and it was only the ending of the
main subject and the subsequent—and, maybe, consequent—unusual-
ness of the clarinet passage that made one listen and think hard, then
the layout of the movement's second large section after the exposition,
the section coming next, would have to be that of a development.

Now this second section undoubtedly begins strangely, rather like the repeat of a first section (see the earlier remarks on the First Symphony). But the discomfiture does not last long, at least not in this passage. After a few measures there comes a working-up of the main theme which merits the name of a development. It is divided into clear-cut paragraphs of varied working-up. The stages are the following:

– mm. 155ff.: main theme in D major, the original form up to its fourth measure, without the continuation in fourths.

– mm. 159ff.: motivic splittings-off from the main theme's first and fourth measures: a semitone/third motif (a motif whose chromatic potential, with all its variants, was exploited so prominently in Beethoven's late quartets) and a chromatic secundal turn determine the development, which revolves around different scale degrees (D minor from m. 159, E minor from m. 163, C-sharp major from m. 165) before finishing.

– mm. 170ff.: head of main theme as unison in the strings and woodwinds, now as an inversion starting out from C-sharp (another little element of irritation?), and with motivic working-up from its third measure onward; again there is a coupling of two derived motifs: the doubly chromatic succession of four quarter-notes looks like an (inverting, and also retrograde) extension of the previous three-note motif (another possible allusion to Beethoven's late quartets), and there is also that motif's eighth-note variant, varied and diminished; both motifs appear in the customary workings-up. An important point is the harmonic level: the C-sharp major clearly corresponds to the important sections in the symphony that are based on F-sharp. Here it is evidently preparing the Tranquillo paragraph of mm. 206ff.

– mm. 182ff.: head of main theme in C-sharp minor (but in its normal form this time), now followed by the rhythmically sharpened fourth-motif (mm. 184–188), and then further Lombard accents, diminished eighth-note motifs. Finally, measures 191ff. correspond motivically, and in content, to mm. 46ff. in the exposition. And indeed, in a similar way to the main subject of the exposition, this developmental paragraph is carried to an intensifying close (one more element to make one think!), out of which—at the point where the clarinet call was heard before—a new idea appears in F-sharp major to provide a contemplative lyrical contrast (mm. 206ff.).

In short, here we have a development, but one that repeatedly reverts to the main subject of the exposition—curious reminiscences.

Equally remarkable is the unexpectedly contrasting Tranquillo. Even the second subject of the exposition was increasingly drawn into the impetus of this onward-rushing finale, and it is surprising to find in the middle of an apparent development section a lyrically loitering contrasted paragraph where the dynamics are *piano* throughout (Example 34). And the emphatic F-sharp major supported by the dominant, al-

contrasting

Relates to 2nd mvt.

though introduced in m. 202 in enharmonic form (thus really a G-flat major in the immediate context), clearly corresponds to the second movement's second idea, to the closing section of the third movement, and to the F-sharp minor of the second theme in the opening movement. Of course even the Tranquillo paragraph is developmental. It depends on the basic motivic material and works up both the semitone motif and the semitone-third motif of the finale's main theme, mediated by the taking up and transforming of this in m. 26 (see Example 31) and in the epilogue (m. 114) (Example 35).

Later on (m. 214), the paragraph takes up the finale theme's fourth-motif. But its basically lyrical stance works in the same direction as the other curiosities already touched on. This development has the decided features of a different formal layout based on the principle of varied repetition, and this jeopardizes the sonata scheme pure and simple.

Tranquillo = ABA

There is also the internal autonomy of the Tranquillo paragraph. In itself it has an ABA layout:

A = mm. 206–214. Alternation between woodwind and strings, in every measure, of successions of notes revolving in triplets, based on the semitonal turn and the semitone-third motif. F-sharp major, then B major, in m. 212 D-sharp minor notated as E-flat minor (retracting again the preceding enharmonic change in m. 202), and then, for the internal middle section, cadencing to B-flat (minor).

B = mm. 214–221. Fourth-theme in the woodwinds, stretto, with eighth-notes elapsing in the end, and two-note figures in the strings with hocket-like turns. B-flat minor, giving the cadence new meaning in the end (again with enharmonic change), with F-sharp major superimposed.

A′ = mm. 221–234. Material of A varied, in the interplay of woodwinds and strings, independent low part on the strings; turn effected from F-sharp major to A major, eventually arriving via G at a C major.

Thus a paragraph that was already separate in expression and motive character now becomes complete in itself, isolating itself from its surroundings in insular fashion, and emerging as a formal element in its own right.

Between Sonata and Rondo

This seems the appropriate point to submit for discussion the question of the formal conception of the entire finale. The starting-point for the analysis was the sonata concept, and this movement undoubtedly is a sonata. But moments such as the ending of the main subject, then chiefly the start of the development with the main theme in the original D major, and now also the independent contrasted section within the development (and perhaps the rather unassuming entry of the reprise as well)—these all modify the straightforward image. Here the sonata form is evidently being permeated or overlaid by rondo elements. And when an intended serenity is the inner expressive form, this is by no means strange or eccentric. Traditionally, the linear necklace-like form of the rondo would be a perfectly suitable garb for a symphony's "last dance." An interpretation of the movement as a rondo (in the more advanced form of the sonata-rondo) would read schematically as in the table below and could be juxtaposed with the sonata scheme given in italics (omitting transitions).

Neither of the two models explains the form of the movement, and the character of its respective parts, completely and without any gaps. The "rondo" model does not, for instance, include the epilogues (mm. 114 and 317), and the "sonata" model ignores the independence of the C couplet (m. 206). To read the section at mm. 155ff. as a varied refrain is to do justice to the tonic beginning, with the main theme, but not to the continuation working it up; conversely, this beginning will have to be

m. 1	78	114	155	206
A	B		A'	C
refrain	1st couplet	[?]	refrain (var.)	2nd couplet
D major	A major		D major (start)	F-sharp major
Exposition			*Development*	
Main subject	*2nd subject*	*Epilogue*		*[?]*

m. 244	281	317	353	
A	B		X	
refrain	1st couplet	[?]	coda	
D major	D major		D minor . . . D major	
Reprise				
Main subject	*2nd subject*	*Epilogue*	*Coda*	

classified as an oddity if the section is defined as a development . . . and so forth. Overall, the sonata model is more accurate and convenient, and one must accept it as being fundamental to a formal grasp of the movement. But without the imagined overlay of rondo elements to supplement this, one would not have an adequate description of the movement's appearance. Perhaps one might reverse the term "sonata-rondo" and refer to a "rondo-sonata" (Stephan; see the Bibliography) in order to typify the interplay of models and to strike the right balance between them. Of course this does not obviate the need to define for each individual model the character of the various formal elements, and the extent of the fluctuation.

The Tranquillo couplet, the strongest rondo element in this movement, is followed by another prominent passage, a short but impressive paragraph that is just as unusual in this movement as the clarinet call before the second theme in the exposition.

A Remarkable Lead-back

Measures 234ff.: extreme pianissimo, very calm tempo as a result of slowing down the motion to half-notes, an octave tremolo in the high strings over a low string pedal as the background sonority, together with the four-note motivic chain of fourths (compare m. 5 of the main theme, although a major second is the linking interval there) on flute, clarinet, and trombone, with parallel leading in octaves, mixing the colors. This is a curious textural pattern with a singular sonority to clothe it in; and it is not only because the trombones are entering for the first time in this finale that it recalls that passage in the slow introduction to the finale of the First Symphony which was so significant in form and content. This constellation appears three times, the harmonic motion proceeding from the quasi-exterritorial, threefold subdominant C major to reach the dominant a in ascending fifth-steps, via g and d, while the filled-in string tremoli in the middle register glide chromatically downward to the secondary dominant leading-note g-sharp, and the motivic chains of fourths gain in intensity and depth of color by a switch of instruments, notably by adding the bass tuba. This all ends in the dominant a, a low pedal-point on basses and kettledrum, a pedal on horns and trumpets, and above it the melodic downward motion on the strings tinged by the flute, using the minor sixth b-flat and the minor third f, over the end-note of d, to achieve a unison minor-key return to the unison main theme in the major, "in tempo" (m. 244).

The bridging function of this extraordinary paragraph is obvious. As a moment that is exceptional in texture, sonority, and rate of motion, it refers to a particular instant in the formal course of the music. An odd phenomenon of reception is also involved here. It concerns this passage's affinity with the start of the introduction to Mahler's First Symphony— the repeated development of the stylized cuckoo call into a chain of fourths, again with the characteristic color of the high flute.[30] After all, Mahler's First is, like Brahms's Second, a work in D major, and it is more than likely that the Mahlerian "entrance of nature" is a conscious ref-erence to the earlier symphony with its nature themes. But this does not even matter in regard to present responses to the two works; for the informed listener, the parallel will be inescapable. And now it is perfectly possible for a situation to arise where the Mahler symphony is seen as the primary work, with its far more elaborate and—as an *initium* of the whole—far more broadly stated chain of fourths, and the Brahms sym-phony, with the episode of only seven measures in the finale, as an anticipation of it: a paradox of current reception whereby the listener's experience reverses the historical positions. But the historical dimension charges the transition episode even more with significance, lends it even more weight.[31]

Recapitulation: The Changes

What the episode ushers in and marks out positionally is, in sonata terms, the recapitulation. This begins smoothly "in tempo" with the

---

30. For another possible reference in Mahler's work to Brahms's Second Symphony (via a Brahms song) see note 19 above.

31. Kalbeck (III, 174) has pointed out the similarity of this "bell motif," as he terms it, to the "motif of the bells" in Wagner's *Parsifal;* Floros (p. 219) calls the two motifs "identical" in spite of the semitone difference.

main theme, eight measures in the original form in D major, the dynamics having been taken right down—a repercussion of the returning paragraph—to pianissimo. (The transitional measures 240–243 are rather casual. We may recall, however, that the recapitulation in the first movement was also arrived at with a totally undramatic bridging figure of this kind in quarter-notes, albeit over motivic trombone chords in that instance.) There are now a number of significant differences to be recorded compared to the exposition. These concern the main subject and the way it is reorganized.

– mm. 252ff.: the continuation of the theme with the threefold fourth-step now appears inverted, which is probably a reference back to, and belated extension of, the second paragraph of the development (m. 170), where the inverted form was only applied to the compressed thematic head; the inverted disposition (lasting from m. 252 to m. 260) stops the main subject's first paragraph from finishing in a low register. Instead there are two simple E minor chords followed, as in the exposition, by the tutti repeat, changed instrumentally, and with fixed chromatic eighth-note figures on the strings and the melodically fragmenting theme on woodwind and horns

– mm. 275ff.: the passage in G minor begins similarly to m. 32 but continues differently after only one measure. In contrast to the exposition, the full range of orchestral devices is not now used to carry the main subject to an animated, jubilant tonic climax, for a passage analogous to mm. 44ff. with the theme continued in fourths is lacking, as is the passage that was introduced by the solo clarinet (mm. 60ff.). Instead there is a very terse and laconic modulation to the dominant A in only three measures, and the movement then leads directly and with broadly bowed triplet motion to the second subject. As usual in the recapitulation this is in the tonic, hence in D major. Here, where the end of the main subject is already modulating, the clarinet call that was so prominent in the exposition—where it started the modulatory transition as a sequel to the curious insistence of the end of the main subject upon the tonic— would be functionally unnecessary. Besides, precisely the extraordinary element that this passage expresses would rule out a repetition of it. Or vice versa: its absence from the recapitulation heightens the importance of its occurrence, which is now confirmed as being unique. To be sure, the recapitulation's laconic six-measure bridge passage is based on a sound which did not occur in the exposition: the entry of trombones and tuba, syncopated, and with marked sforzati.

The second subject and epilogue are quite "normal," showing no notable differences from the exposition. Right at the end of the epilogue, however, with the D minor/B-flat major of mm. 347–348, and thus within the first phrase of a consequent, there occurs a change. It prepares— harmonically first—for a turnabout from possible closure to further development. Unison tutti passages, played fortissimo across the entire orchestra, eventually break out of the realm of the tonic major and demand to be continued via G minor (m. 351) and D minor. This might be because the epilogue, as presented in the exposition, is not conducive to an emphatic close for this brio movement; it would be an ending that lacked a formal climax. Another reason—and the harmonic turn would suggest this—could be that a moment of musing reminiscence has still to be inserted amid the finale's rejoicing. Thus a formal postscript commences.

Coda: The Transforming of the Trombones

And this coda (mm. 353ff.) is presented in a special way, with a tone that is new to the finale. For the first time in this movement the dominant sound is that of the low brass, the three trombones and the tuba. It is hardly surprising that this darkening of the sound goes hand in hand with a harmonic clouding: D minor with a G minor turn, then the turn toward C with F (m. 358), then B-flat (m. 363) and E-flat; harmonic positions from the epilogue's turning-point are being exploited here. Compact chordal writing at a restrained dynamic level, with circling motions of thirds in the two upper parts (a pair of trombones and bassoons respectively) on the motif of secundal turn x, and an accentuated Lombard rhythm at the start, continued with syncopation, succeeded by quasi-imitation (chiefly rhythmic, with harmonic and motivic adjustments) on the three pairs of upper woodwinds—all this against a restless background of a string tremolo of eighth-note triplets, going nowhere harmonically. A dark and also coarse tone, and yet—compared to the first movement's central trombone passages—with a heavy dance pulse that partially cancels out the somber compactness. The trombones, whose "black" potential Brahms called his most personal feature, appear tempered, made to fit in with the character of the finale.[32] This, for all the looking back, might also be already aiming ahead at the trombones' transformed use in the work's conclusion, at mm. 397ff. and particularly, in the end, from mm. 419ff. All the same—along with the clarinet call and also, perhaps, the development's F-sharp major episode—this constitutes an important point of attraction within the finale, and one that is important in the overall context of the symphony as well. It is immensely expanded orchestrally, condensed into the unified process (m. 363), and also enormously intensified dynamically.

The process is continued in a second, very thoroughly thought-out fresh start to the coda. After an abrupt modulation (mm. 373–375), there is a "six over four" combination of the Lombard second theme, as the foundation (low strings, bassoon), and the triplet Tranquillo variant of the main theme in the violins: a quasi-contrapuntal superimposing of the two most important thematic ideas in the finale (though mediated, in the main theme's case, via its transformation). Incidentally, this concentration is prepared in the structure of the second subject in mm. 78ff., where the Tranquillo variant is prefigured by the cello's eighth-note figure transferred from the main theme. Compared to the second subject, the coda combination is, as it were, in double counterpoint. In the process the bass motif remains obstinately fixed, while the violin figure with its extended reach rises in a stepwise sequence. Harmonically, this achieves a repeated alternation of an A major seventh-chord and G major, that is, of the dominant and the subdominant, with the foun-

---

32. Concert experiences are a reminder of the performer's role in such interpretive nuances. When the Boston Symphony Orchestra performed this symphony under Bernard Haitink in the spring of 1990, the compact harshness of the trombones in this passage was particularly prominent, now casting its "shadow" back to the opening of the symphony. Incidentally, Haitink could also be credited with—rare event!—the repeat of the first-movement exposition with that important prima volta and its horn motif.

dation-note g fluctuating in its chordal significance between a dominant seventh and subdominant root. This combination of an ostinato bass figure and melodic upward tension causes a bracing of the music's formal gestures, a mixture of retardation and expanding prolongation. As to retardation, the Tranquillo couplet also had a formally retarding function of this kind before the reprise, but that did not entail an emphatic heightening. And the prolongation, which is reinforced by the orchestral filling-in from m. 379 onward, leads, at m. 387, to the outburst with the main theme's *initium,* still dissonant as a diminished seventh-chord, and thus motivically with the minor third, accompanied by vigorous accents which complement the rhythm, and in which the full brass is involved. And just as it did at the start of the movement, the thematic *initium,* compressed into a 4/8 figure, now "cranks" the movement into activity once more (m. 391). When the motivic minor third then changes to a major third, this is a definitive announcement of the emphatic D-major close, which, using all the instrumental means, and with a supreme effort, is realized in the big orchestral tableau from m. 397 onward. Thus a coda that began pensively turns, in two run-ups, to great, loud, and emphatically unbroken rejoicing.

The coda to the coda, the symphony's goal and culmination. Measures 397–429: thirty-three measures played by the full orchestra, confirming D major with power and brilliance, dashing runs of eighths, and the blaring of brass—the finale's "last dance" is meant to outdo everything that the symphony orchestra had produced so far. One striking thing is the amount of rhythmic regularity through which this is achieved, with simple scales without motivic contours: below the high, static violin trill, mighty quarter-runs on all the bass instruments from m. 397 onward; uniform eighth-scales in the strings, flutes, and bassoons with note repetitions in the other instruments from m. 405 onward, broken off in the fourth measure on three occasions and drawing breath for a fresh start in general rests, first on the tonic (mm. 405–408), then on the dominant-of-the-dominant (mm. 409–412), and finally, with a change of texture, on the dominant (mm. 413–416). This third run-up ushers in—directly so in the case of some instrumental groups—the goal of the coda, of the finale, and of the symphony: the mighty plateau of the pure tonic D major. At this point (m. 417) the composition takes on motivic quality again. And, significantly, it is the finale's more sharply contoured second theme, with its Lombard accent, and not the bustling head of the main theme which now signals the goal in the woodwinds and brass like a fanfare. (In this connection it might not be wholly misguided to think of the blaring horns at the end of Beethoven's Seventh Symphony, although the orgiastic quality of the Beethoven finale is neither attained nor, one supposes, intended here.) The character of the theme has altered strongly, in comparison to the expressively blossoming tone of the low strings in the exposition and recapitulation, being adapted to the impetus of the final tableau. It is important to the symphonic content that finally the low brass, the trombones and tuba, take part in this fanfare as well. In m. 419 they join in the rejoicing. Their change of character, already suggested in the rhythmic pulse at the start of the finale's coda, where it was similarly associated with the Lombard second theme, now provides a signpost, as it were. Like the finale's second subject, the original character of the trombones—so vital to Brahms's symphonic presentation— is consumed by the final optimism as well. Eighth-note figures obtained through diminution from the theme's second measure, and recalling, in their persisting exaltation, the use of the main theme's initial flourish at the end of the main subject (mm. 56ff.), usher in a conclusion stated four times with a volley of chords, played by the full orchestra, fortissimo. It seems as though the rejoicing is meant to go on forever.

But the last important word rests with the three trombones (mm. 425ff.)—calculated very precisely in their significance for the whole of the symphony—and with these alone, not the tuba. Tovey (p. 210) calls this "blast of the trombones" the "most surprising effect of all in the coda." He sees its function as lying in the "sanctioning" of the brilliant and triumphal close, by the trombones as well at long last. Yet there is surely more to be heard in this. At the ejaculation of the long fortissimo chord in the highest register, with its extreme violence, the tone of rejoicing in the trombones suddenly becomes strenuously coarse and boisterous (especially if the conductor is aware of the potential in these measures, as Bruno Walter demonstrates in his 1953 gramophone recording). And an ear that has been repeatedly alerted to hidden depths in this symphony will relate the trombone sound once again, and now for the very last time, to the first, somber entrance of the trombones, and will be able to make the link between the transcending close and the "black wings" that were already casting a profound "shadow" on the first movement's "entrance of nature."

A reflection on the intention and character of the finale seems apposite here, both for the finale itself and with regard to its position in the work as a whole—both of these to be related, ultimately, to analytical judgments and possible preconceptions, to a general prior understanding by the present author.

The interpretation of the final movement began with a characterization that no doubt already involved a value judgment. It referred to the "drive of the willed movement forward," and to the "intention of a euphoria let loose," not to the realizing or even the success of the latter. Such restrained descriptions are partly the reflection of an aesthetic experience which views the first two movements as being essentially richer and more important, and regards the brio tone of the finale, especially, as not reaching the high level of the work's first half. (Compare Knapp's historical explanation, p. 210: "The movement is composed according to the typical classical progression toward decreasing complexity"—an explanation that has only limited validity and does not apply to such classical examples as Mozart's "Jupiter" Symphony.) At the same time, this particular closing movement is by no means an isolated example. A similarly problematic estimation is shared by a number of symphonic finales that want to give a questioning symphonic start a wholly positive turn by surmounting it: the forceful march of triumph as the goal of Beethoven's Fifth, the culmination of sheer figure-work without thematic quality at the end of Schumann's Fourth, the stretta at the conclusion of Brahms's First Symphony (which Clara Schumann, with her fine musical sensibility, already perceived as being only an "outward" climax and a rather "showy close"; see Litzmann III, 349), to name but a few examples. Of course such appraisals are based on a conception that puts "inner" before "outward" effects.

Hence the author of this study is perfectly aware that his concentration on the first two movements has not only a quantitative side. In his understanding of art and in his experience of music, the third and fourth movements are a little too "lightweight" after the profundities of the first two. The sixths and thirds of the Allegretto grazioso are a matter of "taste." And to my own mind's ear, the fourth movement, when compared to the indeed extraordinary opening movement, seems a finale almost devoid of mysteries, without real complications, very directly optimistic. Of course there are the moments of holding back, and there are the somber trombones, even in the coda. And yet at the very end the brass is blaring as though it were the world of the *Academic Festival Overture.* To my ear there is a discrepancy. On the other hand (or maybe for that very reason), the final movement, in relation to the start of the symphony, lacks a "breakthrough," with militant pathos, to that serene world which it seems to envision. Despite the heightened coda in the finale, the symphony does not have a straightforward "plot archetype" structure but seems divided according to movements into two polar halves. Nor does the final movement emulate that of the First Symphony by taking up the start of the opening movement and surmounting it structurally, and the showy close is subsequently even less suited to doing so. But please note: all these doubts and reservations concern a composition of supreme formal accomplishment; they are pointing out those few moments where this very high level does not seem to be fully maintained.

Thus the "top-heaviness" of this study has its basis in the work itself, in its temporal course as also in its different degrees of reflectiveness, the quantitative and qualitative aspects being difficult to separate in the process. One could also say that the reflective first movement necessarily needs more "time" than a "last dance" finale as such could generally lay claim to. A general prior understanding of this kind may, it is true, be kept within bounds through methodical reflection, and can be rendered transparent, but as a subjective element of aesthetic experience it will still be part of the work's historical interpretation. Nor is this something to be afraid of. Methodical counterplay constitutes one of the charms of musical analysis and artistic exegesis.

The judgmental horizon in which this study is grounded can also be discerned from the Second Symphony's early reception—although there, the values are reversed. The Adagio was felt to be not so original, not altogether successful (see Frisch 128–129, and the reviews in Floros 179ff.); Kalbeck's personal hunch (III, 173) that it might have been conceived originally for the tragic world of the First Symphony still represents this view. Only a few early opinions like Ferdinand Pohl's *(Y)* go against such an estimation. The third movement, on the other hand, had the most success of all from the very beginning, and even today it is often regarded as a singularly happy invention in the repertoire of the symphony generally (see Floros 210). Both these points, the lack of appreciation for the second movement and the favoring of the third movement, are bound up with one constant factor in this symphony's reception, already repeatedly cited: the idea of an unbrokenly serene work. In the process, the early statements and reviews referred to that notion of the idyllic that has already been touched on in the section on melancholy. This will be the cue for a summarizing reflection.

In Conclusion:
Idyll, Melancholy,
and Monumental Form

"In ideational content the first movement may be described as the most important: it strikes up such an endearing and cheerful pastoral tone, and although this is supplanted at times by the solemn sounds of trombones, like storms erupting over the calm, magnificent spring landscape, it always regains the upper hand, so that one imagines oneself transported back in time to the age of the idyll, which no savage passions were tearing apart." This is a central sentence in a review of the Leipzig performance of the Second Symphony on January 10, 1878 (*Neue Zeitschrift für Musik,* January 25, 1878, p. 47; see Floros 184). Two aspects of this critique are of interest here. First there is the nature-metaphor of the pastorale, the topic on which Theodor Billroth had already expressed himself to Brahms so enthusiastically *(M).* The metaphor does in fact capture this symphony's essence. In an earlier chapter nature and religion, the two "supra-historical" forces, were perceived as being behind the finale of Brahms's First Symphony and as being its historic identifying mark (in opposition to "history," the principle of "progress," and in contrast to Beethoven). It is as a pastoral metaphor in music, and as the portrayal in sound of Brahms's new symphonic idea, that the Second Symphony starts off. This recourse to "nature" as a formal principle was regarded as one of the signs of Brahms's "melancholic" experience of life, and of the way he internalized it. This leads poetologically to the concept of the idyll as symphonic idea, which is the second interesting aspect of the Leipzig critique. But the interpretation of the symphony in this study does not resolve into that notion of a peaceable "idyll" which is to be discerned as an achieved goal in the review quoted above.[33]

Idyll

For Brahms's symphonic idyll is not—to adopt Schiller's terms— "naive" but "sentimental." "A poet . . . either *is* Nature, or else he will *seek* her. The former is a naive, the latter a sentimental poet" (section on "Sentimental Poets" in Schiller's *On Naive and Sentimental Poetry*). In Brahms's case this seeking, as shown earlier, takes on the intensity of a masterly toiling at the burden of history as well as contemporary hardship. The new philosophical position of "nature" at the end of the First Symphony was achieved compositionally through "unremitting labor." And the idyllic nature-metaphor at the beginning of Brahms's Second Symphony is itself charged with history (through the *Eroica* reference) and highly complex artistically (through the subtly ambiguous interlocking). There is a skeptically broken quality to this music. And insofar as this is bound up with the awareness of a historical loss—thus constituting a latent philosophy of history in an artistic medium—Brahms's idyllicizing expresses that melancholy which is a product of "mourning" for a "lost possession" (see Schelling's definition of melancholy, quoted above). Thus etched on the Brahmsian idyll, with its reflective intensity, is the consciousness of a late period which is excluded from the pure representation of an Arcadian state, and which realizes this consciousness in its art. After the interpretation of the opening movement this was called an idyll broken in melancholy fashion. Poetologically it is, as a genre, what corresponds to the internalizing processes described in the "Melancholy" section.

Here a useful digression can be made. In the City of Vienna Historical Museum there is an oil-painting 49.5 × 73.5 cm in size which the young

---

33. To supplement the writings listed in the section on Melancholy (see note 22), there are also the following studies, dealing mainly with literature and the visual arts: Panofsky 1957, Tismar, Bernhard, Wedewer/Jensen, Empson, and Seeber/Klussmann.

Gustav Klimt painted in 1884.[34] The work is entitled *Idylle*. As a picture
within the picture, two Michelangelesque youths are holding a round
medallion as the center of a grouping in several layers. The medallion
shows an idyllic mother-and-child scene, set in the open air in a classical-
bucolic manner. But the two surrounding youths standing out in sculp-
tural relief are deeply immersed in thought. They are seated on a stone
plinth with an inscription (giving the title, artist's initials, and year), and
this lends the whole scene the appearance of a funerary monument. This
surround-form immediately puts one in mind of the memorial figures
in the Medici Chapel in Florence. (The structural partitioning of the
picture, with its central circle, flanking figures, and pedestal, is even
reminiscent in form of the *ignudi* on the ceiling of the Sistine Chapel,
especially the depiction of "Let there be light." Art historians refer, moreover, to Hans Makart's lunettes on the staircase of the Vienna Kunsthis-
torisches Museum as the model through which Michelangelo was mediated for Klimt.) And since Klimt also decorated his actual picture frame
with ornamental flowers, thus making it part of the picture, the resulting
construction is a complex interlocking of picture and frame. This too,
because of its reception of art history and formal multi-layering, is an
extremely reflective art. Its whole expressive character—introspective,
almost resigned—gives Klimt's painting, like Brahms's symphonic
movement, the appearance of an "idyll broken in melancholy fashion."

– Quite parenthetically, Klimt executed this painting as a study for
one of his contributions to the multi-volume *Allegorien und Embleme,*
whose editor wanted to revive the artistic form of the allegory, and its
mode of thinking, in the name of historicism. Behind this endeavor was
the thesis that, for a reflective late period like the end of the nineteenth
century, allegory was a fitting artistic expression:

> Naive and primitive cultural epochs have no business with the allegory.
> But it becomes indispensable in times of speculation, a philosophical

---

34. See the illustration in the exhibition catalogue *Wien 1870–1930: Traum und Wirklichkeit,* Salzburg and Vienna 1984, Plate 8, p. 92. The following studies elaborate on this
subject and its historical background: Gerlach/Ilg, Schönfelder, Breicha, Frodl, and
Partsch.

world-view, and theories. Its creations are a substitute, unequal but inevitable, for the forms of religious faith and of the crumbling ideals of naive and immediate feeling. Which of the two eras we are living in today is not in question. The allegory is, for our own art, a welcome means of expression. (Ilg, in Gerlach, p. ii) –

Now there can be no doubt that Brahms's Second Symphony matches the foregoing definition of it as a "late, broken idyll" less and less strongly from movement to movement. The description is certainly true of both the first and the second movements, which easily make up the bulk of the symphony, quantitatively speaking. But the third-movement dance—subdued and restrained though this is, with its "waltz tone verging on the sentimental, almost the mournful" (early critique, cited in Floros 184)—comes very close to Arcadian idyll. And the fourth movement with its brio—although this is constantly disrupted, undermined—strives, especially at the end, to be a positive finale. Here the aesthetics of the symphonic genre are quite obviously influencing the formal thinking to a significant extent.

From the second half of the eighteenth century onward, the theory of the symphony was of course related to the aesthetics of the sublime. "Symphony" always meant a large-scale genre in regard to both the form and the impact, the orchestral apparatus and the content. And the symphony continued to stand for something grand, important, and monumental throughout the nineteenth century, at any rate within the Central European tradition and especially the Viennese. (This can be seen both from the actual works and from reflections upon them and the nature of the genre offered by composers, music critics, and within philosophical systems like the aesthetics of F. G. Hand and F. T. Vischer.) The specific formal process arising from, and corresponding to, this idea of the symphony as embracing a whole world was described earlier as a symphonic "plot archetype". Germane to this are the relative proportions of the individual movements within the symphonic whole, particularly the relation of the opening movement and the finale. In this respect Brahms's symphonic compositions come within a network of connections branching off in many directions—a few aspects of which

will be selected for discussion. This includes names (forerunners, contemporaries) as well as formal categories and compositional strategies;
but Brahms's own influence on contemporaries and successors will not
be considered here. As for the composers who influenced and were taken
up in Brahms's symphonic music, the changing and criss-crossing lines
of the tradition lead back above all to Haydn, Beethoven, Spohr,
Mendelssohn, and Schumann. Schubert seems to be involved not directly
but possibly via Schumann, while Berlioz, to whom Schumann owed so
much as a symphonist, appears to take a back seat where Brahms is
concerned. No positive connections are evident in the cases of Liszt, early
Tchaikovsky, and other direct contemporaries like Niels Gade, Joachim
Raff, Anton Rubinstein, or the Bruckner of the 1870s.

Between Apotheosis and "Last Dance": The Finale as Problem

The following thoughts will concentrate on the "finale problem" in the
Viennese symphonic tradition, and this (to look at the problem in general terms) initially concerns the relative weight of the movements.
Robert Schumann in his Moscheles review of 1836, in a passage that has
received little attention, observed a shifting of the center of gravity within
symphonic form since Beethoven, and addressed it as follows:

> A genuine musical structure will always have a certain focal point to-
> ward which everything gravitates, on which all the imaginative strands
> converge. Many composers place it in the middle (as Mozart does),
> others toward the close (like Beethoven). But no matter where it comes,
> the total effect will depend on its force. If one has been listening in-
> tently, and with bated breath, the moment will then arrive when, for
> the first time, one can breathe freely: the summit has been climbed
> and one can cast glances backward and forward, lucid and satisfied.
> (R. Schumann I, 162)

This statement reflects a personal ideal and is at the same time historically developed, and it may be understood as distinguishing concepts
that are oriented more toward architectonics from those that are oriented
more toward process. Haydn and Mozart, it may be argued, were the

exponents of architectonic form (albeit with a pinch of salt; in the "Jupiter" Symphony, for example, with its weighty finale, the formal center of gravity clearly lies with the closing movement, right at the end of the reprise, where the harmonic expansion is greatest, and then in the coda, which shows the greatest thematic and contrapuntal concentration). The main idea is a symmetry in the sequence of movements, with a last movement whose dimensions do not exceed those of the first movement (thought of as being the main one), and which is lightweight, often being constructed as a happy ending and "last dance," and in rondo form. This is the view taken by dictionary definitions of the symphony around 1800, as in Sulzer-Schulz or even with Heinrich Christoph Koch, whose descriptive categories deriving from the theory of the sublime were tested on the opening movement in particular. There then begins with Beethoven the history proper of the "finale symphony" with its forward orientation to the work's close and the transcending of this. The dynamic vocabulary used by Schumann to describe this structure is very illuminating: he writes of "force" and "total effect," of waiting "intently" and "with bated breath," and of an act of deliverance. The "finale symphony" has a summit which has to be climbed and conquered. In an ironically broken form, this general distinction between light and weightier examples of the genre—or, to borrow the language of the end of the eighteenth century, between just a "beautiful" symphony and a really "sublime" one—is preserved in the wording of Brahms's letter to Elisabet von Herzogenberg (document O), stating that his new symphony is not really a *Symphonie*, but just a *Sinfonie*. In saying that when a German spoke of a *Symphonie*, he meant Beethoven, Schumann was confirming that the "finale symphony" in the Beethovenian mold was considered the generic model in this tradition around the middle of the century. The notion of "symphonism," especially the adjective "symphonic," referred to this "great" prototype. (This had concrete repercussions extending to the architectural design of the halls built to accommodate this symphonic music toward the end of the nineteenth century and at the start of the twentieth, even in the New World. Paine Hall, for example, the Harvard Music Department's beautiful little concert hall completed

in 1914, has a frieze of composers' names running around the hall in chronological order. They are so placed that in the exact center above the concert platform, and thus at what was the center of music history around 1910, there stands the name of Beethoven, flanked on the left by Bach, Haydn, and Mozart, on the right by Schubert, Chopin, and Wagner—with the thought-provoking opposition of Bach and Wagner in the two corners of the hall, an opposition also flanking the same central point on the facade of Chicago's Orchestra Hall, built in 1905, over the entrance, where the order is Bach–Mozart–Beethoven–Schubert–Wagner. And in the Boston Symphony Hall dating from 1900, it is exclusively Beethoven's name that appears above the platform, as the avowed fixed point and yardstick of the music played on the podium below.)

Strategies

Recently, Reinhart Kapp has noted the finale strategies of intensification, overstepping, synthesis, concentration, acceleration, broadening, the hymnic tone and especially the chorale, seriousness, and "depth." Already in Beethoven, Kapp finds "the entire arsenal of integration, universality, starting up and breaking up, grandeur, sonorousness, a levying *en masse* and mass effects, a combination of pacifying and gestures of triumph—an arsenal that was meant to inflame a composer's imagination and challenge his productive and synthetic ingenuity" (pp. 242–244). This catalogue can be realized compositionally, and this will involve an interplay of qualitative and quantitative expedients. Inasmuch as a symphonic work is "invented and constructed in the spirit of the orchestra, from the soul of the orchestra" (Adolf Bernhard Marx), all these expedients are related to the historical position and historical development of the orchestral sound-medium.

First, the simplest approach will be to determine Brahms's interest in symphonic finale strategies negatively, by listing those expedients which were available to him but which he did not use. These can then be compared with the expedients he did use.

1. The Choral Finale, Instrumental Choir, and Chorale

Unlike Mendelssohn, with his *Hymn of Praise,* and Liszt (the *Faust* and *Dante* Symphonies), Brahms never wrote a symphony with a choral finale. He may be said to have expressly denied himself the incorporation of the human voice in the symphonic medium, the overstepping of purely instrumental bounds along the lines of Beethoven's Ninth. In that respect he was anticipated by Schumann. Schumann's opinion of Mendelssohn's "symphony-cantata" is equivocal and betrays a decided coolness in its complete form, which the writer suppressed on publication. He views the vocal section, the cantata, as a supplement introduced for a particular purpose, to which he would have preferred a purely instrumental fourth movement, and he recommends that the "actual symphony" and the cantata be published separately. As far as Schumann's own thoughts on form are concerned, the merging of the first three movements into an unbroken continuum seems to be the most important thing about the *Hymn of Praise* from the historical angle; he expressly remarks on its novelty in symphonic composition (and he was obviously following Mendelssohn's example when he composed his D minor Symphony in 1841). Thus Schumann's concert review of 1840 reveals a great deal of what he himself was thinking about the possibilities of the symphony "after Beethoven." He was anticipating his own great symphonies of 1841, preparing his conceptions of them. Here is the central paragraph of his critique of the *Hymn of Praise* in its entirety:

> The actual singing was, however, preceded by three symphonic orchestral movements, so that the form is comparable to Beethoven's Ninth Symphony except for the difference—and this needs stressing, not having been tried in the symphony before—that the three orchestral movements succeed one another without a break. The form of the whole could not have been devised more neatly for this purpose, although we doubt whether it was originally conceived in this way and are almost certain that those orchestral movements, written some time ago, were part of a veritable symphony to which he [Mendelssohn] then appended the *Hymn of Praise*—which seems entirely new to me—

for the particular occasion. However that may be, the composition had an inspiring effect, and this was by virtue of the inner and outward climaxing. The "Hymn of Praise" was the summit to which the orchestra was, as it were, lifted by the human voices, and there was also an organ for the supremely vigorous close. But if we are right in our supposition that the symphony movements came about earlier, independently of the "Hymn of Praise," we would prefer the two works to be published separately, to the obvious advantage of both. The symphony movements assuredly contained things that are extremely lovely in themselves, in the first movement and especially the Allegretto; but to my mind they were wrought too subtly and delicately to go with the ceremony and splendor of the "Hymn of Praise," and a cheerful conclusion is more what they call for—not unlike, say, Beethoven's [Fourth] Symphony in B-flat major, which is also the home key of these pieces. And just as these three movements, when rounded off by a finale, would provide a complete symphony for the concert hall, so the "Hymn of Praise," too, stands as a complete work in itself, and even as one of Mendelssohn's most successful in my opinion, one of his freshest, most charming, most brilliant. (R. Schumann I, 486; II, 436)

Schumann's text may also have drawn on the intensive aesthetic debate regarding the suitability of the choral finale in Beethoven's Ninth that was on many musicians' minds at that time. The debate was carried on primarily in the pages of the *Neue Zeitschrift für Musik* for 1838 (but also 1834, 1836, 1837, and as late as 1847), and Schumann himself as editor was not afraid of commenting on his authors' Beethoven critiques in footnotes. It was as late as 1847 that Adolf Bernhard Marx entered the debate "On the Form of the Symphony-Cantata" (*Allgemeine Musikalische Zeitung,* July 21 and 28, 1847).

Such discussions, of course, also prepared the ground for later on, when Brahms's First Symphony was instantly perceived as a confrontation with Beethoven's Ninth. Chrysander's aforementioned reference to a *Gegenbild,* an antithesis to the final sections of the Ninth Symphony, and the postulation of a "return of the symphony that mixes playing

and singing to the purely instrumental symphony," were influenced by
the previous attuning of people's minds to this proposition.

But Schumann's text is also the continuing expression of a belief which
he had already stated years before, and which is a very typical mixture
of admiration for Beethoven's Ninth and dissociation from it. There is
a comment in Schumann's influential Berlioz critique of 1835, whose
wording and substance are a very neat illustration of this ambiguity. The
original passage (which Schumann again suppressed on publication)
reads:

> After Beethoven's Ninth Symphony, outwardly the greatest instru-
> mental work in existence, moderation appeared to have had its day. A
> gigantic idea needed a giant's body, a god a universe to operate in. But
> art has its limits. The Apollo of Belvedere, were it several feet taller,
> would give offense. The later composers of symphonies noticed this,
> and some of them even took refuge in the cozy Haydn-Mozartian
> forms. (R. Schumann I, 70; II, 378)

Schumann's definition of himself as a symphonist, in an endeavor that
went on for years, ruled out any escape from the consequences of the
standard set by Beethoven; at the same time it was striving for autonomy
and self-reliance. And it was these very attributes which Schumann, with
palpable relief, was praising in 1839 in Schubert's newly discovered
"Great" C major Symphony: "Assuredly he never thought of trying to
carry on Beethoven's Ninth Symphony." Schumann located the individual character of Schubert's purely orchestral composing in the "idiosyncratic treatment of the instruments and also the mass of the orchestra
..., whose discourse is often like that of human voices and a chorus"
(Schumann I, 461/463). Here he was already expressing the view that it
was perfectly feasible for the vocal element to take an instrumental form.
The actual addition of the human voice (described in Schumann's Mendelssohn review as an "outward climaxing" toward the "summit to
which the orchestra was meant to be lifted by human voices") is not
necessary.

Brahms evidently agreed with Schumann in this kind of critique. He
banished the human voice from the symphonic genre, and (in works

like the *Alto Rhapsody, Song of Destiny, Naenia, and Song of the Fates*)
reserved other orchestral-vocal areas for this combination. Like Schumann, however, he exploited the purely instrumental representation of
the human voice: through the chorale inflection, the intonation of the
hymnic, of collective song. And once again one may put it more forcibly
and say that, without these resources, he could not manage from the
standpoint of content. Yet there is, significantly, no instrumental recitative in Brahms.

The First Symphony in particular features "instrumental choirs" as a
means of formal and contentual heightening. In the opening movement,
the first climax in the development is a chorale-like tutti (mm. 232ff.)
which is then integrated thematically; the finale of the symphony uses a
brass chorale in the slow introduction and for the coda triumph, while
its main theme, which is suppressed later on, is a choric song for strings.
This goes back as far as Beethoven (the *Eroica* Symphony with its singing
out, involving all the orchestral voices, of the main theme in the first-
movement coda and in the slow episode preceding the close of the finale;
the *Pastoral* Symphony with the chorale-like epilogue to the storm at the
end of its fourth movement, leading to the instrumental "shepherds'
song" of the finale). The same device occurs in the chorale arrangements
of Spohr's Fourth Symphony *(Die Weihe der Töne),* and it appears as a
direct quotation of the "Dies irae" in the finale of Berlioz's *Symphonie
fantastique.* Mendelssohn's Second Symphony, the *Hymn of Praise,* places
an instrumental chorale in front of the vocal cantata; the goal of his
Third Symphony, the *Scottish,* is an orchestral finale-hymn, a festive
Allegro maestoso in A major; the earlier Fifth Symphony *(Reformation)*
is, on account of its very subject and its designation, full of chorales—
both the chorale "tone" and the symphonic working up of concrete
models. Schumann, finally, is interested far less directly in the chorale
as such. But in his *Overture, Scherzo, and Finale,* he used a hymnic broadening of the theme in the brass to extend the third movement into a
finale to the complete work. And both Schumann's Second and Third
Symphonies feature an instrumental hymn as the apotheosis of the cycle
of movements. Within the Second Symphony's comprehensive thematic
joining of all the movements, this hymn forms a contrast to the lyrical

new theme, which is drawn into the hymnic upswing; moreover, it is combined with the festive fifth-motto of the entire symphony, a figure which strikes the work's "grand" tone in the *stile antico* of the slow introduction—probably a double homage to Haydn (the *London* Symphony, No. 104) and Mendelssohn (the *Reformation*). The coda to the finale of Schumann's *Rhenish* Symphony brings a chorale with written-out line fermatas, dominated by the full brass, before turning head over heels in a stretta. By blending a brass chorale with the stretta close, Brahms's First Symphony combines the two elements that Schumann kept separate. Both Schumann and Brahms seem to stress that "the intentions and effects pursued with a choral finale can also be realized . . . with purely instrumental means" (Kapp 247). Of course the instrumental allusion to the vocal domain is not, in essence, abandoned. It guarantees the representation of the symphonic meaning. This meaning has a strong religious component; in the First Symphony's union of nature-metaphor and chorale intonation it would be classifiable as a nature religion. (And it was no accident that the old Brahms rounded off his composing on a religious note with the biblical Four Serious Songs and the organ chorale "O Welt, ich muss dich lassen," "last" works that were evidently the result of conscious planning. In this perspective it is the First Symphony that sets the turning point.)

Even the Third Symphony of Brahms features a chorale, although here, of course, the expressive standpoint and function are totally different. The chorale is prepared in the slow second movement's contrasting section for winds (mm. 41ff.) and the same section in the last movement's bridge passage (mm. 19ff.). In the coda to this finale, quite untypically, it induces the ebbing away at the symphony's conclusion. Although the instrumental chorale is again a choric summing-up, followed by a brief final upswing, it enters *piano* and *dolce* and eventually fades mildly away before the first movement's main theme does what it did at the end of that movement and leads to the symphony's ultimate dying away. In regard to what this conclusion is expressing, it is particularly telling that the chorale does not perform its usual function of a hymnic heightening; this gentle, rather lyrical chorale emphasizes the historically important change, in this work, in the character of the finale.

(In the first movement of Berlioz's *Symphonie fantastique* the "religios-amente" conclusion that he composed as an afterthought, with its ec-clesiastical plagal cadence, constitutes a similar movement-ending, but the overall function is relativized by the fact of its coming within the work, and not right at the end of the finale.)

2. Separate Movements and Continuum

Brahms did not compose any direct transitions between movements (the whole formal range of which, from simple joining-on to independent status, Beethoven had already outlined in exemplary fashion in his C-sharp minor Quartet). He persisted with the classical separation of the four traditional movement-types and their modifications. With Brahms there is never the simple instruction "attacca" between inherently au-tonomous movement units (as there is with Mendelssohn in the *Hymn of Praise* and the *Scottish* Symphony, and with Schumann after him, in the first three movements of the D minor Symphony; in his First Sym-phony, Schumann had joined the two middle movements together with a dominant link and "attacca" heading). Neither does Brahms use a fully composed transition passage (like Beethoven between the closing move-ments of his *Pastoral* Symphony)—and certainly not in the form, so effective in regard to the finale apotheosis, of a climactic linking passage (as in Beethoven's Fifth, a passage that Schumann's D minor Symphony emulates in function and form). This also rules out the formal model of a superimposing of single-movement and multi-movement structure as realized by Schumann in the D minor Symphony (affecting the form of the individual movements, especially the first and third), before it be-came historically prevalent through Liszt's formal experiments (piano concertos, Sonata in B minor, symphonic poems), and with Strauss (*Don Juan,* for instance), Schoenberg (First String Quartet, First Chamber Symphony), and Schreker (Chamber Symphony). Liszt's ap-proach, incidentally, was the opposite of Schumann's: Schumann unified the four-movement symphony as a one-movement continuum whose units functioned as both individual movements and sections of the prin-cipal movement, whereas Liszt enriched and enlarged the single-movement overture by incorporating the four symphonic movement-types. The most important incentive for this, apart from Schumann's Fourth Symphony, was probably Schubert's *Wanderer* Fantasy, which Liszt arranged as a piano concerto prior to 1852.

Brahms, on the other hand, was fond of playing tricks by his interchanging of the formal patterns of individual movements, especially in closing movements. The rondo allusion in the First Symphony's sonata finale, the superimposing of rondo and sonata in the last movement of the Second (as in Schumann's Second before it), the Fourth Symphony's passacaglia variations and sonata, which is possibly even a sonata cycle: these are evidence of a tendency toward a complex multiplicity of meanings within traditional forms.

3. Thematic Concentration, Motto, Device

Similarly, Brahms never composed a last-movement introduction that recalled and summed up the preceding movements—as Berlioz, borrowing directly from Beethoven's Ninth, did in *Harold in Italy*. Nor did he combine movements by means of quotations along the lines of Beethoven's Fifth (the finale's scherzo quotation, with the fresh link to the apotheosis of the triumphant march). But there was one occasion when Brahms, like Mendelssohn in the *Hymn of Praise,* did take up the start of a symphony at the end of the work to round it off (a principle outlined in Schubert's "Great" C major Symphony, if only in regard to the first movement). As was shown earlier, however, the intrinsic purpose of this expedient in Brahms's Third Symphony is, all through the thematic transformation at the close of the first movement, completely different. With Brahms, moreover, there is no concentration of themes from the symphony during or toward the end of the finale (something that is particularly marked in Schumann's Second), whether the themes are brought together one after the other or superimposed in counterpoint, all at the same time. And there is no Berliozian *idée fixe,* a device which Schumann converted in his Second Symphony into a motto linking the movements. On the other hand Brahms repeatedly uses the motto technique for individual movements, as in the opening movements of his First and Third Symphonies. The Second also has a motto in its first movement, but embedded in a complex web of thematic derivations, and because it is their starting point it has a structural function on several levels right across the work. Beethoven's motto movements (the opening movements of his Fifth and Sixth Symphonies) used a fermata to isolate the emblem, or motto, from the "real" start of the movement. Schumann did the same in the closing movement of his First Symphony. Conversely, in both the finale of Schumann's Second and the opening movement of Brahms's Third the motto is connected to the start of the movement by serving as a "curtain." In Schumann's First and Fourth Symphonies, the motto is introduced as the start of a slow introduction (and provides the basis for the genesis of the allegro's main theme). Brahms's First Symphony combines the two: the motto opens the slow introduction to the first movement and is also a curtain for the allegro theme.

4. Introductions

Brahms only composed slow introductions for the first of his symphonies; as Tovey noted, it is one of the few examples in his entire output. Moreover, even though the introduction to the first movement sets the tone for the whole, Clara Schumann testifies that it was written later (letter of June 1, 1862, to Joseph Joachim, Litzmann III, 123), being preceded genetically by the motto's allegro version. For this imposing way of opening a work Brahms had, of course, many possible models from Haydn to Schumann. If we permit ourselves a cautious typologizing along the lines of Peter Gülke's, the introduction to Brahms's First Symphony is one of the "portal" type (Haydn, Mozart, Beethoven II and VII) and not the evolving, processual type of introduction (Beethoven I and IV, Schumann IV). But what is significant and special about Brahms's First is the provision of a slow introduction to the finale. True, this was prefigured in the Viennese tradition by the placing of a slow movement before the finale (Beethoven's Ninth Symphony, where the adagio and scherzo are transposed; Mendelssohn's *Scottish*, where the order of the middle movements is again reversed; or Schumann, who similarly transposes the inner movements in his Second Symphony, and provides the *Rhenish* with an extra slow movement), or by the formal dispositions of chamber music, as in Beethoven's piano sonatas. Nonetheless the expedient is relevant dramaturgically to the specific content of this finale, as the foregoing analysis has demonstrated. (Hence Gounod's First Symphony of 1855, whose final movement begins with an Adagio, was not a model for Brahms.) The finale's antithesis of initial gloom and a subsequent brightening, which is built into it on several compositional levels and sums up the symphony's ideational program, is repeated in the opening of the Second Symphony; here, however, with the pastoral beginning and its gradual clouding over, the events happen in the reverse order, and within the basic tempo. Accordingly, the contrast takes a dramatic form in the First Symphony, whereas the expression is resigned and restrained in the Second. Incidentally, the two inner movements do not come in the order fast-slow in any of Brahms's four symphonies, but this does occur in the (symphonically four-movement) Second Piano Concerto.

Neither did Brahms adopt the type of opening seen in Beethoven's Ninth: the inclusion of a progressively evolving introduction in the *a tempo* start of the movement (that is, the paradox of the slow introduction as an allegro)—later to be Bruckner's model with the unison breakthrough of its main theme. (This was adopted—mirrored through Beethoven's Fourth—by Brahms's friend Heinrich von Herzogenberg in 1885 for his Symphony No. 2 in B-flat major.) The opening of Brahms's Second Symphony is, as explained above, only seemingly derived from this formal disposition. Nor does Brahms's First feature a repeat of the slow introduction as such in the further course of events, as occurs at the join between the first and second movements of Mendelssohn's *Scottish* Symphony (or also, much earlier, in Haydn's Symphony No. 102, the one with the drum-roll, before the coda). The transforming procedure in the finale of Brahms's First has a different status.

It is part and parcel of this approach that in his symphonies, Brahms never inserts the "slow episode" just before the end of the movement. (This certainly occurs elsewhere in his works, for example as a closing ritornello in the First Piano Concerto, and before the end of the Double

Concerto.) In the finale of Beethoven's *Eroica* it is an effective method of delaying the climax, and the way Haydn takes up the slow introduction again before the coda to the first movement of his Symphony No. 102 served the same purpose. (And, certainly, the trombone passage in the first movement of Schubert's last symphonic fragment D 936a could also be mentioned here.) Now in symphonies this technique usually goes hand in hand with the laying out of the finale as a set of variations, as can be seen in the final movements of Beethoven's Third or Ninth. Brahms, of course, composed only one variation finale, the passacaglia in his Fourth Symphony. But this movement's slow variations 13–16, with their E-major brightening, blend sonata-cycle elements into the passacaglia in such a way as almost to perform the function of a lyrical middle movement. Of course the idea of a slowing down before the end, as a penultima, and a speeding up of the ending itself can also be suggested by prescribing ritardando and accelerando, or through the sheer note values. Here one could mention the transition from slowed-down quarter triplets to scampering eighth-note runs at the end of Brahms's Second; it has the effect of a stretta.

5. The New Theme

One important strategy that Brahms adopted from Schumann is the introduction of a "new" theme (which often is not really all that new and presents hidden contours of material already stated as though they were new ones). For the nineteenth century, the precedents were set, once again, by Beethoven, in whose Third and Fourth Symphonies the new theme encroaches on the form at an unexpected place in the sonata convention—namely within the first-movement development section. In the *Eroica* this is the moment of regeneration after the main thematic material has been worked off and used up, and the coda takes it up again to create a balance. In the Fourth Symphony it is an extended melodic gesture. And this seems to have been Schumann's source of inspiration. In the first movement of his D minor Symphony (this already applies to the first version of 1841), the propulsive new idea appears in the middle of the development (mm. 147ff.) and subsequently becomes the theme of the coda upswing hurtling to D major with which the movement closes. There is, in the process, a causal connection between the deployment of the new theme, its function, form, and character, and the double modification to this movement's sonata form—a movement which, being "exposition" in the sense of the overriding single-movement structure, has no real recapitulation. Formally and dynamically the place of the recapitulation is taken by the new theme. In the same symphony Schumann goes on to outstrip Beethoven by transferring the same technique to the finale, where he again uses it twice, in the development and just before the coda. Schumann's Second Symphony extends this in the illustrated manner, the main theme being "replaced" where the recapitulation would normally come. And in the finale of Schumann's Third Symphony, a little before the end of the development section, the captivating verve of a new theme effectively swallows up the ensuing recapitulation. Brahms, as shown in detail earlier, was able to link up with such Schumannesque procedures in his First Symphony, with its horn call and its chorale. Of course, he changed around the formal idea of the "new theme" to suit his own purpose.

6. Apotheosis

It is surprising that Brahms of all people did not—except in his Third Symphony—forgo the rather superficial, so to speak quantitative methods of the finale apotheosis. (In creating an instant effect they are, to be sure, extremely handy.) This involves a whole bundle of expedients with the same objective. In both the First Symphony and the Fourth, Brahms saves the forceful sound of the trombones for the enhancement of the last movement, following the example of Beethoven in the Fifth Symphony and of Schumann in his five-movement Third, with the trombones in the two closing movements. And not for one moment does Brahms disdain, in his First and Second Symphonies, the crowd-pulling stretta; even the Fourth Symphony's passacaglia has a Più allegro coda. (As has been mentioned earlier, Clara Schumann in her critique of the First Symphony thought this an unwarranted externalization.) Again, Brahms's models were Beethoven's Fifth and Ninth, along with

Schumann's Fourth Symphony. Also part of this is the dramatic major-key brightening of a symphony starting in the minor, which is what gives the conclusions to Beethoven's Fifth and Ninth Symphonies, Mendelssohn's Third, and Schumann's Fourth their final power and final glory, whether in a major-key coda or an entire movement in the major. As in Schumann's D minor Symphony, the light of the parallel major in Brahms's First already appears at the end of the opening movement, before Brahms takes it up within the introduction to the finale, as an antithetical world, and then for the entire Allegro. The same applies to the Third Symphony's mild-sounding close. The Fourth Symphony, which makes use of contrapuntal rigor, of the rich trombones as also the stretta, remains in the unalleviated darkness of E minor both in the opening movement and in the finale. It thereby repudiates the positive ending.

Brahms's Second Again

If we now place the Second Symphony within the framework of this tradition and consider its choice of means in comparison with Brahms's other symphonies, particularly the First, the result will be a very characteristic picture. The finale of the First Symphony stands wholly within the tradition of the pathos-filled "plot archetype." It makes use of the existing strategies of musical language and programmatic content, and it adds new ones in order to demonstrate seriousness, dignity, and "depth." At the same time it operates the finale process with "all the available technical means," the chorale apotheosis that makes an all-out effort being its goal and its victory. In sharp contrast to this is its symphonic "sister," the Second Symphony with the happy ending, a final rondo in thematic character and formal persuasion. Here there is a good parallel with the rondo movements of Mahler's middle period, in his Fifth and Seventh Symphonies, after the finale strategies in his first three. On a new level, and using a later man's historical experience, Mahler made a very similar journey to the final word of the *Song of the Earth* and the Ninth Symphony. Brahms's Second occupies an analogous central position in his (slimmer) symphonic oeuvre.

Brahms's Second contains less of the formal arsenal of the finale weighed down with dignity. There is the trombones' transformation and the orchestral brio at the close. But compared to the First, and against the symphony's historical background, Tovey's reference back to Haydn (p. 210; see also Knapp, pp. 158–159)—and thus back to the symphony before Beethoven, with what Schumann termed the more symmetrical and architectonic layout and its more lightweight final movement—is quite appropriate. (In his letter of October 1886 to Heinrich von Herzogenberg, Brahms preferred the first version of Schumann's D minor Symphony to its thematically condensed, more ponderous revised version, saying of the former that it was "a pleasure to see something invented cheerfully and easily being expressed just as easily and naturally" [Letters II, 2, p. 127], and even comparing it to Mozart. This may be a signpost showing what he ultimately wished to achieve with his D major Symphony, since it has many affinities with Schumann.) Now, as already mentioned, Brahms's Second Symphony is curiously "top-heavy." Even quantitatively, the two "lighter" and shorter movements III and IV hardly manage to counterbalance movements I and II.

The third movement (this too was mentioned earlier) initiates something of a turnabout. But from the standpoint of large-scale form this movement lasting just five minutes is no more than an intermezzo, after which the symphonic "plot" could revert perfectly well to the tone and expression of the symphony's first half. Hence the finale becomes all the more crucial to the formal idea and the content. In terms of formal dramaturgy the movement remains a hybrid. On the one hand it is meant to preserve the melancholic tones by virtue of the movements' interdependence, the pensiveness of the first two being essentially carried over via the restraint of the third into the symphony's ending as well. But on the other hand (and this is more emphatic), the finale is meant to be the symphony's crowning point in itself, with the coda's stress on the "plot archetype," changed into rondo gaiety. The situation is not, however, the same as it was in the First Symphony. Because of the opening movement's subtle expressive stance, there is no possibility here of a dramatic culmination and clash of ideas in the final movement, no positing of a contrary principle. Brahms does in fact want a happy ending, which is already announced in the rondo character of the finale's main theme, and he wants to have it right at the close, a monumental triumph sounded by the orchestra in all its brilliance and richness. But what was given formal conviction by the great rush of ideas in the finale of the First Symphony becomes superficial in the Second after m. 379. Here the themes are less pregnant throughout the finale, and with the full orchestra entering fortissimo, the ear is left with a sense of discrepancy. This affects not only the trombone sound which has been a hallmark of the symphony, and which is now completely subordinated to a mercurial brilliance (lacking conviction even if one sees the semi-dancing trombones in mm. 353ff. as having a consciously intermediary position and hears in the drastically fulminating final chord of the three trombones an eloquent coarseness). The melodic lines themselves eventually become devoid of any thematic quality, with sheer figural passagework remaining, and even the second theme's characteristic gestures in mm. 417ff. are smoothed out again directly afterwards. Not unfairly, Clara Schumann had already criticized the stretta at the end of the First Symphony as being an unnecessary piece of externalizing; at the end of the Second the gaiety becomes almost violently brilliant and seems stagemanaged. (Let us once more recall Schumann's Fourth, where the conclusion wins through with a similarly problematic D-major brio and the instrumental lines are similarly reduced to mere passagework without pregnant themes.) This is by no means a question of something idyllically "simple" but a matter of exaggeration, of a positivity deliberately unleashed after the symphony has been dominated by a rich spectrum of intermediate tones. This mighty, unequivocal conclusion cannot efface the melancholic ambiguity of the first two movements and the shadow it cast on the third movement. For all the mastery of the orchestral writing, it does not quite live up to the earlier movements, either as a formal idea or in the practical realization. Here Brahms is relying not so much on structural tautness, on the appropriate tone and means as integrating factors that would take up ideas in a quasi-retrospective way, as on the extreme effect of the final moment, which was meant to be overwhelming. Ultimately the attempt to unite the internalizing idyll and an extensive monumentality is not altogether successful. Therein—a

philosopher of history might solemnly say—lies the historical truth of
this symphony: the sensitive artist whose person and whose life appear
to be threatened by "black wings" can no longer attain to limitless rejoicing.

To recapitulate: Brahms's attempt at another climactic finale at the
end of his Second Symphony could be connected with the view of the
genre, with expectations regarding the topos of a symphonic finale with
which this close fits in—or, rather, still fits in.

The Symphonic Ending: "The Taking Back"

Another option—one that was markedly different from the above
topos—was composed by Brahms later on, in his Third Symphony, and
from this angle it seems a continuing reflection on the situation of the
Second. (The way both finales begin with a unison theme on the strings
is another indication of this.) In the Third Symphony the music ebbs
away at the close with its chorale, which Brahms introduces "piano" and
"dolce," and with its first movement's downward-directed main theme,
here transformed in "tone" (as it already was at the end of the opening
movement). The symphony withdraws into a reflective restraint, and the
close becomes an *Abgesang,* a valediction. Incidentally, Carl Dahlhaus
rightly thought that this main theme, which paraphrases Schumann, was
inherently already a closing idea in structure and character: "not until
the diminuendo epilogues of the first and fourth movements does it reveal
its true character, and the direction it then takes is one of introspection,
where the subject immures itself to the world and turns ultimately to
silence" (1989, p. 269). Hermann Kretzschmar had previously proposed
this formal intention for the Third Symphony in its entirety, interpreting
it as a historically important departure from the Beethovenian plot archetype. His commentary reads like an inversion of Schumann's idea,
which was quoted above: "Perhaps this Third Symphony of Brahms constitutes, in the later history of the arts, the starting point of a new period
in the symphony. For it seems to inaugurate a break with the Beethovenian
type of structural design by transferring the compositional center of
gravity back from the development section to the thematic group, from

working-out and skillful continuation back to the realm of the initial invention" (pp. 299–300). This quite unheroic "ending" to a symphony (one which curiously enough is usually called Brahms's "Heroic Symphony") was eventually followed, in the fourth and last, by an uncompromisingly "negative" symphonic finale with its passacaglia, which is as though hewn from granite. Here again the close of the movement, the coda, is so set apart as to break the pattern, but this is now effected structurally, as a departure from the orderly, four-square metricality of the groups of measures in the passacaglia. And the close, with its either chromatic or canonic but always cogent voice-leading and its powerful trombone intonations, is neither given a positive shimmer, nor does it transfigure the music or lapse into a resigned silence; it persists in its negativity. Felix Weingartner, writing in poetic language, interpreted the last movement in terms of the history of ideas:

> The outer movements, however, are of downright monumental force, especially the finale. Here it is usual for people to praise Brahms for his feat in adapting the old form of the passacaglia to a modern symphony movement in a positively subtle way. This is certainly astonishing, but for me the real miracle is the tremendous emotional content of this piece of music. Here I cannot get away from the impression of an inexorable fate implacably driving some great creation, whether it be an individual or a whole race, toward its downfall. The latter resists and fights with all its strength, and once there is briefly a glimmer of hope, but all is in vain. Its extermination has been decreed and presses on with irresistible giant's steps. This movement is seared by shattering tragedy, the close being a veritable orgy of destruction, a terrible counterpart to the paroxysm of joy at the end of Beethoven's last symphony. (pp. 58–59)

Both the content and the language of this judgment are noteworthy. The finale of Brahms's last symphony is an "orgy of destruction," the depiction of "a whole race" heading "irresistibly" toward its "extermination," and is regarded both aesthetically and philosophically as the "terrible counterpart to the paroxysm of joy" in Beethoven's Ninth. (Chrysander had already spoken similarly of the first Brahms symphony as forming a *Gegenbild,* an antitype, to Beethoven's Ninth Symphony, although in a purely internal aesthetic sense.) The vocabulary brings to mind the words used by a later composer to define his self-imposed historical task—again in contrast to Beethoven and to the form, expression, and message of the finale of the Ninth. The final work by this creator of modern music, a cantata of truly symphonic dimensions with great orchestral interludes and an "orchestral closing movement . . . into which the choir disappears," is described as follows by the person who knows it best, quoting the composer himself: "The conclusion is purely orchestral: a symphonic adagio movement into which the chorus of lament powerfully commencing after the infernal *galop* gradually passes— it is, so to speak, the return trip from the Ode to Joy, the negative companion piece to that passing of the symphony into vocal rejoicing, it is the taking back." It is Adrian Leverkühn's final work on which Thomas Mann's narrator Serenus Zeitblom is reporting, here in Chapter 46 of the novel *Doctor Faustus.* And this "hymn to mourning" which "prophetically anticipates so much ruin" was written "with an eye to Beethoven's 'Ninth' as its counterpart, in the word's most mournful sense." The musical models for a symphony with an adagio instead of a triumphant finale are Mahler's Third and Ninth Symphonies (in the latter of which, as in Leverkühn's work, "one instrumental group after another withdraws," and Mahler directs the movement to "die away" at the end), and especially Tchaikovsky's *Pathétique* with its "almost frightening conclusion" (Klaus Mann) on cellos and basses by themselves— if not, as in Leverkühn's piece, with "the high g" of a solo cello, "the final hovering sound, slowly dissipating in a fermata, pianissimo." (And here the model clearly is the end of the first "Night Music" from Mahler's Seventh Symphony, with the isolated high g of the cello group playing harmonics, briefly accented by the harp but indeed fading away in a fermata, *lange* and *morendo.*)

In his Tchaikovsky novel of 1935, Thomas Mann's son Klaus described that Sixth Symphony's "Adagio lamentoso" in words that must have echoed in his father's ears when, in his own novel, he was invoking "coldness" as a principle of modern art and the "tone" of the "lament" as its ultimate statement. Klaus Mann writes in the tenth chapter of his

novel: "There emanated from this pain-wracked finale a breath that sti-
fled all gratitude, all enthusiasm: on hearing this tone of farewell and
lament, which already seemed to come almost out of another world, the
audience of St. Petersburg art lovers shivered, and many felt a chill running down their spines." Chrysander and Weingartner, Tchaikovsky and
Brahms: nineteenth-century critics confirm, and artists of that same century were stating in their music, that the idea of a counter-plan to
Beethoven's Ninth Symphony stemmed from the century itself. Thomas
Mann's novel gives it a far-reaching historical and philosophical perspective for the twentieth century, but toward the end of the nineteenth
it already existed in an artistic form (first in Berlioz, as a grotesquely
ironic archetype, then as an anti-archetype in the later Brahms,
Tchaikovsky, and Mahler) and in critical terminology (Chrysander's
"leading back" and "antitype," Weingartner's "orgy of destruction" and
"counterpart to the paroxysm of joy"). It took the novelist's collabora-
tion in exile with Theodor W. Adorno to establish these ideas and words,
which were already at hand, on the philosophical basis of negativity, and
"to realize in imagination" (Thomas Mann's phrase) these same ideas
as an artistic design in a musical work, as a "symphony-cantata" (the
term used by Mendelssohn). The idea of what Thomas Mann called "the
taking back" does in fact stem from the nineteenth century. And it is
interesting to note the symphonic works that Mann was discussing while
working on Chapters 45 and 46 of *Doctor Faustus,* or hearing on disc
during his daily gramophone soirées. His diary records a "conference
with Adorno about the 'Symphonic Cantata' ... discussion about
Tchaikovsky" on November 25, 1946; "in the evening *Harold in Italy* ...
The 4 Serious Songs" on November 27; "in the evening Mahler's 4th
Symphony" on November 30. Although Mann listened to the last-named
work "with doubts," it still belongs (with its "morendo" close) to a
symphonic "taking back," along with Tchaikovsky's *Pathétique* and,
from even earlier, Berlioz's *Symphonie fantastique* and *Harold in Italy.*[35]
By expanding this idea into a historio-philosophical category and a po-

35. On Berlioz compare the discussion above and the study by Bonds (see the Bibliography).

litical thesis, *Doctor Faustus* works up the experiences of German history in the twentieth century. But such an expansion is already implicit in Weingartner's description of Brahms's passacaglia finale: "fate implacably driving some great creation, whether it be an individual or a whole race, toward its downfall."[36]

The actual expression "taking back" (in Mann's account of "The Genesis of Doctor Faustus" *Zurücknahme* appears in quotation marks, while in the sketch for the novel's Chapter 46 it is underlined for emphasis) is one that might have been coined by Adorno. In the first, typescript version of the text which Adorno later expanded into his *Philosophie der neuen Musik,* there occurs the sentence: "Nevertheless, *Wozzeck* takes back its own initial position" (p. 3; the sentence remains unchanged in the final German text). Here the expression occurs in the form of a verb. The meaning, however, is not the same. The fact that Alban Berg's *Wozzeck*—which Adorno calls a "great opera," a "masterpiece" that "suffers from sophistry"—"takes back" its critical "impulses" (as a "portrayal of anxiety," and in the "undemonstrative sympathy of the tone") is a critical diagnosis from Adorno's viewpoint and represents a failing, albeit on the highest artistic level. Thomas Mann's interpretation of "taking back," on the other hand, would in Adorno's post-Hegelian thought be read as "determinate negation." Part of this, as Adorno adopted it, is the act of preservation (of art, of the Absolute) through uncompromising negativity. As reported by both Mann and Adorno, the dialectical interpretation of negativity led to a final correction of Chapter 46 of *Doctor Faustus,* where the first version seemed to Mann's adviser on the philosophy of music to have made the religious element of hope too positive. Here Mann adjusted the balance, although with initial reluctance. Thus right at the end of Leverkühn's *Weheklag* symphony, his Symphony of Lamentation, there comes "the high G of a cello, the final hovering sound," "the note hanging in the silence as it goes on oscillating"—and

36. According to Claudia Bernini (Thomas-Mann-Archive, Zurich; letter of March 23, 1991), Thomas Mann did not have Weingartner's book on the symphony since Beethoven in his library; nor does the name occur in Mann's diaries for the period when he was working on *Doctor Faustus.*

it dies away as a "light in the darkness," as the "miracle that passes belief"—almost like the "message in a bottle" already mentioned in the typescript of Adorno's *Philosophy of New Music,* except that Mann, typically, makes it more positive. But here his novel takes us beyond Brahms's Third Symphony, as did Mahler's Fourth and Ninth Symphonies in their approach, and of course Tchaikovsky's *Pathétique,* works that no longer wished to use the chorale, and hence the directly religious element, as a means of "preservation."

When these backgrounds have been outlined, the discussion of melancholy contained in the present book also lends conviction—and all the more strongly because its author is receptive to verbal mirrorings—to Thomas Mann's reference to *Schwermut,* mournfulness, as part of the "taking back." And let us not forget that earlier—in Chapter 27 of the novel, to be precise—Leverkühn had set Keat's *Ode on Melancholy* to music, as an "extremely elaborate" set of variations for voice and string quartet. "With an eye to Beethoven's 'Ninth' as its counterpart, in the word's most mournful sense" is how Leverkühn's symphony-cantata was supposedly written. An anti-triumphal, dissipating finish is also to be found in Brahms's Third Symphony, although without the explanatory "morendo" of Mahler's Fourth, the *ersterbend* ("dying away") of Mahler's Ninth, or the "slowly evaporating" directive in Leverkühn's *Weheklag.* All these works are a late era's artistic confessions. Even the concept of Leverkühn's *Faustus* symphony belongs aesthetically to the nineteenth century. Proceeding from this situation, let us go over Brahms's four symphonies once more. The chorales in the First and Third Symphonies resound with "hope," directly and positively, although this is no longer triumphal in the Third but a kind of melancholy internalization. With its negative ending, the Fourth Symphony denies this hope; it is the composed revocation of it.

In the two-plus-two order of the Brahms symphonies the finale of the Second occupies a central position. Despite the melancholic tinge to the work's overall outlook, it *still* retains elements of the triumphal strategy of the First Symphony, and it does *not yet* realize the Third's final fading away into silence, or the sharply delineated negativity of the Fourth. Yet as a "late idyll," this Second Symphony's "overall outlook" adopts the historical position which Adrian Leverkühn so neatly describes as "the taking back." Thomas Mann derived this category from the experience of exile in the mid-twentieth century, so to apply it to Johannes Brahms may seem surprising. But it was the musing, melancholy Brahms—Ernst Bloch's "passionate, deep and somber Brahms" (*Essays*, pp. 29–30)— who had already *composed* the artistic "taking back" in the nineteenth century, and who did so from right within the Viennese tradition. And it is Brahms's skeptical, broken mastery that needs to be affirmed, in the face of a reception of his music which misplaces the accents because it is listening, and revising, with academic ears.

Bibliography

Index

Bibliography

Sources

No sketches or drafts for Brahms's Second Symphony are extant. The following is a brief account of the sources providing clues for the symphony's analysis and interpretation, either because they retain earlier readings or through autograph corrections or other entries by Brahms.

Autographs and Copies

1. Autograph of the full score. Signed, undated. Belongs to an American private owner, deposited in the Pierpont Morgan Library, New York. Evidently the complete manuscript was originally divided into three: movements I, II + III, and IV are on different manuscript paper, and Brahms has numbered them separately. Movements I and III are both followed by a blank page (sheets 25 verso and 45 verso), and after movement IV there are three blank pages (68 verso, 69). For movements II–IV the autograph served as the printer's copy. It contains a series of corrections, most of the major ones being in movement I (such as the trombones in mm. 44ff., the parts accompanying the horn in mm. 454ff., the horn part itself in mm. 477–478), and at the end of the second movement. These corrections are discussed in this study in the appropriate place, insofar as they have a bearing on the analysis of the symphony. (A copyist's version of the score of the first movement, which was the printer's copy for the first edition and includes numerous corrections in Brahms's hand, is in German private ownership. The source could not be inspected for the purposes of the present study.)

2. Autograph of the piano reduction for four hands. Signed, undated. Music Collection of the Stadt- und Landesbibliothek, Vienna. Formerly owned by Clara Schumann. (See document T.)

3. Fair copy of the four-hand piano reduction, in the hand of two different copyists (NN1: movements I–III, NN2: movement IV). Unsigned. End of movement I dated 17. 12. 1877, end of movement III dated 22. 12. Staats- und Universitätsbibliothek,

Hamburg (Brahms Archive). Formerly owned by N. Simrock. Used as printer's copy for the first edition of the reduction.

Author's Copies, Printer's Proofs

4. Author's copy of the first edition of the full score, formerly owned by Brahms (published by N. Simrock in Berlin, plate number 8028, issued August 1878). Archive of the Gesellschaft der Musikfreunde, Vienna. Contains no corrections but some conductor's markings, one of the points to be singled out for attention being the big violin melody in the coda to movement I (mm. 477ff.).

5. Printer's proof of the first edition of the four-hand piano reduction (published by N. Simrock in Berlin, plate number 8030, issued 1878), formerly owned by Brahms. Archive of the Gesellschaft der Musikfreunde, Vienna. The proof contains corrections in Brahms's hand which were then included in the first edition. There is an interesting change in m. 477 of the first movement.

Publications

Günter Bandmann, *Melancholie und Musik,* Cologne-Opladen: Westdeutscher Verlag, 1960.

Daniel Beller-McKenna, "Johannes Brahms's Later Settings of Biblical Texts," Ph.D. diss., Harvard University, 1994.

Walter Benjamin, *The Origin of German Tragic Drama,* trans. John Osborne, London: Verso, 1985.

Hector Berlioz, *Treatise on Instrumentation,* enlarged and revised by Richard Strauss, trans. Theodore Front, New York: Edwin F. Kalmus, 1948.

Klaus Bernhard, *Idylle: Theorie, Geschichte, Darstellung in der Malerei* 1750–1859, Cologne and Vienna: Böhlau, 1977.

Peter Betthausen et al., *Adolph Menzel: Master Drawings From East Berlin* (exhibition catalogue, Frick Collection, New York, 1990), Alexandria, Virginia: Art Services International, 1990.

Billroth und Brahms im Briefwechsel, ed. Otto Gottfried-Billroth, Berlin and Vienna: Urban & Schwarzenberg, 1936 [Billroth].

Ernst Bloch, *Das Prinzip Hoffnung,* Frankfurt am Main: Suhrkamp, 1959.

———— *Essays on the Philosophy of Music,* trans. Peter Palmer, Cambridge: Cambridge University Press, 1985.

Harold Bloom, *The Anxiety of Influence: A Theory of Poetry,* Oxford: Oxford University Press, 6/1975.

Mark Evan Bonds, "*Sinfonia anti-eroica:* Berlioz's *Harold en Italie* and the Anxiety of Beethoven's Influence," *The Journal of Musicology* X, 4, Fall 1992, 417–463.

Renate Böschenstein-Schäfer, *Idylle,* Stuttgart: Metzler, 1967.

Johannes Brahms, *Briefwechsel,* vols. I–XVI, Berlin 1907–1922, reprint Tutzing: Hans Schneider, 1974 [Letters].

Johannes Brahms und Fritz Simrock: Weg einer Freundschaft: Briefe des Verlegers an den Komponisten, ed. Kurt Stephenson, Hamburg: Augustin, 1961 = Veröffentlichungen der Hamburger Staats- und Universitätsbibliothek VI [Simrock].

Brahms-Analysen, ed. Friedhelm Krummacher and Wolfram Steinbeck, Kassel: Bärenreiter, 1984 = Kieler Schriften z. Musikwissenschaft XXVII. (Includes Peter Gülke, "Sagen und Schweigen bei Brahms," pp. 12–32; Reinhold Brinkmann, "Anhand von Reprisen," pp. 107–120; Wolfram Steinbeck, "Liedthematik und symphonischer Prozeß. Zum ersten Satz der 2. Symphonie," pp. 166–182.)

Otto Breicha (ed.), *Gustav Klimt: Die Goldene Pforte: Werk-Wesen-Wirkung,* Salzburg: Galerie Welz, 1978.

"Briefe von Brahms an Ernst Frank," ed. Alfred Einstein, in *Zeitschrift für Musikwissenschaft* IV, 1921–1922, 385–416 [Frank].

Reinhold Brinkmann, "Brahms und die 'Mächte der Massen.' Über Struktur und Idee der 1. Symphonie," in *Berliner Philharmonisches Orchester: Philharmonische Programme 1983/84,* No. 40, June 19–20, 1984, 815–825.

———— "Wirkungen Beethovens in der Kammermusik," in *Beiträge zu Beethovens Kammermusik: Symposium Bonn 1984,* ed. Sieghart Brandenburg and Helmut Loos, Munich: G. Henle Verlag, 1987 = Veröffentlichungen des Beethovenhauses in Bonn, Neue Folge IV, 10, 79–110.

———— "Die 'heitre Sinfonie' und der 'schwer melancholische Mensch.' Johannes Brahms antwortet Vincenz Lachner," *Archiv für Musikwissenschaft* 46, 1989, 294–306.

———— "The Lyric as Paradigm: Poetry and the Foundation of Arnold Schoenberg's New Music," in Claus Reschke and Howard Pollack, eds., *German Literature and Music: An Aesthetic Fusion: 1890–1989,* Munich: Fink, 1992 = Houston German Studies 8, 95–129.

David Brodbeck, review of the Brahms *Thematisch-Bibliographisches Werkverzeichnis* by Margit L. McCorkle, *Journal of the American Musicological Society* 42, No. 2, Summer 1989, 418–431.

Peter Brooks, *Reading for the Plot,* New York: Vintage Books, 1985.

Elmar Budde, "Johannes Brahms' Intermezzo op. 117, Nr. 2," in *Analysen: Festschrift für Hans Heinrich Eggebrecht,* Stuttgart: Franz Steiner, 1984, 324–337.

Jacob Burckhardt, *Reflections on History* ("Weltgeschichtliche Betrachtungen"), trans. M. D. Hottinger, London 2/1950.

Günter Busch, "Menzels Grenzen," in *Adolph Menzel: Realist, Historist, Maler des Hofes* (exhibition catalogue, Kiel et al., 1981), Schweinfurt: Sammlung Georg Schäfer, 1981, 11–12.

Carl Dahlhaus, "Beethovens 'Neuer Weg,' " *Jahrbuch des Staatlichen Instituts für Musikforschung Preußischer Kulturbesitz* 1974, Berlin 1975, 46–62.

———— "La Malinconia," in Ludwig Finscher, ed., *Ludwig van Beethoven,* Darmstadt: Wissenschaftliche Buchgesellschaft, 1983 = Wege der Forschung 178.

———— *Nineteenth-Century Music,* trans. J. Bradford Robinson, Berkeley: University of California Press, 1989.

Wilhelm Dilthey, "Rede zum 70. Geburtstag (1903)," in *Die Geistige Welt.* 1. Hälfte = Gesammelte Schriften, vol. 5, Leipzig: Teubner, 1924, 7–9.

Joachim Draheim, ed., *Johannes Brahms in Baden-Baden und Karlsruhe: Eine Ausstellung der Badischen Landesbibliothek Karlsruhe und der Brahmsgesellschaft Baden-Baden e.V.,* Karlsruhe: Verlag der Badischen Landesbibliothek, 1983.

Gustav Droysen, *Historik: Vorlesungen über Enzyklopädie und Methodologie der Geschichte,* ed. Rudolf Hübner, Munich: Oldenbourg, 1937.

William Empson, *Some Versions of Pastoral,* London: Chatto & Windus, 1935.

David Epstein, *Beyond Orpheus: Studies in Musical Structure,* 2/Oxford: Oxford University Press, 1987.

Anna Ettlinger, *Lebenserinnerungen für ihre Familie verfaßt,* Leipzig: C. Grumbach, n.d. (?1923).

Ludwig Finscher, "Kampf mit der Tradition: Johannes Brahms," in *Die Welt der Symphonie,* ed. Ursula von Rauchhaupt, Braunschweig: Westermann, 1972, 165–174.

Constantin Floros, *Johannes Brahms: Symphonie Nr. 2 D-Dur op. 73: Taschenpartitur, Einführung und Analyse,* Mainz: B. Schott's Söhne, 1984 = Goldmann Schott pocket score No. 33110.

Theodor Fontane, *Wanderungen durch die Mark Brandenburg,* ed. Gotthart Erler and Rudolf Mingau, Part 1, Frankfurt am Main: Insel Verlag, 1989 = insel taschenbuch 1181.

Françoise Forster-Hahn, "Authenticity into Ambivalence: The Evolution of Menzel's Drawings," in *Master Drawings* XVI, No. 3, London 1978, 255–283.

Sigmund Freud, *Trauer und Melancholie,* in Gesammelte Werke, vol. 10, London-Frankfurt: S. Fischer, 1946.

Walter Frisch, *Brahms and the Principle of Developing Variation,* Berkeley: University of California Press, 1984 = California Studies in 19th-Century Music 2.

Gerhart Frodl, "Begegnung im Theater: Hans Makart und Gustav Klimt," in *Klimt-*

Studien = Mitteilungen der Österreichischen Galerie 22–23, No. 66/67, Salzburg: Galerie Welz, 1978–1979.

Martin Gerlach, ed., *Allegorien und Embleme,* Vienna: Gerlach und Schenck, 1882ff., with commentaries by Albert Ilg.

Jean Granier, "Nietzsche's Conception of Chaos," in David B. Allison, ed., *The New Nietzsche,* Cambridge, Mass.: MIT Press, 4/1985, 135–141.

Peter Gülke, *Brahms Bruckner: Zwei Studien,* Kassel and Basle: Bärenreiter, 1989.

Eduard Hanslick, *Concerte, Componisten und Virtuosen der letzten fünfzehn Jahre. 1870–1885,* Berlin: Allgemeiner Verein für Deutsche Literatur, 1886.

———— *Fünf Jahre Musik.* 1891–1895, Berlin: Allgemeiner Verein für Deutsche Literatur, 1896.

Erich Heller, *The Importance of Nietzsche,* Chicago: University of Chicago Press, 1988.

Kurt Hofmann, *Die Bibliothek von Johannes Brahms,* Hamburg: Verlag der Musikalienhandlung Karl Dieter Wagner, 1974.

Werner Hofmann, *Menzel der Beobachter* (exhibition catalogue, Kunsthalle Hamburg, 1982), Munich: Prestel, 1982.

Georg G. Iggers, *Deutsche Geschichtswissenschaft,* Munich: Deutscher Taschenbuch Verlag, 2/1972.

Gustav Jenner, *Johannes Brahms als Mensch, Lehrer und Künstler,* Marburg an der Lahn: Elwert, 1905.

Jens Christian Jensen, ed., *Brahms-Phantasien* (exhibition catalogue, Kunsthalle Kiel, 1983), Kiel: Kunsthalle, 1983.

Max Kalbeck, *Johannes Brahms,* Berlin: Deutsche Brahms-Gesellschaft, vol. I, 4/1921; vol. II, 3/1921; vol. III, 1910/1912; vol. IV, 1914.

Reinhart Kapp, "Lobgesang," in *Neue Musik und Tradition: Festschrift Rudolf Stephan,* Laaber: Laaber Verlag, 1990, 239–249.

Rudolf Klein, "Die konstruktiven Grundlagen der Brahms-Symphonien," *Österreichische Musikzeitschrift* XXIII, 1968, 258–263.

Raymond Klibansky, Erwin Panofsky, and Fritz Saxl, *Saturn and Melancholy,* London: Nelson, 1964.

Raymond Knapp, "Brahms and the Problem of the Symphony: Romantic Image, Generic Conception, and Compositional Challenge," Ph.D. diss., Duke University, 1987 (Ann Arbor, University Microfilms International).

Karl Michael Komma, "Das 'Scherzo' der 2. Symphonie von Johannes Brahms," in *Festschrift Walter Wiora zum 30. 12. 1966,* Kassel: Bärenreiter, 1967, 448–457.

Werner F. Korte, *Bruckner und Brahms,* Tutzing: Hans Schneider, 1963.

Reinhart Koselleck, *Vergangene Zukunft: Zur Semantik geschichtlicher Zeiten,* Frankfurt am Main: Suhrkamp Verlag, 1979.

Hermann Kretzschmar, *Führer durch den Concertsaal I: Symphonie und Suite,* Leipzig: A. G. Liebeskind, 2/1891.

Stefan Kunze, "Johannes Brahms oder: Das schwere Werk der Symphonie," in *Johannes Brahms: Leben und Werk,* ed. Christiane Jacobsen, Wiesbaden: Breitkopf & Härtel, 1983, 111–113.

Michael Landmann, *Anklage gegen die Vernunft,* Stuttgart: Klett, 1976.

Wolf Lepenies, *Das Ende der Naturgeschichte,* Munich and Vienna: Hanser Verlag, 1976.

—————— *Melancholy and Society,* Cambridge, Mass.: Harvard University Press, 1992.

David Lewin, "On Harmony and Meter in Brahms's Op. 76, No. 8," *19th Century Music* IV, 3, Spring 1981, 261–265.

Berthold Litzmann, *Clara Schumann: Ein Künstlerleben nach Tagebüchern und Briefen,* vol. III, Leipzig: Breitkopf & Härtel, 4/1920 [Litzmann].

Karl Löwith, *From Hegel to Nietzsche: The Revolution in Nineteenth-Century Thought,* New York: Doubleday, 1967.

Thomas Mann, "Der alte Fontane," in *Adel des Geistes,* Stockholm: S. Fischer, 1959, 470–495.

Margit L. McCorkle, *Johannes Brahms: Thematisch-Bibliographisches Werkverzeichnis,* Munich: G. Henle Verlag, 1984.

William J. McGrath, *Dionysian Art and Populist Politics in Austria,* New Haven: Yale University Press, 1974.

Herman Meyer, *Das Zitat in der Erzählkunst,* Stuttgart: Metzler, 1967.

Paul Mies, "Aus Brahms' Werkstatt," in *Simrock-Jahrbuch* I, 1926, 43–63.

Anthony Newcomb, "Once More 'Between Absolute and Program Music': Schumann's Second Symphony," in *19th Century Music* VII, 2, 1984, 233–250.

Friedrich Nietzsche, *Werke in drei Bänden,* ed. Karl Schlechta, Munich: Hanser Verlag, 1955.

Alfred Orel, "Ein eigenhändiges Werkverzeichnis von Johannes Brahms," in *Die Musik* XXIX, 1936–1937, 529–541.

Erwin Panofsky, "Et in Arcadia ego," in *Meaning in the Visual Arts,* Garden City, N.Y.: Doubleday, 1957, 285–320.

Susanne Partsch, *Klimt: Leben und Werk,* Munich: International Publishing Verlagsgesellschaft, 1990.

Peter Petersen, "Brahms und Dvořák," in *Brahms und seine Zeit: Symposium Hamburg 1983* = Hamburger Jahrbuch für Musikwissenschaft VII, 1984, 125–146.

Walter Rehm, "Jacobsen und die Schwermut," in *Gontscharow und Jacobsen,* Göttingen: Vandenhoeck und Ruprecht, 1963.

Rudolf Reti, *The Thematic Process in Music,* New York: Macmillan, 1951.

Max Rychner, *Welt im Wort: Literarische Aufsätze,* Zurich: Manesse, 1949.

Carl Schachter, "The First Movement of Brahms's Second Symphony: The Opening Theme and Its Consequences," in *Music Analysis* II, 1983, 55–68.

Erich Schenk, "Zur Inhaltsdeutung der Brahmsschen Wörthersee-Symphonie," in *Ausgewählte Aufsätze und Vorträge*, Graz Vienna and Cologne: Böhlau, 1967, 133–142 = Wiener musikwissenschaftliche Beiträge 7.

Christian M. Schmidt, "Von Zeitarten tonaler Musik," in *Archiv für Musikwissenschaft* XLII, 1985, 287–299.

Paul Schönfelder, review of Martin Gerlach, *Allegorien und Embleme, Kunstchronik* XIX, 1884, 37–41.

Giselher Schubert, *Johannes Brahms: Symphonie Nr. 1 c-Moll op. 68: Taschenpartitur, Einführung und Analyse*, Mainz: B. Schott's Söhne, 1981 = Goldmann Schott pocket score No. 33031.

Clara Schumann and Johannes Brahms, *Briefe aus den Jahren 1853–1896*, ed. Berthold Litzmann, 2 vols., Leipzig: Breitkopf & Härtel, 1927 [Schumann/Brahms].

Robert Schumann, *Gesammelte Schriften über Musik und Musiker*, ed. Martin Kreisig, 2 vols., Leipzig: Breitkopf & Härtel, 5/1914.

Hans Ulrich Seeber and Paul Gerhart Klussmann, *Idylle und Modernisierung in der europäischen Literatur des 19. Jahrhunderts*, Bonn: Bouvier Verlag Herbert Grundmann, 1986.

Charles Seeger, "On the Moods of a Music Logic," in *Studies in Musicology* 1935–1975, Berkeley: University of California Press, 1977, 67–69.

Susan Sontag, "Under the Sign of Saturn," in *Under the Sign of Saturn*, New York: Noonday Press, 1980, 103–134.

Philipp Spitta, "Johannes Brahms," in *Zur Musik*, Berlin: Gebrüder Paetel, 1892, 385–427.

Jean Starobinski, *Die Erfindung der Freiheit*, Geneva: Skira, 1964.

Rudolf Stephan, "Zu Beethovens letzten Quartetten," in *Vom musikalischen Denken*, Mainz: Schott, 1985, 42–51.

Wilhelm Szilasi, *Macht und Ohnmacht des Geistes*, Freiburg im Breisgau: Alber, 1946.

Richard Taruskin, "Resisting the Ninth," in *19th Century Music* XII, 3, Spring 1989, 241–256.

Jens Tismar, *Gestörte Idyllen*, Munich: Hanser, 1973.

Ernst Toch, *The Shaping Forces in Music*, New York: Dover, 1977.

Donald F. Tovey, *Essays in Musical Analysis I*, Oxford and New York: Oxford University Press, 1989.

Manfred Wagner, *Geschichte der österreichischen Musikkritik in Beispielen*, Tutzing: Hans Schneider, 1979 (pp. 218ff.: reviews of the first performance of Brahms's Second Symphony).

Richard Wagner, *Sämtliche Schriften und Dichtungen: Volks-Ausgabe,* 16 vols., Leipzig: Breitkopf & Härtel/C.F.W. Siegel, o.J.

James Webster, "The General and the Particular in Brahms's Later Sonata Forms," in George S. Bozarth, ed., *Brahms Studies: Analytical and Historical Perspectives,* Oxford: Oxford University Press, 1990, 49–78.

Klaus Wedewer and Jens Christian Jensen, eds., *Die Idylle: Eine Bildform im Wandel: Zwischen Hoffnung und Wirklichkeit: 1750–1930,* Cologne: Dumont Buchverlag, 1986.

Peter Wegmann, *Von Caspar David Friedrich bis Ferdinand Hodler* (exhibition catalogue, Nationalgalerie Berlin, 1993), Frankfurt am Main/Leipzig: Insel Verlag, 1993.

Felix Weingartner, *Die Symphonie nach Beethoven,* Leipzig: Breitkopf & Härtel, 3/1909. (English edition: "The Symphony since Beethoven," trans. H. M. Schott, in *Weingartner on Music and Conducting,* New York: Dover, 1969.)

Günter Weiß-Aigner, "Die instrumentalen Zyklen der drei Kärntner Schaffenssommer von Johannes Brahms: Thematisch-figurale Affinitäten im kompositorischen Entwicklungsstrom," in *Augsburger Jahrbuch für Musikwissenschaft* 1984, Tutzing 1984, 73–124.

Karl Heinrich Wörner, *Das Zeitalter der thematischen Prozesse,* Regensburg: Gustav Bosse Verlag, 1969.

Index of Names and Musical Works